A Psychological Strategy for Alternative Human Development

A Psychological Strategy for Alternative Human Development

India's Performance Since Independence

Prayag Mehta

Sage Publications
New Delhi/Thousand Oaks/London

First published in 1998 by

Sage Publications India Pvt Ltd
M-32 Market, Greater Kailash - I
New Delhi-110 048

Sage Publications Inc
2455 Teller Road
Thousand Oaks, California 91320

Sage Publications Ltd
6 Bonhill Street
London EC2A 4PU

Published by Tejeshwar Singh for Sage Publications India Pvt Ltd, typeset by Siva Math Setters, Chennai and printed at Chaman Enterprises, Delhi.

Library of Congress Cataloging-in-Publication Data

Mehta, Prayag, 1926–
    A psychological strategy for alternative human development:
  India's performance since independence / Prayag Mehta.
        p.   cm.   (alk. paper)
    Includes bibliographical references and index.
    1. Rural development—India. 2. Manpower policy—India. 3. Human capital—India. 4. India—Economic conditions—1947– 5. India—Politics and government—1947– I. Title.
HN690.Z9C664182   307.1'412'0954—dc21   1998   98—7051

ISBN: 0–7619–9257–X (US–HB)   81–7036–711–5 (India–HB)

Sage Production Team: Ritu Singh, N. K. Negi and Santosh Rawat

Dedicated to the Golden Jubilee
of
India's Independence

CONTENTS

LIST OF TABLES

PREFACE
A Personal Account

This book has evolved over a fairly long time. During this period, I have had the privilege of interacting with a large number of people at the grassroots level: village level meetings, participatory workshops and training programmes in small group discussions as well as in formal and informal individual interviews in various parts of the country, from some very remote villages unconnected by rail, even by road, to some located near big cities and towns. Let us go on a tour of some areas to meet and talk with some people there.

What do they say; what message do they give to the state and our political parties; what do they suggest as an alternative to the usual development paradigm? Let us start the journey with Karnataka and take the case of recently 'liberated' bonded labourers in the rich paddy areas of the State. It is early 1978. Their grievance: 'Why have they "freed us"; we have lost our huts and work; there is now no place to live and there is nothing to eat'. 'Surely you received some cash compensation for your rehabilitation?' 'What money we have seen none'. We have nothing now; we have lost everything'. They were eager to go back to their masters—to their huts and to the safety of bondage.

Move now to a city in Tamil Nadu, famous for its medical education and *beedi*-making. The time: early 1982. You are face-to-face with bonded (mortgaged) child labourers—barely 8 to 10 years old, with baskets hanging round their necks and their nimble fingers busy rolling *beedies*. They have come to school for the midday meal. 'Why do they not stay in the school to study?' we asked their mothers. 'What study? What would we eat? All women and children roll *beedies* for the *thekadar* (contractor); The males pull rickshaw sometimes. Occasionally, they may get some other casual work. And, the arrack takes all this away'.

Let us now go to the East. The Santhal Parganas in Bihar and Sundergarh in Orissa. Illiterate tribal women. Time 1980–81. They would very much like to work; to have skill training; use the local forest resources; have production facilities: But want no government control. They want everything to be managed by their own autonomous organisation. 'But why not a government department?' 'Because everything would be taken away'.

Take this small tribal village in Ranchi district. Period—1978–82: Almost everyone is illiterate; children not going to school; women walking miles to sell headloads of firewood; men having or doing very little work. The moneylender and arrack are the masters. They would not talk to you. They mistrust all outsiders. They are afraid of everything—even their own shadow. Any petty government functionary can extract favours and money from them. All this changed, rather radically, as they succeeded in organising themselves under the aegis of their *gram sabha*—the village council. The youth succeed in enforcing total voluntary prohibition; the village council involves the members in planning and implementing several socio-economic projects; all children in school and the adults, both men and women, throng the night literacy classes; they dig new wells, build new cooperative irrigation facilities, get additional crops. Practically everybody has work. They now want more and better education for their children, technical training for themselves and plan to launch several new economic projects. They successfully confront the moneylenders, the police, the trader, the officials and the corrupt among themselves. They now look forward to the future with hope. In a way, they have changed the economy of the village and also their own mind-set.

Go now to Rajasthan. A remote village in Udaipur district. Time: February 1979. Working in small groups, somewhat educated to illiterate tribal youth tell you that: They have practically no land; no irrigation, not even drinking water; no work in the village or in the neighbourhood, they have to be away from home in search of work for 6 to 8 months in a year; no medical facilities, have to physically carry their sick crossing the hills to the *tehsil* hospital where there may be no doctor; not even a primary school in many villages. At times they have no food as there is no income. The same story is repeated at Banswara and Pratapgarh. They add ruefully, 'Nobody listens to us, neither the Minister, nor the *Surpanch* nor the *Patwari*'.

Moving next to western Rajasthan: Barmer. Period: 1990. The district has the dubious distinction of having the lowest female literacy—about 8 per cent—in the country, perhaps in the world. The government adult education field functionaries and the volunteers enlighten you about the '*safha*' (patron–client kind of feudal relationship) culture and the '*paripatra*' (proforma) culture of the senior officials. The policy talks of debureaucratisation and decentralisation in implementation. In reality, the programme has, however, become much more bureaucratised, more centralised and 'feudalised'. The officials are interested more in numbers and 'ceremonies' than in performance. Despite such odds, the volunteers/

instructors, just somewhat educated youth, seem determined to use the literacy projects to make the people more aware of their 'rights'.

Let us now see what the rural women have to say in the context of a non-government organisation (NGO)-run government development programme. Sonebhadra is mineral-rich but a very backward district. The people are illiterate, unskilled and are considered unexposed to the 'modern' stimuli. Period: 1991–92. At meeting after meeting, the people, particularly the women, articulate their needs and problems. These are almost the same as commonly mentioned by the people elsewhere. One distinguishing feature here is their deep resentment and overt anger. At one such meeting held in front of a newly constructed building, the NGO Director wants to know why they do not send their children to the school. No response. Total silence. He again prods them, 'After all, we have constructed the school for you. You should send your children here'. Then slowly, a young mother stands up and tells him in her idiomatic Bhojpuri— the local language, 'Whenever children ask for water, the teacher sends them home', saying, "Bring some water for me also". And where is the water? Not a drop at home also'. At another meeting, another woman says, 'You tell us to keep food covered, what should we cover, we do not have a single grain of food'. In another village, an old woman remarks, 'You ask us about our problems. Here no work is possible without *lehnden* (bribes). They are not releasing my widow pension, but I am also determined not to pay them anything'. At yet another meeting, held to discuss problems regarding vocational training for women, the Director asks them as to why they do not bring materials, such as wool, etc., for such programmes. Again a pregnant silence. He further reminds them, 'After all, these courses have been specially organised for your benefit. Your children will get the knitwear'. Then a middle-aged woman breaks the silence in her powerful Bhojpuri, 'Why should we bring the material? Why should we come? Go to the *Mukhiyaji* (village head)'. Prior to this, at several other meetings, the women repeatedly gave vent to their anger that no effort was made to give them technical training so that they, and particularly their children, could get employment in the emerging power plants and industrial enterprises in the area. Instead, the organisation persists in giving them training in *khadi* spinning, knitting, sewing and such other traditional courses.

The journey does not end here. The above are only a few samples of deeply felt, living and penetrating insights of the marginalised labouring people—men and women—from across the country. These add up to tell the stark story of development, particularly human development, in the country. Such experiences lead us to raise questions as to where and what has gone wrong.

The present work owes much to the ideas generated by these large number of struggling people—small and marginal farmers, landless rural workers, artisans and others about our human development, reasons for poor performance and also towards a broad framework of an alternative strategy to alter the situation. I am grateful to all of them, too numerous to be named here, for enriching my understanding of development issues and this book.

Despite Fundamental Rights and Constitutional directives for equality of opportunities, protection of life, protection of children and for primary education, and despite 50 years of Independence, human development in the country has been very poor. This reality, long experienced by the people, is now widely discussed and recognised. It also came out clearly in the debate at the special session of the Parliament to mark the golden jubilee of Independence. The performance has lagged far behind the promises made from time to time, including those in the historic 'Tryst with Destiny' speech by the first Prime Minister on 14 August, 1947, and which was replayed at the golden jubilee session of the Parliament. However, what has not been discussed so much is why the state in India has failed to discharge its duties to the people.

Reviews of development programmes show some dysfunctional systemic tendencies in their implementation. Besides policy factors, such tendencies and behaviours have significantly contributed to distorting programmes like those for poverty alleviation, health care, literacy, primary education, forests and environment on the ground. Instead of pursuing the stated objectives of social development, the programmes have tended to alienate the people from the state. Such 'development' behaviours are obviously not motivated by the egalitarian and democratic values projected in the Constitution but by the traditional hierarchical values of superordination and subordination entrenched in the social system as well as in the system of administration. Without a proper understanding of the factors responsible for poor human development performance, we are likely to repeat the same situation over and over. This book provides a conceptual framework for understanding such behaviours and values and also the reasons for the state failures resulting in the denial of basic needs and rights to the people.

Field experiences and the insights provided by the concerned people underlie the urgency for not only meaningful state interventions, but more importantly, for enhancing the morale and motivation of the common people. We suggest a psychological strategy for enhancing their self-esteem, personal efficacy, capability and empowerment in order to accelerate both economic and social development in the country.

Various portions of the book were presented at seminars from time to time for several organisations, generating very valuable ideas. I am grateful to the faculty and the students of the Zakir Hussain Centre for Educational Studies, Jawaharlal Nehru University; Department of Social Sciences and Humanities, Indian Institute of Technology, Delhi; Division of Agricultural Extension, Indian Agricultural Research Institute, New Delhi; Centre for Research in Rural and Industrial Development (CRRID), Chandigarh; Indian Association of Social Security, New Delhi; Institute of Research and Management in Agriculture, Hyderabad; Department of Psychology, Sukhadia University, Udaipur; and Tribal Research Institute, Udaipur in this connection.

Discussions with T.V. Rao, B.P. Sinha, Udai Pareek, J.M. Ohja, Purnima Mathur, Sushila Singal, B.L. Abbi, Rashpal Malhotra and Martin Zuberi on various portions of the book have been enriching. I am grateful to all of them for their contributions. I am also grateful to Ms Omita Goyal, the anonymous reviewer and other members of the editorial team for their help in processing the manuscript for publication.

The book was completed at the Participation and Development Centre, with a visiting fellowship from the Centre for Research in Rural and Industrial Development (CRRID), Chandigarh for part of the period during which the book was under preparation. I am grateful to CRRID, and particularly its Director, Rashpal Malhotra, for this facility. The book owes greatly to Jagdish Singh for providing continuous secretarial assistance and for processing the various drafts of the manuscript.

New Delhi   Prayag Mehta
September 1997

CHAPTER 1

HUMAN DEVELOPMENT IN INDIA

I

Human Development as a Duty of the State

In 1950 the people of India resolved to constitute India into a democratic republic in order to secure to all citizens socio-economic and political justice; liberty of thought, expression, belief, faith and worship; equality of status and opportunities and to promote in all fraternity, assuring dignity of the individual and the unity of the nation.

Fundamental Rights of Citizens

The Constitution of India guarantees several Fundamental Rights to its citizens, as summarised in Table 1.1. These rights are inviolable in the sense that no law, ordinance, customs, usage or administrative order can abridge or take them away. In several important landmark judgements, the then Chief Justice, Shri P.N. Bhagwati, held in 1984, that 'it is the right of every one in the country to live with human dignity, free from exploitation. This right to live with human dignity, enshrined in Article 21, derives its life-breath from the Directive Principles of the State Policy' (SSC 608 : IAR 1984 SC 802 quoted in Singh 1994: 165).

The Right to Human Dignity

Article 21, read with the Directive Principles of the State Policy enshrined in Articles 39, 41, 42 as well as the Bonded Labour System (Abolition) Act 1976, obligates the state* to identify, release and suitably rehabilitate

---

* 's' with lower case is used to indicate state in India, the power of which is held by the Government at the Centre and 'S' with upper case to indicate States of the Indian Union, except in headings.

Table 1.1
Summary of Fundamental Rights*

Article	
14	Equality before law.
15	Prohibition of discrimination on grounds of religion, race, caste, sex or place of birth.
16	Equality of opportunity in matters of public employment.
17	Abolition of untouchability.
21	Protection of life and personal liberty.
23	Prohibition of traffic in human beings and forced labour.
24	Prohibition of employment of children in factories etc.
31(c)	Grant complete immunity from judicial scrutiny if the President certifies that a given legislation has been enacted to promote the policy laid down in Articles 39(a) and (b). (See Table 1.2). The Constitution was amended to facilitate land reforms.

*Summarised version of some of the Fundamental Rights, in Part III of the Constitution of India.

bonded labourers. Everyone has the right to live with human dignity, as enshrined in Article 21. Article 23 prohibits traffic in human beings and forced labour. Begging and other similar forms of forced labour are punishable offences in accordance with the law. In People's Union for Democratic Rights Vs. Union of India, popularly known as the *Asiad Workers Case*, the Supreme Court held in 1982 that, all unwilling labour is forced labour, whether paid or not. On the specific question of minimum wages, the Court held that where someone works for less than the minimum wages, the presumption is that he is working under some compulsion. The Court concluded that 'any factor which deprives the person of choice of alternatives and compels to adopt one particular course may probably be regarded as "forced" and if labour or service is compelled as a result of such "force", it would be a forced labour' (182, 3 SSC, 235 : IAR SC 1473 quoted in Singh 1994:203).

Following this decision, the Supreme Court, in 1983, invalidated the provision of the Rajasthan Famine Relief Works Employees Act, 1964 which exempted the application of Minumum Wages Act, 1948 to the employment in famine relief works. The Court further declared that bonded labour is a crude form of forced labour prohibited by Article 23 and that the failure of the state to identify the bonded labourers, to release them from their bondage and to rehabilitate them as envisaged by the Bonded Labour Abolition Act, 1976, violates Article 21 and 23 (3 SSC, 243, 1984 as quoted in Singh 1994:203–04).

Article 24 prohibits employment of children in hazardous factories and employment. Article 31, concerning egalitarian policy, was amended to include Article 31-C in order to grant complete immunity from judicial scrutiny to any law if the President certifies that it was enacted to promote the policy laid down in Articles 39(a) and (b). This was done to facilitate implementation of the Directive Principles as enshrined in these Articles, i.e., Article 39(b) and (c) which call upon the state: (*a*) to direct its policy towards securing to the citizens, men and women equally, the right to adequate means of livelihood; (*b*) to distribute the ownership and control of the material resources of the community to best subserve the common good; (*c*) to operate the economic system in such a way so that it does not result in concentration of wealth and means of production in hands of the few to the common detriment.

Constitutional Obligations of the State

The Directive Principles of the State Policy impose certain obligations and duties on the state. These are briefly summarised in Table 1.2. It was charged specifically to ensure universal education of children up to 14 years of age and to fulfill this task in 10 years after the promulgation of the Constitution, i.e., by 25 January 1960. In a recent judgement, the Supreme Court has held that the state must make arrangements for free education for all children up to 14 years of age because it is one of the Fundamental Rights of the individual under Article 21, read with the Directive Principle as laid down in Articles 41 and 45 (*UniKrishnan Vs. State of Andhra Pradesh*, 1993, 1 SC, 645, 732; see Singh, 1994: 166).

The Constitution of India, thus directed the state way back in 1950 and obligated its various organs and institutions to formulate policies and to take appropriate steps for ensuring proper quality of life to all citizens. This could include universal education, proper health, adequate income, adequate nutrition, humane conditions of work and promotion of a facilitative social and economic environment to enable the people to lead a dignified life.

Duty of the State

The Fundamental Rights and the Directive Principles of the State Policy together form the conscience of the Constitution. These impose on the state,

Table 1.2
Directive Principles of State Policy*

Article	
39(a)	Securing to citizens adequate means of livelihood.
39(b)	That material resources would be owned and distributed to sub-serve the common good.
39(c)	That economic system does not result in concentration of the means of production to the common detriment.
39(d)	Equal pay for equal work.
39(e)	That workers, men and women and children, are not forced to enter vocations not suited to their age and strength.
39(f)	That children are given opportunities and facilities to develop in a healthy manner and that childhood and youth are protected against exploitation and against moral and material abandonment.
40	Organisation of village *Panchayats* as units of self-government.
41	Right to work, to education and to public assistance.
42	Provision for just and humane conditions of work and maternity relief.
43	Living wages etc. for workers.
43(a)	Participation of workers in management of industries.
45	Provision for free and compulsory education up to 14 years. (The state was directed to fulfill this task by 25 January 1960).
46	Promotion of educational and economic interests of SCs/STs; protecting them from social injustice and exploitation.
47	To raise the level of nutrition and standard of living and to improve public health.

*Summarised version of some of the Directive Principles of State Policy in Part IV of the Constitution of India.

the obligation to take positive action for creating social and economic conditions in which there will be an egalitarian social order with social and economic justice to all so that individual liberty will become a cherished value and the dignity of the individual will become a living reality. The Constitution imposes duties on the state to take affirmative action in favour of weaker sections in political and socio-economic spheres.

The Constitution, thus, envisages that the Fundamental Rights of the citizens cannot be obtained by letting the individual alone. The state has been directed to take appropriate collective steps and public action in order to ensure these rights to them.

The state in India and its various organs have thus been made duty-bound to formulate and create conditions for fulfilling the various Fundamental Rights of its people. It has been directed to intervene and implement programmes designed to: provide universal education; adequate health services including child and mother care; appropriate employment opportunities for adequate purchasing power; and to ensure: that, children and youth are not exploited; that workers get the minimum living wage; that adequate nutrition is available to children, mothers and others; that, land-reforms are carried out for equitable distribution of means of production and other material resources: that humane conditions of work are available to workers to promote good health, sanitation and personal development for them; and that adequate affirmative actions are launched to ensure socio-economic justice to the weaker sections, such as SCs/STs and other backward classes.

The state and its various organs are obliged, therefore, to create a suitable environment to enable all citizens to enhance their capabilities and put these to best use in all fields—economic, social, cultural and political. 'The real foundation', as the *Human Development Report* (UNDP, 1994:13) has put it, 'of human development is universalism in acknowledging the life-claims of everyone'. The Constitution of India not only recognises such claims, but directs the state to try and fulfill such life-claims of all citizens—particularly the weaker sections of the society.

The philosophical foundation for many contemporary policies of human development, as of the Constitution of India, underlies the search for meeting basic human needs. 'It demands a world where no child goes without education, where no human being is denied health care and where all people can develop their potential capabilities' (UNDP, 1994:14). The Indian Constitution obligated the state and its various administrative and other organs, at the time of the launching of Indian Republic in 1950, to initiate policies and programmes to fulfill such human development goals. It would be worthwhile to take stock of our performance and achievements in this regard.

II

The Indian Situation

Appendix Table 1 reports some select social indicators of development in India since 1950—the year in which the Indian Republic was inaugurated and the various state organs were called upon to launch planned interventions for ensuring adequate quality of life for its people, particularly the weaker sections. How does the state fair after more than 45 years of the republic? Let us briefly map the profile of human development, as it has emerged over these years.

Health

Health occupies a crucial position in everybody's life. People's productive labour and quality of life greatly depend on their health. 'An investment in health,' as one of the government working groups noted, 'is investment in man and on improving the quality of life' (GOI, 1981: Preface). Let us, therefore, first take a look at the health status of our people as indicated by mortality rates and life expectancy at birth.

Mortality (death per thousand)

One of the positive gains of the state policies and interventions in India is the declining death rate in its population over the various Plan periods. The combined (rural and urban) death rate (per thousand) was 22.8 in the pre-Plan period of 1950–51 which gradually declined to 10 in 1991–92. Although the total death rate has declined uniformly both in the rural and urban areas during these years, the urban–rural and gender gaps have been persisting (10.8 in rural and 7.0 in urban areas in 1991–92).

Infant Mortality Rate (IMR)

Like the overall death rate, the infant mortality rate (per thousand live births) has also shown a declining trend over the years since the pre-Plan period of 1950–51. It was 182.5 per thousand live births in 1950–51 which gradually declined to 79.0 in 1991–92. Despite the decline, the gender difference has persisted in favour of male children. The urban–rural difference has persisted even more strongly. Thus, the combined IMR in rural and urban areas was respectively 138 and 82 in 1970–71, 114 and 66 in 1984–85 and 85 and 53 in 1991–92. Such disparity is further compounded for women as indicated by the decreasing sex ratio (number of females per thousand males) in rural areas from 965 in 1950–51 to 939 in 1990–91.

U-5 Mortality Rate

Another important indicator of health is the U-5 mortality rate (percentage of mortality among children up to five years of age). It was 51.9 per cent in 1970–71 which gradually decreased to 33 per cent in 1989–90 thus showing the same trend as recorded for other indicators of the mortality situation.

Maternal Mortality Rate (MMR)

Mother's health is another very important indicator of human development. During 1970–71, MMR (per one thousand live births) ranged between 376 and 418, which increased to 500 in 1979–80 and further to 550 in 1989–90. Thus, maternal health showed a reverse trend. As we will see later in this chapter, it has been a crucial indicator of development-performance in the country over the years.

Life Expectancy at Birth

How long does the new born child expect to live? In other words, what is the life expectancy? In 1950–51 the life expectancy at birth was 32.1 years for the combined population which gradually increased to 58.2 years in 1991–92. The Eighth Five Year Plan further projected it to increase to 60.6 by 1996–97. Biologically, females are expected to live longer than males. However, in our country, the situation showed a reverse trend up to 1993–94, as seen in Appendix Table 1. Females showed a somewhat higher life expectancy in 1980–81 and again in 1988–89 and 1991–92, although the difference was marginal. However, females expect to live almost as long as males. As we shall discuss later, life expectancy at birth is also a crucial indicator of health and social development of the population in a country. While it is a positive achievement that life expectancy has increased from approximately 32 years to 59 years in about 40 years , we would get a clearer picture regarding the pace of such progress on comparing it (in Section II which follows) with other developing countries.

Nutrition

The net availability of foodgrains has increased over the Plan years from 52.4 million tonnes in 1950–51 to 150.2 million tonnes in 1992–93. However, during the same period, the net availability of foodgrain through public distribution system (PDS) has shown an erratic but generally a declining trend. The quantity available through PDS was 15.3 per cent of the net availability of foodgrains in 1950–51 which came down to 12.5 per cent in 1991–92 and further declined to 10.1 per cent in 1992–93. A particularly alarming trend is reflected in the decline in net availability of pulses over these years. The per capita net availability of pulses was 60.7 grams in 1950–51 which came down to 34.3 grams in 1991–92. This figure increased slightly to 36.6 grams in 1992–93.

In rural areas, the total per capita household consumption expenditure was Rs 15, including Rs 9.9 on foodgrain, in 1954–55, which respectively increased to Rs 189.5 and Rs 121.8 in 1989–90. In urban areas, these were respectively Rs 24.7 and Rs 13.7 in 1954–55 and Rs 298.00 and Rs 165.5 in 1989–90. Thus, about two-thirds of the total per capita household consumption in the rural areas and more than half in the urban areas continued to be taken away by food alone all these years. Moreover, while the daily calorie per capita intake increased from 2,111 in 1965–66 to 2,283 in 1989–90, it decreased to 2,139 in 1991–92. The per capita daily protein intake decreased from 63.6 grams in 1973–74 to 61.8 grams in 1989–90 and decreased further to 54.1 grams in 1991–92. Thus, the share of protein—the main source of nutrition, has tended to gradually come down for the general population over the Plan periods. This would amount to a much greater decline in the nutritional status of the weaker sections. As we will see later, it does. That is why, the nutritional status of the people in India is amongst the lowest in the world.

Water and Sanitation

The overall access to supply of safe drinking water in rural areas has improved over the years—with the number of people getting this benefit going up from 31 per cent in 1980–81, to 78.4 per cent in 1991–92. During this period, the percentage of rural people enjoying access to sanitation increased from a low of 0.5 per cent to another low of 2.7 per cent. Such amenities were available in much greater proportion in urban areas. In simple terms, a large majority of our people in the rural as well as urban areas were forced to live under unhygienic and insanitary conditions even after the full implementation of seven Five Year Plans. And even amongst them, millions of people did not have access to safe drinking water, thus posing very serious hazards to public health.[1]

Medical Care

Availability of medical care is an important, albeit indirect indicator of the importance attached to health care in society. Availability of qualified allopathic doctors and also the availability of nursing personnel together constitute availability of medical amenities. There were 17 such doctors per 100,000 population in the country as a whole in 1950–51, which gradually increased to 47 in 1990–91. The availability of doctors in rural areas has been rather dismal—only 6.9 doctors per 100,000 population in 1960–61 and 13.8 per 100,000 population in 1980–81.

The availability of trained nursing personnel was no better. There were 5 such nurses per 100,000 population in 1950–51, going up to 32 nurses in 1989–90, in the country as a whole. For the rural population such availability was very low. Thus, there were only 4.9 such nurses for 100,000 rural population in the beginning of the Second Five Year Plan, progressing to 11 by the Fifth Five Year Plan, in 1980–81.

Basic Health Infrastructure

Availability of the number of hospital beds of all types is another important indicator of the importance attached to people's health. In 1950–51, 32 beds were available per 100,000 population which increased to 95 beds in 1990–91. The rural population, however, continued to suffer much more, with only 11 beds available per 100,000 population in 1950–51, increasing to just 17.7 in 1989–90.

Primary Health Centres

The weaker section of the population, particularly the rural population, is supposed to be served by primary health centres and rural dispensaries. There were on an average 0.22 primary health centres per 100,000 persons in rural areas in 1950–51 which increased to 3.45 in 1990–91. The number of rural dispensaries per 100,000 people increased from 1.8 in 1950–51 to 2.1 in 1988–89 and the number of rural hospitals from 0.40 to 0.49 during the same period. Despite this increase, progress on the whole has been very tardy. The foregoing profile indicates very dismal progress, *almost zero in large cases*, regarding the availability of health infrastructure and qualified medical care in the country. This was particularly so for the rural areas, where three-fourth of the country's population lived. The same is true for access to clean living conditions and safe drinking water. Under such unhealthy conditions of life, as a recent UNICEF study has shown, 2 million children out of 25 million born every year die before they reach one year of age. The majority of such deaths are caused by avoidable infections and malnutrition (UNICEF, 1993a). As can be easily anticipated under such conditions, child and mother care gets largely neglected, resulting in high infant and maternal mortality rates and in relatively lower life expectancy.[2] As discussed further in Section III, the performance of the state and its various public systems in the field of public health towards providing a dignified life to its people, as mandated by the Directive Principles of the State Policy, has left much to be desired.

Work Participation, Employment and Income

The quality of life of people is intimately linked with their income, i.e., purchasing power, in a market economy. This in turn depends on whether or not they have productive work to do. Without work/employment, most people would have no source of income, and therefore, no purchasing power. Under such conditions of life, it would become difficult for them even to survive, what to say of a dignified quality of life.

Total Labour Force

With increase in the population of the country, the total labour force (i.e., age specific labour force based on the usual status in proportion to the population aged five years and above) has also been increasing. Thus, it was 140 million in 1950–51, gradually increasing to 328.9 million in 1991–92. The Eighth Plan had projected it to increase further to 383.6 million in 1992–93 and to come down to 364.3 million by 1996–97. The rural population has continued to provide the major share of the country's total labour force—being 79.2 per cent in 1990–91. There has thus been an increase in the urban labour force from 16.5 per cent in 1970–71 to 20.8 per cent in 1990–91.

Work-Participation Rate

What proportion of the labour force has actually been involved in work? As per the census and Planning Commission estimates, 43 per cent of the total population were either main or marginal workers in 1960–61, which decreased to 34 per cent in 1970–71 and increased to 36.8 per cent in 1980–81 and further to 37.6 per cent in 1990–91. The gender bias has been obvious—with male participation rates much greater than females. The difference could also be due to the cultural bias in enumerating female work participation. Keeping this in mind, the census of India did try to sensitise the enumerators as well as the respondents in an effort to remove the gender bias in enumeration (Registrar General and Census Commissioner, 1992). It did not, however, change the situation in any substantial way during the 1981–91 period and women continued to show a lower rate of work-participation in both urban as well as rural areas. On the whole, work-participation has tended to decrease over the various Plan periods, with 43 per cent of the people participating in 1960–61 to 37.6 per cent in 1990–91. This was true for both the urban as well as rural population—and for all, i.e., both males and females. Obviously more and more people have been left without any work—not qualifying even as marginal workers.

Employment Rates

The declining trend in the rate of labour force participation is matched by an increasing trend in unemployment. Thus, it was estimated that 12 males per thousand of labour force were unemployed in 1973–74 in the rural areas which increased to 20 in 1991–92. Similarly, the rural female unemployment rose from 5 to 8 (per thousand labour force) during the same period. Urban male unemployment, which was 48 per thousand labour force in 1973–74 rose to 54 during 1978–79 and then gradually fell to 43 in 1990–91. Urban female unemployment fell from 60 to 56 per thousand of labour force during the same period. It is interesting to note here that there was greater unemployment reported among urban females than their counterparts in rural areas. On the whole, there was much greater unemployment among them during the various Plan periods with, however, some declining trend in this respect. This was not the case with the rural population where unemployment tended to increase among both males and females, with males reporting more.

Unemployment Estimates

The various estimates clearly show the massive extent of worklessness among the eligible people (age group 15+), both in urban and rural areas. Such results indicate the spectre of continuous chronic unemployment in the country. Increasing unemployment among the rural population has tended to drive people from villages to urban areas in search of work, compounding the problem there.

Different concepts and measures yield different estimates of unemployment. It is necessary to understand these as, taken together, these reveal the real nature and structure of unemployment. The following concepts narrate the scenario of unemployment in the country:

Unemployment in Usual Status: If a person was not working but was either seeking or was available for work for relatively longer time during the reference year, then it is considered unemployment on the basis of usual principal status (UPS).

Unemployment on Current Weekly Status: If a person had no work for even one hour during the week but was seeking or available for work, then it is considered unemployment on the basis of current weekly status (CWS).

Unemployment on Current Daily Status: This unemployment is in terms of total person-days of unemployment, i.e., the aggregate of all unemployed days of all persons in the labour force during the week. The current daily status (CDS) is a comprehensive measure of unemployment which includes both chronic unemployment and underemployment on a weekly basis.

Thus, unemployment, as percentage of labour force, in 1987–88 worked out to be 3.77, 4.80 and 6.09 according to UPS, CWS and CDS respectively. In absolute terms, unemployment in that year was estimated respectively at 11.53 million persons, 14.35 million persons and 6,508 million person-days according to the three levels of status (GOI, 1992b: Table 6.7 and p. 118).

Summarising the growth and structure of unemployment in the country, particularly over the 10-year period ending with 1987–88, the Eighth Five Year Plan (GOI, 1992a: 116–17) summarised it as follows (based on NSS survey for this period):

1. Employment had grown at about 2 per cent per annum during the 10-year period—about the same as the rate of growth of labour force. However, it was not possible to absorb the backlog of unemployment of about 10.8 million that existed in 1977–78.

2. During this period, i.e., 1978–88, all major sectors except agriculture, showed over 3.0 per cent growth of employment per annum. Agriculture registered a growth of only 0.92 per cent which was also the rate in the last two quinquenniums.

3. The organised sector had suffered a sharp deceleration in the rate of employment growth from 2.48 per cent during 1977–83 to 1.3 per cent during 1983 and 1987–88. Employment in the organised manufacturing sector had virtually stagnated during the latter period. Thus the unorganised manufacturing sector contributed more to the growth of employment than the organised sector.

4. Employment in organised sector was primarily contributed to by the public sector.

5. Relatively speaking, employment in the educated sector showed some growth, particularly for women.

Employment thus, somewhat shifted away from agriculture in this decade, from 71 per cent of the workers in 1977–79 engaged in agriculture and allied occupations to 64 per cent in 1987–88. Though not strictly comparable with the NSS estimate, the 1991 Census put it at 64.9 per cent for 1991. Additionally, the proportion of casual labour increased while that of self-employed decreased during this period. The share of the unorganised sector in non-agricultural employment had, thus, increased from 72 per cent in 1977–78 to 77 per cent in 1987–88. The Planning Commission, thus, came to the conclusion that a 'relatively higher growth of population and labour force had led to an increase in the volume of unemployment from one period to another' (GOI, 1992a: 119).

Employment has thus continued as a major and formidable challenge for the state and the population. The labour force is projected to increase by about 35 million during 1992–97 and by another 36 million during the ensuing period of 1997–2002. Thus, 58 million persons would require employment during 1992–97 and a staggering number of 94 million persons during the entire period of A.D 1992–2002 (GOI, Ministry of Labour, 1994c). The new economic policy and its structural adjustment programme, instead of mitigating the problem, has been contributing to further worsening of the situation. The job loss in the organised sector was unprecedented in the first three years (1991–94) of reforms. There has been a virtual stagnation in industrial employment and the pattern of investment is likely to generate further unemployment (Chapter 5).[3]

Low Productive Labour

The unemployment data tend to hide a vital fact about work in the country. The situation of invisible unemployment or under-employment forces people to take up jobs with very low levels of productivity and income. As the Planning Commission has remarked, 'the latter is a problem of much larger magnitude in India' (GOI, 1992a: 118). Persons belonging to low income households are forced to engage in any casual work even if it yields very low income. As per the Supreme Court judgements, such employment may amount to forced labour which is violative of the Fundamental Right enshrined in Article 23. Such forced labour is one of the reasons why statistical rates of unemployment in India are reportedly low, particularly when compared to the need for productive and dignified work in the country.

Income Generation

Conditions of worklessness and unemployment tend to adversely affect per capita GNP and the compounded growth in per capita income per annum (See Appendix Table 1). The per capita income per annum grew by 1.9 per cent in 1960–61 (at 1980–81 prices) and showed negative growth during 1973–74, a substantially higher negative growth in 1979–80 and again in 1991–92. Such negative growth could only lower the purchasing power of the people, particularly the weaker sections, both in urban and rural areas. Declining purchasing power of people directly lowers the quality of their life.

The Poverty Line

The depressing unemployment situation and low or negative growth in per capita income were likely to accentuate the poverty conditions in the country. Though the overall percentage of people living below the poverty line tended to fall over the plan periods, it was clear that a large number of people—ranging from 33.4 per cent to 48.7 per cent of the total population in the rural areas (as per various estimates)—lived in poor conditions in 1989–90. Comparatively speaking, the proportion of people living below the poverty line tended to be lower in urban areas as compared to the rural areas (Appendix Table 1). However, as per the estimates of the Planning Commission Expert Group, a greater proportion of people in urban areas (about 40.12 per cent) were living below the poverty line than the proportion (39.06 per cent) in rural areas. Thus the number of people living below the poverty line was 3,127.48 lakhs (2,293.96 in rural and 833.52 in urban areas) in 1987–88 (GOI, 1993a).

It is thus clear that one-half to one-third of India's population has been living below the official poverty line—many of them perpetually throughout the various Plan periods. Not only has development not helped them, but in many cases, it has adversely affected their quality of life, forcing them to live under abject and dehumanising conditions. The Planning Commission (GOI, 1992a:116) thus, came to the conclusion that the 'incidence of poverty is much higher than of unemployment and overwhelming majority of the poor are thus not apparently unemployed but are engaged for a major part of their time in some activity, albeit, at very low levels of productivity and earnings.'

The growing unemployment, lack of productive work, casualisation of labour and very poor conditions of life have retarded the quality and rate of human development in the country.

Literacy and Primary Education

Education is another very crucial indicator of social and human development. Its progress is indicated by the extent of literacy and the years of schooling of children in a given society. At the dawn of independence, the new Republic inherited a huge backlog of illiteracy in the country. Thus, only 18.3 per cent of the population was literate in 1950–51, which gradually increased to 52 per cent by 1991–92 (*Unless otherwise mentioned, for all data in this chapter, see Appendix Table 1*). Simultaneously, there has been, however, an increase in the number of illiterates in the country over the years. While the population aged seven years and above increased by about 138 million, the number of literates increased only by 120 million during 1971–81 period, thus adding 18 million to the number of illiterates (Premchand, 1993:3).

Female literacy is still a more sensitive (than the total literacy rate) index of social development. In India, it has lagged far behind male literacy. Against 27.2 per cent of the male population, only 8.9 per cent of the female population was literate in 1950–51 (Appendix Table 1). This gender difference has persisted all these years, staying at around 25 percentage points right from 1961—with 25.06 per cent in 1961 and 24.84 per cent in 1991. While male adult literacy increased to 64.2 per cent, female literacy could go only up to 39.2 per cent by 1990–91 (Premchand, 1993:3).

As per the UNESCO estimates, out of 948.1 million adult illiterates of the age 15 years and above in the world in 1990, as much as 30 per cent (280.7 million) were in India. It is noteworthy that, in the prime productive age group of 15–35 years, 97 million youth were illiterate in 1971; 110 million in 1981; and some 121 million in 1991 (Premchand, 1993:8).

As in the case of health services, the urban–rural disparity in education has also continued unabated. Such disparity has stayed around 30 percentage points all these years. The literacy rates respectively were 27.89 per cent and 60.22 per cent of rural and urban population of 5 years and above in 1971 and 44.69 and 73.1 per cent of population of 7 years and above in 1991 (Premchand, 1993:4). However, the urban–rural (and regional) difference in female literacy has further increased—with just 8 per cent in Barmer district of Rajasthan to 94 per cent in Kottayam district of Kerala (GOI, 1993a:30). Thus, the rural women have been the victims of double discrimination, first because of gender and second due to their rural status.

School Enrolment

For children to complete their primary education, it is essential that they enrol in some school (formal or non-formal) in the first place. School enrolment could thus be one broad indicator of the extent of schooling in the country. Thus, by 1991–92, 117 per cent of male children (6–11 years) and some 88 per cent of female children were enrolled in primary schools. If enrolment was the sole criterion, India could have taken the credit for almost universal elementary education. There are, however, other more dynamic factors which affect the extent and quality of schooling. So much so that only about 43 per cent children in the age group of 10–14 years (the younger ones were excluded) could be considered as literate in 1961. By 1981, this ratio had increased to about 56 per cent (Premchand, 1993: 7). The data for 1991 were then not available but the percentage could not have been very high in view of widespread illiteracy among the youth of 15–35 years, as mentioned before.

Pupil–Teacher Ratio

The pupil–teacher ratio can be considered as an index of the strength of school infrastructure, including classroom and teachers. This ratio is an indirect index of quality of education and extent of schooling of children. Interestingly, such a ratio has been uniformly increasing over the years at all school levels but more at the primary school level, where, on an average, there were as many as 42 children for one teacher in 1990–91. Such over-crowding at the elementary level would have several significant implications for both the quality and quantity of schooling. This is reflected in high school drop-out rates.

School Drop-Out Rates

The high rate of school drop-outs has been one of the most persistent maladies of the school education in the country (Mehta, 1995:25–67). As many as 65.3 per cent of boys and 75 per cent of the girls enrolled at the primary level in 1960–61 dropped out without completing school, most of them in Class 1 itself. Though the drop-out rate has tended to somewhat decrease over the years, about 46 per cent of the boys and 50 per cent of the girls dropped out without completing their primary education in 1989–90. The same situation prevailed at the middle school level where almost two in every three children dropped out without completing their full education (GOI, 1993a : 12). Such high rates of school drop-outs, therefore, rendered the enrolment data almost infructuous and misleading.

High rate of school drop-outs is indeed a very sad commentary on our school system and on the functioning of the state, which was (is) directed by the Constitution to provide universal education to all children of 6–14 years as early as 1960. Besides being a drain on meagre resources, drop-out is one of the major factors in perpetuating mass illiteracy in the country. Failures of primary education have very adversely affected the entire human development scenario, as education is a very significant correlate of health, employment and skill development.[4]

Quality of Primary Education

The quality of primary education in the country has been a subject of continuing discussion over the years. From time to time, educational surveys have revealed startling facts in this respect. Some such short-comings and failures were highlighted by the Department of Education while formulating their New Education Policy (GOI, 1986). Five years later, the Ministry of Human Resource Development reported that thousands of schools were still lacking in terms of basic facilities. Quoting the fifth All-India Education survey, it concluded that, infrastructure at the elementary school was poor and that 27 per cent of all primary schools, were held in open space. (GOI, 1990a, 1990b).

A recent survey (NCERT, 1994) has once again drawn attention to the continuing poor quality and deteriorating health of primary education in the country. Such studies, covering several districts in several states such as Assam, Haryana, Karnataka, Kerala, Madhya Pradesh, Maharashtra, Orissa and Tamil Nadu, reiterated the persisting problems such as low levels of learning, low quality of teaching and teachers, and high rate of school drop-outs. Assessment of achievement revealed low levels of learning and inadequate basic skills such as reading skills. In some districts, such as Sehore and Panna in Madhya Pradesh, not even five words could be read correctly by some children in Class 2. Further micro analysis showed that 47.6 per cent of them in Panna (Madhya Pradesh) and one-third of pupils in Sirsa (Haryana), Nanded (Maharashtra) and Karvi-Along (Assam) could not read even a single letter correctly.

Pupils (of class 2) were expected to have mastery over basic numerical skills of recognition, simple addition and subtraction. No district achieved the average score of 80 per cent in recognition of single digit, while two-third of them in Dubri in Assam, 25 per cent in Phulbani (Orissa) and

67.7 per cent in Parbhani (Maharashtra) could not do a single addition or subtraction exercise correctly. In Tamil Nadu and Kerala, only about one-third of the pupils could achieve the mastery level of learning in these basic skills.

The quality of teachers was no better than the quality of learning. Though the minimum qualification for primary school teachers is 10 years of schooling, in all the districts, except those in Kerala, Haryana and Tamil Nadu, there were a large number of unqualified teachers. More than half of the teachers had not received any in-service training during the previous 5 years in many areas. Teachers found mathematics a difficult subject to handle. A mathematics test conducted on some teachers showed that most of them could not even correctly do a question of LCM and 64 per cent could not correctly give a title to a paragraph in the language comprehension test. With the exception of Tamil Nadu and Kerala, it was widely reported that teachers did not take classes and that they did not correct the home-work regularly.

Unqualified Teachers

The situation created by recruitment of unqualified and untrained trainers was further compounded by the fact that there was practically no super-vision of their work and no guidance given to them. Only one-third of the teachers reported guidance from their head teachers and more than two-third said that there was no supervision by their block level education officers, who, in some cases, had not even visited the schools for many years. In many cases, supervisory officers themselves did not even know the location of schools under their charge. Interestingly, the officers them-selves attributed their non-visits to non-availability of TA and DA funds and/or delay in payment of such dues for years together. The quality of literacy instruction under the National Literacy Mission was also found to suffer from similar administrative problems.[5]

Quality of Overall Human Development

Thus, the progress regarding availability of basic services of health, nutrition, employment and education since Independence has not only been slow, but disappointing in several other ways, such as in terms of gender and urban–rural disparities. The performance has been much below the expectations and obligations put on the state by the Constitution of the country. It has failed miserably to provide universal elementary education, a reasonably healthy and conducive socio-economic environment, particularly regarding child and mother care, nutrition for physical and mental development of children and youth, and employment and income for the working people. Such wide gaps between what was expected of the state and what has actually been achieved (or not achieved) indicate a very disquieting human development scenario in the country.

Such non-performance in various fields of human development is dramatically highlighted when compared with the progress achieved by other similarly placed developing countries. We present a brief comparative analysis in the next section in order to underline not only our slow and disappointing performance but also shortcomings and failures in the functioning of our state organs and public systems.

III

India's Human Development in International Perspective: Comparison with Some Similar Countries

India's rank in human development was 135 among 173 countries in the world, against China's rank of 94, Malaysia's 57 and Sri Lanka's 90 (see UNDP, 1994: 129–31, Table 1). India's situation was more or less similar to that of China and some other developing countries in the late 1940s and early 1950s—the period when several developing countries emerged free from the erstwhile colonial regimes. We, therefore, get important insights about our performance by comparing it with other similarly placed developing countries such as China, South Korea, Malaysia and Sri Lanka. Where do we stand in comparison to such countries in respect to various indices of human development?[6] This comparative picture is seen in Appendix Table 2.

Life Expectancy at Birth

The life expectancy at birth of people of India has certainly improved as compared to what it was in 1950, but, when compared with that in other developing countries, it comes out as the shortest. For instance, China recorded life expectancy at birth of 70.5 years in 1992 as compared to India's 59.7 years. Similarly, Sri Lanka, Malaysia, Republic of Korea (i.e., South Korea) and several other developing countries showed life expectancy of over 70 years. Some trends in human development over the last few years in these countries are seen in Appendix Table 4. For instance, life expectancy in India was 44 years and in China 47.1 years in 1960. In a 32-year period (1960–92), we were able to improve it by 14 years whereas China showed an improvement of more than 23 years. Similarly, other developing countries like Republic of Korea and Malaysia also showed faster achievement during the same period in this regard.

Adult Literacy

Here also, several developing countries, including China, showed a much higher rate of adult literacy by 1992 as compared to India's 49.8 per cent. South Korea showed adult literacy rate of 96.8 per cent, Malaysia 80 per cent, Jamaica 98.5 per cent, Cuba 94.5 per cent and Sri Lanka 89.1 per cent. India's performance was the lowest. In fact, these countries were much more literate than India by 1970 and improved much faster. It is noteworthy for discussion of our performance that as much as one-half of India's population had continued to be submerged in illiteracy as late as in 1992.

Mean Years of Schooling

Our tardy progress is also indicated by the extent/length (in terms of mean years) of schooling obtained by the people in the country by 1992. As compared to China's average of 5 years, we were able to provide on an average only 2.4 years of schooling to our people. Several other developing countries succeeded in providing much longer years of schooling. For example, by this period, South Korea was able to provide 9.3, Malaysia 5.6, Cuba 8.0 and Sri Lanka 7.2 years of schooling. We again ended as lowest in this respect (Appendix Table 2).

Literacy and Schooling: Low Educational Attainment

It is clear that the state in India, and its various organs and public systems failed to carry out their responsibility for providing compulsory and universal elementary education. The achievement was not even near this goal. Thus, India's educational attainment[7] (as indicated by literacy and mean years of schooling or literacy index and schooling index in which the former has two-third weightage and the latter one-third) was 1.16 as compared to China's 1.93, South Korea's 2.5, Malaysia 1.97 and Sri Lanka's 2.26.

Income and Purchasing Power

The standard of living of people is shown by their purchasing power. Cross-country comparisons in this respect is rather a complex matter as economic conditions, wage levels and pricing vary from country to country. The UNDP have used the real GDP per capita PPP $, i.e., purchasing power parity dollars and the adjusted real GDP per capita (adjusted for local cost of living) to indicate standard of living in a country.[8] India's real GDP per capita (PPP $), as well as the adjusted real GDP per capita in 1991 was 1,150 as compared to adjusted real GDP per capita of 5,233 for South Korea, 5,215 for Malaysia, 2,650 for Sri Lanka and 2,946 for China (Appendix Table 2). Trends of progress (increases) over three decades in this respect are instructive (Appendix Table 4). For instance, the real GDP per capita (PPP $) for South Korea in 1960 was 690 which increased to 8,320 in 1991. During the same period, Malaysia jumped from $ 1,783 to 7,400, Sri Lanka from 1,389 to 2,650 and China from 723 to 2,946 whereas India's real GDP per capita improved only from 617 to 1,150. Though the Republic of Korea, China and India were more or less at the same level of real GDP in 1960, their economic performance in this respect, in the next three decades, was much higher. Not only did these countries progress much faster but were able to distribute the income more equitably and provide much better purchasing power to their people than India.

India's poor performance has thus placed the country much lower on the various indicators of human development (Appendix Table 3). Except for the daily calorie supply in 1989–90, we were placed towards the bottom on the various scales. As compared to several developing countries, our achievements were glaringly low—particularly regarding access to safe drinking water, infant mortality, child nutrition, adult literacy and people's purchasing power. Absence of proper public health, sanitation, literacy, elementary education and purchasing power greatly impair the sense of self and collective pride of the people. Such dismal performances put a big question mark on the functioning of the state and the related policies and management of programmes[9] (Chapter 2).

Progress in Human Development

India's dismal performance is succinctly indicated by its low progress on human development index (HDI) values over the decades since 1960, as seen in Table 1.3. In 1960, South Korea was placed at HDI of .398 and India at .206, which was more or less equal to China's and Indonesia's HDI value of .248 and .223 respectively. However, by 1992, South Korea was able to jump to the HDI value of .859, China and Indonesia respectively achieved values of .664 and .586 and we were still stuck at just .382. It is noteworthy that our human development level in 1992 was even much lower than the levels obtained by several developing countries way back in 1960.

Table 1.3
HDI Values, 1960–92, for India and Some Other Developing Countries

Countries	1960	1970	1980	1992
Republic of Korea	0.398+	0.523	0.666>	0.859
Chile	0.584	0.682	0.753>	0.843
Costa Rica	0.550	0.647	0.746>	0.848
Malaysia	0.330	0.471+	0.687	0.794
Jamaica	0.529	0.662	0.654	0.749
Sri Lanka	0.475+	0.506	0.552	0.665
China	0.248	0.372	0.475+	0.644
Indonesia	0.223	0.306	0.418+	0.586
India	0.206	0.254	0.296	0.382

Source: UNDP (1994), *Human Development Report, 1994*, Annex Table A5.3, p.105

Notes: > Country moving from medium to high human development.
+ Country moving from low to medium human development.

India's human development performance, particularly when put in an international perspective, thus raises a number of questions, regarding the nature and extent of elementary deprivation in the country. Some recent estimates identify 52 countries with a combined population of 1,685 million where the expectation of life at birth was below 60 years. Except six smaller countries with combined population of 59 million, all countries are concentrated in South Asia and Sub-Saharan Africa. Even in these countries, there are some privileged sections of population having life expectancy much above 60 years. However, nowhere else is elementary deprivation as endemic as in South Asia and Sub-Saharan Africa.

India alone accounts for more than half the combined population of the 52 deprived countries. Taking the country as a whole, it may not be the worst performer, having life expectancy very close to 60 years; However, within the country, there are wide regional variations Such disparities are highlighted when we compare the levels of infant mortality and adult illiteracy for three worst-performing countries of Sub-Saharan Africa, three worst-performing Indian States and the worst-performing districts of each of these States (Table 1.4). The districts of Ganjam in Orissa and Barmer in Rajasthan respectively come out as regions having the highest infant mortality rate and the lowest female literacy rate in the world. Each of these districts has a larger population than countries like Botswana or Namibia. Even the entire State of Uttar Pradesh, having a population as large as that of Brazil or Russia, shows worse perfor- mance in terms of female literacy rate than Sub-Saharan Africa as a whole and this cannot be much better than the least developed countries in this region.

Taking India and Sub-Saharan Africa as a whole, the two regions are not very different in terms of either adult literacy or infant mortality. Such comparisons assume greater significance in view of the fact that India has been relatively free from internal armed conflicts for the last 50 years unlike Sub-Saharan Africa where many countries have been periodically ravaged by divisive wars, famines and other calamities which make it difficult to improve living standards. The States in India have not been able to take advantage of their good fortune in escaping such calamities. If anything, social and economic inequalities are, in some respects, acute in India. These inequalities indicate the presence of some strong social and administrative tendencies which are negative to the well-being of the disadvantaged sections of the population (Chapters 2 and 3).

Persistence of endemic illiteracy thus emerged a common factor in India and Sub-Saharan Africa. Failure to achieve basic education for masses of people in India is all the more striking as it is in sharp contrast with a relatively good record in higher education—a benefit which largely goes to the elite. A failure, on the one hand, and an achievement on the other, thus work towards widening the traditional gap between the rich and the poor, between the powerful and the weak in society. Such gaps are also reflected in the widespread gender, urban–rural and regional disparities.

These comparative analyses of human development achievements show the functioning of the state in India and the behaviour of its political leadership and the civil services, i.e., the total administration, in rather an unflattering light. The dismal performance and the weak base of human development assume greater importance in view of the new market-oriented economic policies. Such economic reforms are likely to further dilute and dampen human development efforts in the country as discussed in Chapter 5.

IV

Under-Achievements and Non-Performance

India's achievement in the various fields of human development such as health, literacy and quantum of schooling for children, can be rated as only very meagre, comparing quite unfavourably with other similarly placed developing countries. Why has the state in India failed to satisfy even the basic needs of its people? Why has it also not been able to discharge obligations placed on it by the country's Constitution? In the chapters which follow, we analyse and discuss some issues relating to such questions. We discuss some aspects of the state functioning and management of programmes in Chapter 2; some historical antecedents of political processes and administrative behaviour in Chapter 3 and some structural, behavioural and policy issues in subsequent chapters. These could help us in understanding some underlying factors responsible for poor human development performance and also in suggesting an alternative development strategy for improving the situation in the country.

END NOTES

1.   Lack of proper sanitation and preventive health programmes has been demonstrated rather repeatedly and dramatically in the last few years. The outbreak of deadly epidemics like cerebral malaria, dengue, haemorrhagic fever, Japanese encephalitis and resurgence of T.B. in various parts of the country have been making headlines. About 14 million people are reported to be suffering from active tuberculosis, of whom about 1.5 million die annually. The national health management information system and surveillance of the health situation seem to have also collapsed. Newspapers have been repeatedly highlighting various aspects of the deteriorating health situation. For example, see reports in *Times of India*, September 25, 26 and 27, 1994 and also editorial comments in this newspaper on 28 and 30 September, 1994. *India Today*, October 15, 1994 carried a cover story on the plague situation. The situation has, however, continued unabated despite wide public disaffection. See reports by Kalpana Jain in *Times of India**, September 1, 1995; November 1, 1995 and 4, 5, and 6 January, 1996; an editorial comment in *Times of India*, March 30, 1996. Interestingly, the editorial laments that 'India's political elites, are singularly unconcerned about the impending catastrophy.'

2.   Government interventions towards enhancing nutrition for children and for providing some related health care measures through various schemes, like mid-day meal and integrated child development, though most urgently needed, have not been able to help children much in improving their health condition. One of the reasons is lack of attention to improving public sanitation and quality of drinking water for children.

---

*All are New Delhi editions, unless specified otherwise.

In the absense of such measures, even nutrition fails to yield the full benefit and the high infant mortality rate continues. See Shukatme (1993).

3. It has been reported in the press from time to time that the actual growth of employment tends to lag behind the targetted growth. For example, the target for generating jobs was 6.62 million per annum during the 1991–96 reform period whereas the actual employment generated was only 2.24 million per annum. For decline in employment rate, see *Times of India*, February 2 and 5, 1996.

4. The mean years of schooling and IMR have been identified as the main determinants of life expectancy. The IMR itself is influenced by mean years of schooling, literacy rate and the population–doctor ratio. The mean years of schooling emerge as the most critical variable in determining the level of human development. For a factor analytical study, see Prabhu and Sarkar (1994).

5. Poor quality of primary education has been a subject of continuing discussion in various reports of the Department of Education, Ministry of Human Resource Development. Such annual reports as well as other research reports have also been widely commented upon in the press. See, for example, *Times of India*, April 2, 1994. Another more recent report (GOI, Ministry of HRD, 1994b) reviews the quality and level of achievements obtained in primary education in various parts of the country. One of the main findings was, which is well known, that the conditions and quality of the government schools have been persistently deteriorating.

6. The UNDP revised its methodology for computing human development index (HDI) in 1994. It used 85 and 25 years as the maximum and minimum years respectively for longevity, 10 per cent to 0 for literacy and 15–0 per cent for the range of mean years of schooling for determining the respective indices. It also suggested revised approach for determining income. See UNDP (1994, Technical Note: 108–10). Also see, UNDP (1990, 1992, 1993, 1995, 1996).

7. In determining the level of educational attainment, literacy has been assigned two-third weight and mean years of schooling, the remaining one-third. Thus greater importance has been given to literacy for determining the level of educational attainment in a given country. See UNDP (1994).

8. Computation of income and estimation of correct purchasing power of people in one country is a complex question as conditions widely differ from country to country. The *Human Development Report*, 1994 takes into account the local conditions in computing such purchasing power. See UNDP (1994: 108–9) and for discussion see pp. 90–92.

9. The quality of private health care facilities like private dispensaries, etc., is very pathetic. People are forced to go there because of the poor conditions prevailing in the government hospitals. For instance, it has been reported that even bare minimum diagnostic equipments were either not available or were out of order at several important government hospitals in Delhi. See, *Times of India*, January 6, 1997. People have expressed strong resentment at the functioning of private health facilities particularly during the crisis situation as, for example, happened in case of plague in Surat and other cities. See, *Times of India*, September 27, 1994. For comments on the quality of private health care, see a piece by Jayati Ghosh, *Frontline*, December 27, 1996: 103–4.

CHAPTER 2

BEHAVIOURAL TENDENCIES IN STATE FUNCTIONING AND IN MANAGEMENT OF PROGRAMMES

Human development is essentially development of human capability. It also seeks to promote participatory skills and empowerment of people. In other words, social/human development programmes seek to actualise and maximise human potential and create conditions to enable individuals to exercise various choices (Sen, 1990, 1992a). Such programmes should, therefore, help people develop a positive self-concept including a sense of self-efficacy and self-esteem (See Chapter 4 for further discussion).

I

Adverse Impact on People's Self-Esteem

As is now well known, our human development performance in various fields has been slow and low as compared to other similarly placed countries.[1] As discussed in Chapter 1, there has been slow progress in attaining universal elementary education and full literacy and in providing adequate health and employment services which is bound to affect the self-concept of the people.[2] Such effects are likely to be accentuated at the workplace and elsewhere in view of the primacy now being given to market forces in the macro-economic policies in the country (Mehta, 1994a). People with inadequate purchasing power and skills are not able to take advantage of market opportunities. Such economic policies would, therefore, further bypass the already marginalised people. Such a situation is likely to further injure their self-concept, particularly their sense of pride and self-esteem.

Importance of Processes in Programme Implementation

Poor human development underlines the urgent need for taking a searching look at policies and at the nature and manner of state functioning and management of programmes in various social sectors. Reviewing of state functioning and various social development policies helps us understand the underlying socio-political and psychological processes in this respect and in identifying some important systemic tendencies and behavioural factors in the management and implementation of public programmes.

As has been discussed earlier, the relatively greater success in human development in countries like South Korea and Malaysia is due to their very effective implementation of various policies and programmes. The quality of economic management has been identified as one of the major achievements in South Korean transition to maturity (Esho, 1992; Leipziger, 1988a, 1988b). The same has been reported for Malaysia and Japan where state interventions were effectively implemented for enhancing the capabilities of the people. It has been noted in this connection that 'improvements in quality of life are sometimes seen simply as a result of increase in overall affluence per se. In fact, the expansion of public support might have been a crucial intermediatory' (Drèze and Sen 1989:18).

The experience of East Asian countries, therefore, suggests that it was not the interventionist strategy which was at fault in India but rather the absence of political will to formulate and push through appropriate policies coupled with the absence of flexibility within the bureaucracy in administering the system that ruined the development process. As has been shown (Kawakami, 1992), the tendency towards heavy government control in Japan was equally strong, if not more, as in India under the influence of 'socialist' policies. However, in countries like Japan and South Korea, the administration showed remarkable flexibililty and quick entrepreneurial response to constant changes unlike the bureaucracy in India.

Experience, therefore, suggests that it is not only low per capita expenditure that leads to poor outcome but the pattern of expenditure and efficiency with which programmes are implemented that are crucial in promoting human development. As is common knowledge now, despite the reported stress in the various Five Year Plans, and once again in the Eighth Five Year Plan, (GOI, 1992a), on social transformation and on development of human resources in the country, the performance on the ground has not matched such promises.

Criteria for Evaluation of Programmes

Since capability development is an important, if not the primary, goal of human and social development, it is appropriate to evaluate various development programmes and activities for their social and psychological impact in this respect. Low HDI shows that our various public policies and programmes to improve literacy, education, health, employment and income generation, skill training, etc., have not been effective in improving people's quality of life and in enhancing their capability and empowerment. The end results suggest that these have not been successful towards inculcation of a sense of personal and social efficacy and sense of self-esteem, i.e., towards the inculcation of positive self-concept and a sense of power and purpose in the people.

The individual's sense of potency, i.e., self-confident behaviour, is often the result of successful action in the social and political domain (Friedmann, 1992:34). The functioning of public systems and programmes, therefore, assumes great significance as their effects have powerful implications for the functioning of our society and the democratic polity. How far have they been able to facilitate people's participation and involvement in public affairs and motivate them for development action? Do they promote people's self-confidence in this regard? Or, do they inculcate a sense of alienation and cynicism in them? How effective and successful have our public functionaries been in enhancing people's morale and motivation and in protecting their rights and welfare? In other words, how effective have they been in discharging their Constitutional obligation?

Inadequate human development could have been due to faulty policies as well as due to ineffective and distorted implementation of the related programmes. In this chapter, we propose to take, first, a brief look at the functioning of our public policies and programmes on the ground and then at some critical systemic tendencies and behaviours manifested by public functionaries during their implementation. Such socio-psychological characteristics seem to emerge as inhibiting factors in the functioning of policies and management of programmes.

II

State Functioning in Practice

A large proportion of our people has been left behind socially and economically due to various socio-political reasons, particularly due to the pattern of age-old social organisation obtaining in the country. The Indian Constitution has, therefore, directed the state to accord preferential treatment to the marginalised people belonging mostly to lower castes and tribal groups for their socio-economic development. How far have such Constitutional guarantees and directives been implemented in the last several decades and what has been the performance of the state organs in providing conducive conditions to the oppressed people in order to enable them to lead a dignified life?

Civic Rights and Dignity of Life

Articles 15(iv) and 16(iv) of the Indian Constitution provide for protection and promotion of weaker sections like Scheduled Castes, Scheduled Tribes and Backward Classes, and for reservation of seats for them in educational institutions and in public employment. Besides these Fundamental Rights, Article 46 directs the state to protect the SCs/STs from social injustice and exploitation. Laws have, thus, been enacted, such as Protection of Civil Rights (PCR) Act of 1976, to implement various Constitutional provisions. However, implementation of such legal and other related provisions has been too ineffective, as has been brought out by various reports of the Commissioner and Commission for SCs/STs.[3]

The Untouchability (Offences) Act was enacted in 1955 to prevent and eradicate the practice of untouchability. However, out of 6,778 cases registered by the police during the 20-year period, i.e., between 1955 and 1975, in the country as a whole, only 1,779 or 26 per cent ended in conviction. Both the number of cases registered in the country as a whole and the proportion of cases resulting in conviction over this period, clearly show the failure of these legal and administrative measures in protecting the civic rights of the weaker sections and in eradicating the inhuman practice of untouchability. These continue almost unabated.[4]

The Protection of Civil Rights (PCR) Act was promulgated in 1976 after the Untouchability Act of 1955 proved totally ineffective. The new Act was targetted at eradicating untouchability totally within five years of its implementation. However, analyses of various reports of competent authorities showed that the practice was widely persistent in all states except West Bengal. Between 1977 and 1985, only a small number of cases got registered under the PCR Act with the police. Of these, a mere 62.1 per cent were *challaned*; out of which only 31 per cent were brought before any court; of which only 20 per cent cases ended up in conviction. Thus, on an average, not even in 10 per cent of the cases registered with the police in the 8-year period were the offenders convicted (Radhakrishnan, 1991). In this connection, the Commissioner for SCs and STs remarked thus, 'examination of the judgements delivered by the special courts in respect of atrocity cases revealed a high rate of acquittals' (Commissioner's Report, 1988:222).

The fact of the matter was that social atrocities on the weaker sections of our people not only continued unabated, but increased during 1981–86. Thus, the number of reported cases of murder increased from 493 in 1981 to 564 in 1986; cases of rape from 604 to 727 and for other offences from 10,434 to 11,715 during the same period (Commissioner for SCs/STs, 1988: 238). Commenting on the case of Bihar, in this connection, the Commissioner remarked, '... the administrative and political leadership in Bihar is known to be partisan as most of their members belong to higher castes and have vested interest in the status-quo'(ibid.: 250). No wonder the oppressed people continue to suffer the denial of access to wells, temples, hospitals, restaurants, barber shops and such other places in several states of the country specially in Andhra Pradesh, Bihar, Karnataka, Madhya Pradesh, Orissa, Rajasthan, Tamil Nadu and Uttar Pradesh (ibid.).

The Persisting Practice of Bonded Labour

The practice of bonded and forced labour is a glaring example of atrocities being committed on weaker sections. Bonded labourers represent the most vulnerable section of the landless agricultural labourers in the rural economy. The practice of bonded labour was abolished by the Bonded Labour System (Abolition) Act of 1976 and the state was made responsible for identifying, freeing and rehabilitating its victims. A sample survey (NLI, 1979) identified an estimated 21.7 lakh bonded labourers in the country in 1977–78. This represented about five per cent of all agricultural labourers in the country. Senior officials, however, tended to deny even the existence of such bonded labour.[5] A decade later, two lakh bonded labourers had reportedly been identified and freed, of whom only 1.6 lakhs were rehabilitated during the period ending March 31,1986.[6]

The employers have continued to deny that they had given any loans and that they had kept any person as 'bonded'. The Commissioner for SCs and STs remarked in this connection, 'what can be said about the above situation in which even today after 14 years of the enforcement of that Act, such exploitation is continuing in such an extensive area which is within the knowledge of administration.... The violation of human rights is not a matter of regret but is a matter of shame for everyone in the nation' (Commissioner of SCs/STs, 1988:80–81).

The number of bonded labourers has thus tended to increase over the years after the promulgation of the Act in 1976. As reported in the press, there were about three million bonded labourers in 1993–94. An ILO study, however, put it at 15 million of whom 5 million were adults and 10 million were children engaged in sectors like agriculture, quarrying, carpet weaving and domestic work. The traditional debtor-moneylender-cum-landlord relationship was mainly responsible for pushing these labourers into slavery. Low wages rendered it impossible to secure their release. The debt tends to increase and burden of repayment is passed on to their children. There are cases where people have to slave away to repay their grandparents' debts.[7]

The state authorities are Constitutionally responsible for the liberation and rehabilitation of bonded labourers. However, such measures are not taken by them wholeheartedly. On the other hand, labourers themselves are not aware of their rights under the Bonded Labour (Abolition) Act of 1976. Corruption deprives them of their dues. For instance, there were reports that they got only Rs 450–500 instead of Rs 6,250 for which they were entitled under the Act. The rest is paid in kind, which means a rocky piece of land or useless animals. It is no wonder that such an impoverished existence pushes them back into bondage.[8] Additionally, their children may get mortgaged as bonded labourers in various vulnerable unorganised sectors like *beedi* manufacturing (Mehta, 1983).

It is thus clear that the state and its public administration have not only been unsuccessful in eradicating untouchability and in protecting the civic and fundamental rights of the people, but also have been quite unwilling to abolish the practice of bonded and forced labour—a patently un-Constitutional and inhuman practice about which the Supreme Court has repeatedly given directives.[9] A large section of our people is thus forced to lead a life of indignity and semi-serfdom.

Agricultural and Rural Development

The intensive agricultural development strategy sought to increase productivity by improved technology and high yielding varieties of seeds. Such a strategy has resulted in enhanced income from land. However, such benefits accrue only to those who own land. Such land-owners not only get the benefits but also manage to increase their wealth without yielding any direct benefit to the landless agricultural labourers. In fact, the number of poor households increased from 30 per cent to 35 per cent during 1961–71, a period of intensive agricultural development. Such development therefore promoted further concentration of economic power in the hands of few, leaving the majority, the landless agricultural labourers, and small and marginal farmers, in a state of increased pauperisation (Kurien, 1987). The Sixth Five Year Plan (1980–85) studies showed that in 1976–77, 73 per cent of the rural people had either no land or possessed less than 2 ha of land. The remaining 20 per cent owned about 76 per cent of the land, of whom 3 per cent households owned more than one-fourth of the total land (GOI, 1980a:8).

Increasing Agricultural Labour and Poverty

Prior to the intensive agricultural development strategy, the focus was on development of infrastructure like roads, etc. This also tended to benefit not only the wealthier residents within the village but also wealthier villages and regions (Myrdal, 1968:134). Such a strategy failed to enthuse the people. The Sixth Plan, therefore, came to the conclusion that programmes over the years had achieved their objectives only partially. The bottom deciles of the rural poor, i.e., the landless and the rural artisans—the poorest in most cases—were left untouched (GOI,1980a:169).

It was, therefore, not surprising that during the periods of such development strategies, the proportion of agricultural labourers increased from 19.7 per cent to 26.2 per cent. It was clear that a large number of peasants lost their land and were pushed down on the socio-economic ladder, into the category of landless agricultural labourers. Their number increased from 31.53 million in 1961–65 to 51.6 million in 1974–75. Employment and rural earning declined and large masses of rural people—about 51 per cent fell below the poverty line as estimated in 1978–79 (GOI, 1980a:7).

It was not that benefits did not result from the various agricultural development strategies. These did result in income generation and other achievements. For instance, food production increased from 55 MMT (million metric tonne) in 1950–51 to 170 MMT in 1990. Dairy production also increased rapidly from 17 MMT in 1947–48 to 52 MMT in 1990, making India self-sufficient in this respect. Similarly, sugar production increased from 11.5 MMT to 110 MMT. Also output of tea, coffee, rubber, cotton, jute, tobacco, etc., increased during the same period. Such achievements, however, did not produce the desired impact on the lives of the rural poor. The moot point, therefore, is that all these achievements did little to benefit the large and growing mass of our rural poor and much less to enhance their capability to improve their lot in the long run (Shah, 1993).

Anti-Poverty Programme: Integrated Rural Development Programme (IRDP)

The feedback from various plans and programmes and increasing poverty and destitution led to the new policy of direct attack on poverty by replacing multiple agencies with an integrated programme. Thus, the Integrated Rural Development Programme (IRDP) came into being. This was conceived primarily as an anti-poverty programme. The IRDP was extended to all the 5,011 blocks in the country by October 2, 1982.

Subsequently, several review studies came to the conclusion that the quality and the general impact of the IRDP left much to be desired (NABARD, 1984:11). The NABARD studies confirmed the findings of other similar studies that the IRDP adopted a uniform strategy resulting in providing dairy even in drought-prone districts and that the officials insisted (against the wishes of the beneficiaries) on advancing credit on such items. The study pointed out several problems in identification of beneficiaries resulting in substantial mis-classification.

Other intensive case studies of block and district-level administration indicated several lapses in implementation of the programme. It was concluded that failure to assess the beneficiary-oriented schemes against the availability of needed resources in the area, its possible use by people other than the poor, commitment for the product in the market, persuading members to accept loans and subsidies, has led to widespread wastage and failure (Rath, 1985:234).

Other Anti-Poverty Schemes

There have been reports of massive corruption in other anti-poverty programmes like Employment Guarantee Scheme (EGS), Rural Landless Employment Guarantee Programme (RLEGP) and Jawahar Rozgar Yojana (JRY). Dantawala's simulation model of investment and income in such programmes has been widely quoted to explain this phenomenon. Thus, according to him, the spill-over effect of net injection of one rupee to rural bottom class would result in overall increase in income of Rs 1.916 in rural areas distributed in Re 0.213 to the bottom class, Re 0.520 to the middle class and Rs 1.183 to the top class (apart from the income-generation of Re 0.640 to the urban class) (Dantawala, 1987).

Field studies of JRY have tended to confirm the malfunctioning of employment-generation and anti-poverty programmes. One of the distinguishing features of JRY is that funds are released directly to the village *panchayats*, by-passing the bureaucracy. The governments have also issued detailed guidelines for functioning of the JRY in which stress has been put on associating the village community and on people's participation at all levels (GOI, 1988c, 1989). In a case study of JRY in Uttar Pradesh (Shankar, 1994), it was found that the government guidelines, particularly about people's participation were glaringly flouted by *pradhans* and other officials. It was further found that only 60 per cent of the funds were actually used and 40 per cent represented the leakage. In backward, drought-prone blocks having low agricultural productivity and very low literacy, such leakage was as high as two-third. The government directives that 60 per cent of the funds were to be used on wages and only 40 per cent on materials were nowhere followed. On the contrary, two-third of the funds were used on purchase of materials. Scant attention was given to the repair and renovation of drinking water wells, again in violation of the government directives. As per the records of the *panchayats*, on an average, 19 days of employment per worker was created. A similar finding was reported by the Planning Commission (GOI 1992b).

In view of the large-scale leakage and in absence of social control, the quality of assets thus created was not, by and large, up to the mark. The drought-prone areas continued to suffer acute water shortage. No irrigation facilities were created. Despite the importance attached to social forestry, less than 3 per cent of the expenditure was incurred on such schemes. Out of 39 *panchayats* surveyed in the case study, as many as 30 incurred no such expenditure and the remaining nine spent a total of Rs 23,453. The field investigators, therefore, nowhere found trees planted under the scheme. The interesting point to be noted here, which is very relevant to the functioning of public systems, is that the scheme was being implemented in gross violation of government directives.

The story is partly explained by the social background of the *pradhans*. Out of 39 *pradhans* surveyed, 10 were from high castes, 19 from OBC, 8 were Muslims and 1 each was from SC and ST. Asset-wise, 41 per cent of them belonged to asset category of Rs 2.5 to 5 lakhs and another 36 per cent to over Rs 5 lakh category. Thus, more than three-fourth of the *pradhans* possessed assets of about Rs five lakhs or more. Most of the *pradhans* were agriculturists, three were teachers, two were shopkeepers, one a contractor and one public worker. It was, therefore, not surprising that during the three years of the JRY in operation, *pradhans* acquired new tractors, jeeps, motorcycles, scooters, additional land and buildings (Shankar, 1994).

It was thus clear that the various anti-poverty schemes had been implemented in a distorted manner to directly benefit the rich and the implementing officials themselves. The functionaries—the administrative personnel and even the public functionaries like *pradhans*—came from the affluent and the influential section of the rural society and were able to distort the programmes. Such programmes, therefore, hardly enhanced the individual and collective capability of the marginalised people and the quality of their life continued to be poor.

Progress of Land Reforms

The successive Five Year Plans have been emphasising the need for land reforms for effective agricultural and rural development in the country. The Sixth Five Year Plan (GOI, 1980a), however, conceded that the progress of land reforms has been less than satisfactory, not due to flaws in the policy but due to indifferent implementation. Often the necessary determination to effectively undertake action has been lacking particularly in the matter of implementation of ceiling laws, consolidation of holdings and in not vigorously pursuing concealed tenancy and having vested with tenancy/occupancy rights as enjoyed under the laws (ibid.). The intensive agricultural development strategy, as mentioned earlier, in fact resulted in concentration of economic power in the hands of the few, leaving the majority, particularly the landless agricultural labourers, small and marginal farmers in increasing pauperisation. Land got concentrated in the hands of the few, as the Sixth Plan studies showed.

Increasing Landlessness and Pauperisation

In the absence of effective land reforms, the agricultural development strategy continued to favour the strong. A large number of peasants lost their land and were pushed down the socio-economic ladder as landless agricultural labourers, as discussed before.

Laws: A Mockery

As the existing laws proved ineffective, Parliament enacted a special Act in 1960 which took away the power of the judiciary to slow down the implementation of land ceiling laws. However, despite such special legal provisions, land reforms have largely failed in the country. The state has helplessly watched the administrative and political elite making a mockery of laws. As Dantawala (1987: 152) remarked, 'except Zamindary and tenancy legislation (that too in only in some States), on all India scale, the land reforms have not been effective. This is particularly true of ceiling legislation.' As Bandyopádhyay (1986) has argued, the bureaucracy tends to imbibe the dominant ethos of the state in the market economies where the propertied class has been controlling the state apparatus. It was natural that the basic laws, administrative and judiciary have been weighted in favour of the existing social order. In such a situation, the bureaucracy would develop a bias against any concerted action which aims at alteration of existing social arrangements.

Reviewing the land reforms experience in the country, Rao (1992) noted that the socio-economic context exerted a strong dampening influence on the political will and administrative efficiency with which progress of land reforms have to be formulated and implemented. The Department of Rural Development, Government of India has also identified the lack of political will as the main reason for poor implementation of land reforms. The state is not able to act against the rural rich who maintain their position through use of muscle power and manipulation of administrative and judicial processes. Such political ambivalence is matched by an administrative style where 'token' implementation and efficiency on paper are appreciated as good practices (GOI, 1988b).

Forests and Environment: Conflict between the People and the State

Forests serve a double interest in the lives of the people. On the one hand, they have a crucial ecological importance in preserving the atmosphere and in the very survival of human beings on the earth. On the other hand, their produce, including minor produce like leaves, seeds, gum, wax, dyes, resins, bamboo, cane and grass, has been the basis of livelihood and survival of people who live in and around them. It has been estimated that collection of such produce creates about two million person-years of employment (Gupta and Guleria, 1982).

The history of forest management in India has been a battle between the state and the people over the control of forests. Over the last 100 years or more, several forest Acts have been enacted from time-to-time to consolidate the position of the state and to enable it to forcibly take over all forests. Such Acts reflect, on the one hand, the state's lack of faith in the people to manage or protect their forest areas and, on the other hand, the state's tendency to give priority to commercial aspects of forests (Arora, 1994).

The genesis of the conflict lies in the enormous commercial value of forest goods and environmental services. The social forestry programme has been motivated by commercial interest. Initiated in 1970, this had incurred an expenditure of over 60 million rupees by 1988. This, however, failed to make any dent in the worsening crisis of fuel, fodder and food for the people despite huge investment.[10]

A set argument, given routinely for various programmes including the anti-poverty programme, has also been given for forest-degradation, i.e., increasing pressure on forests because of increasing population. However, it is now admitted that one of the main reasons for the worsening state of forests is the government policy itself which gave primacy to revenue in disregard of people's needs (Arora, 1994).

The primacy of commercial interest in forest policy management has been at the cost of the livelihood needs of forest dwellers. The neglect of the people's needs and their upliftment was already evident in a Fourth Plan document with emphasis on large-scale plantation of quick growing species of economic and industrial value, especially for forest-based industry (GOI, 1970 : 207). Under such a policy and commercially-oriented management, the local people were bound to get alienated. Such policies created seething discontent among the people resulting in militant movements such as the Chipko movement in Uttar Pradesh hills and the Appico movement in Karnataka (DGSM, 1982; Agarwal, 1985; Mies, 1986).

People's Participation and Joint Forest Management

The new forest policy (SPWD, 1992) recognises the value of people's participation in management of forests. However, the success of such a policy greatly depends upon the extent of empowerment of people, development of their capability to initiate and manage their affairs and enhancement of their autonomy and self-efficacy. The experience of the functioning of state policies (and legal measures) for safeguarding civic rights and dignity of weaker people, implementation of agricultural and rural development programmes and land reforms does not provide any such optimism. The policy of participation, like the schemes for release and rehabilitation of bonded labourers and the organisation of the rural poor, may itself be bureaucratised. This is indicated by the concern of the forest officials for attaining high targets in respect of formal forest protection committees. (This has resulted in formation of a large number of people's committees on paper which are in reality non-existent.) In some cases, contractors have taken up leadership in such committees (Arora, 1994). A similar situation existed in the implementation of literacy programme where also the government requires people's participation through village committees, which were either dominated by the local powerful elite or were defunct.

Adverse Impact on People's Morale

As we have noted before, although the various development programmes including agricultural development, rural development, forest and environment preservation and development, and other similar programmes generated a substantial income and some growth, they have not really benefitted the marginalised and the poor people. In the absence of effective land reforms and fair and equitable distribution of income, the economic power has unabatedly remained in the hands of the already entrenched and powerful sections in the society. Wherever land reforms have been, even partially, implemented, as in the case of West Bengal, people have gained in self-esteem and in morale (Das Gupta, 1987 cited in Rao, 1992). Success of land reforms, thus, not only enhances the sense of self-respect of the poor people but also develops in them a sense of efficacy and a belief in their own capability which, in turn, releases their energy for further empowerment. Interestingly, effective land reforms also help in energising the administration and reforming their attitudes toward the people(Bandyopadhyay,1986). On the other hand, wilful non-implementation of the Constitutional directives for land reforms and inadequate income-generation tend to damage the people's self-esteem and demoralise them.

Effective land reforms along with proper agricultural and rural development strategies, therefore, have a very important role in promoting human development of vulnerable people. The state has a Constitutional obligation in their respect. However, the above brief evaluation of the various programmes suggests that the concerned state organs and the public functionaries have not been effective in this respect. Failure on agricultural and rural development fronts would inevitably have an adverse impact on the progress of education, health and employment programmes in the country, as the following brief review indicates.

Literacy and Elementary Education Shifting of Achievement Targets

The Directive Principle contained in Article 45 of the Constitution, enjoins that 'the state shall endeavour to provide, within a period of ten years from the commencement of the Constitution, for free and compulsory education for all children until they complete the age of fourteen years'. Further, the Constitution provides for protection and promotion of the interest of the under-privileged sections of the population, making it an obligation of the state. Under Article 46, it states that, 'the state shall promote with special care the educational and economic interests of the weaker sections of the people, and in particular, of the Scheduled Castes and Scheduled Tribes ...'.

What has been the response of the state to such Constitutional directives? Following the recommendations of the Education Commission, 1964–66, the Government of India, in its statement on National Policy on Education, stated that, 'strenuous efforts shall be made for the *early* fulfilment (emphasis added) of the Directive Principle under Article 45 of the Constitution. Suitable programmes should be developed to reduce the prevailing wastage and stagnation in schools and to ensure that every child who is enrolled in school successfully completes the prescribed course' (GOI, 1966/1971: XVI). The Education Commission itself had recommended that five years of good and effective education should be provided to all children by 1975–76 and seven years of education by 1985–86. Further, it was to be ensured that no less than 80 per cent of the children entered Class I reached Class VII in a period of seven years (ibid.: 315). It was further recommended that expansion at the primary stage should be accompanied by qualitative improvement (ibid.: 316).

In addition to primary education, the Commission had recommended that, 'every possible effort should be made to eradicate illiteracy from the country as early as possible and in no part of the country, however backward, should it take more than 20 years. The national percentage of literacy should be raised to 60 by 1971 and 80 by 1976' (GOI, 1966/1971:806). The programmes, however, continued to drift and the Government of India shifted the target dates. It was restated that, Adult Education and elementary education form part of Minimum Needs Programme in the Sixth Five Year Plan. One of the objectives indicated under MNP is '100 per cent coverage of adults in the age group 15–35 years by 1990 through non-formal education' (GOI, 1984:1).

The New Education Policy, 1986

The Government of India introduced another new education policy in 1986 and it made a firm resolution that 'it should be ensured that all children who attain the age of 11 years by 1990 will have had five years of schooling or its equivalent through the non-formal stream. Likewise, by 1995 all children will be provided free and compulsory education up to 14 years of age' (GOI, 1986: 12). Following the new policy, the National Literacy Mission was launched in 1988. Its main objective was to impart functional literacy to 80 million illiterate persons in the age group 15–35 years—30 million by 1990 and additional 50 million by 1995. The functional literacy would include: 'self-reliance in numeracy and literacy; awareness about causes of deprivation and preparedness to ameliorate their conditions through organisation and participation; acquisition of economic skills to improve status and well-being and acquisition of values of national integration, conservation of environment, women's equality and acceptance of small family norms etc.' (GOI, 1988a: 14).

Education for All by A.D. 2000

The deadlines were, however, once again shifted to A.D. 2000. It was stated that a place would be ensured for every child in a school or an appropriate education programme according to his/her capabilities; disparities in access to basic education would be eliminated and that relevance and quality of basic education would be improved (GOI, 1994b: 10). Further, efforts would be made for drastic reduction in illiteracy, particularly in the 15–35 age group, in order to bring the literacy level in the age group to at least 80 per cent in each gender and for every disadvantaged group. Besides, it would be ensured that the levels of the three R's, relevant to the living and working conditions of the people (ibid.: 16) are achieved.

Thus the deadline for education for all children up to 14 years of age which was to be achieved by 1960, got shifted, for five years of education to 1975–76 and seven years of education by 1985–86; shifted further respectively to 1990 and 1995 and now, once again, has shifted to the year A.D. 2000. Similarly, the deadline for total literacy, at least for those in 15–35 age group, was shifted to 1976, then to 1990, again to 1995 and now it is set for the year A.D. 2000. It is unique for educational development in the country that the time period for fulfilment of the Constitutional directive has repeatedly been postponed.

Shortfalls in Progress

The progress of elementary education and literacy programmes has thus been quite slow in the country. The growth of literacy (percentage wise) was 10.4, 6.4, 7.1 and 8.6 for the decades 1951–61, 1961–71, 1971–81 and 1981–91. Despite some improvement in literacy rates over the various decades, the magnitude of illiteracy tended to increase because of a backlog of illiterate population over time. Thus, 241.64 million people were illiterate in 1951, 240.37 in 1961, 274.87 million in 1971, 314.15 million in 1981 and 335.85 million in 1991 (GOI, 1991a, 1991b, 1994a). The total number of illiterate people (aged seven years and above) was stated to be 320.41 million in 1993 (GOI, 1994b: 19). The drop-out rates for children continued to be as high as 47.9 per cent for Class I–V and 65.4 per cent in Class I–VIII in 1988–89 (GOI, 1993a: 12, details in Annexure Table 7).

The Elusive Goal of Education for All

The main reason for unabated mass illiteracy in the country has been the failure of elementary education. The Department of Education has noted that the need for literate population and universal education for all children in the age group 6–14 years was recognised as crucial for nation-building and was given due consideration in the Constitution as well as in successive Five Year Plans. This has resulted in manifold spatial spread of infra-structural facilities and increased coverage of various social groups, but the goal of providing basic education to all continues to be elusive (GOI, 1993a).

Our Educational Programmes

The functioning of our public education system and implementation of such programmes is in sharp contrast with the functioning of similar pro-grammes and public systems in other developing countries like China, Malaysia, Indonesia, Thailand and South Korea. The failure on this front has resulted in lack of capability in people to improve their own lives which is the main aim and measure of development. Nothing could contri-bute more directly to the achievement of this goal than education and literacy. As the World Bank has noted, improving people's confidence in their ability to create and innovate, it multiplies their opportunities for personal and social achievement (World Bank, 1991: 55–56). Thus, the failure on the front of education is a basic failure of our public systems in promoting the desired developmental capability in our people, thereby hampering their human development. The vulnerable groups of people, such as those belonging to SCs/STs and other backward sections of society, have to bear the brunt of such failures. The drop-out from school of such children has been continuously high. The rate of literacy has also been very slow and low in these groups. Females as a whole, and more if they belonged to the vulnerable social groups such as SCs/STs, have been suffering an additional handicap in this respect.[11]

Health Programmes

Like education, the health programmes in the country have also come under close scrutiny in media, academic circles as well as internationally. Taking life expectancy at birth as the overall indicator, we have been lagging behind several developing countries in Asia and elsewhere in this regard. As compared to China's life expectancy at birth of 70.5 years, Sri Lanka's 71.2, Malaysia's 70.4 and South Korea's 70.4, ours is about 60 years. A more glaring shortcoming in our health performance relates to nutrition for children, mothers and others; availability of safe drinking water; access to public sanitation as well as to medical infrastructure including doctors, nurses, etc. We have been lagging far behind developing countries in these areas. The implementation of even stated health policies and programmes has been very tardy, as repeatedly acknowledged by the Planning Commission, particularly with regard to the functioning of the programmes for health for all and primary health facilities. It has been candidly recognised that it would be difficult to provide a healthy environment to all by the year A.D. 2000.[12]

One of the devastating failures in this respect relates to preventive health and public sanitation. This was dramatically highlighted by the outbreak of plague, malaria and other deadly epidemics in several parts of the country during 1994.[13] Even the target for providing safe drinking water to all could not be fulfilled and was shifted to the end of Eighth Five Year Plan, i.e., 1997. Other similar targets have been set from time-to-time and these have not been fulfilled.[14]

Misreporting and Unused Foreign Aid

One of the interesting aspects of inadequate implementation of health programmes is a continuing tendency for misreporting. It has recently been reported that at least some such data are doctored and put out for publicity.[15] Another symptom of such gross failure in implementation of important programmes is the reported information about unused foreign aid which stood at Rs 72,945 crore by the end of August 1994. The major chunk of unused aid has been in the social sector. All assistance was project tied, therefore the poor project implementation was obviously a major factor in under-utilisation of external assistance.[16]

Failure of the Public Health Programme

Outbreak of various epidemics in 1994 have highlighted the neglect of public health, sanitation and health programmes in the country. Such epidemics indicate the continuing apathy of the concerned public functionaries as well as the policy makers regarding the vital task of providing healthy life conditions for the people in the country. Such social conditions have an adverse impact on empowerment of people (Wallerstein, 1992).

Employment and Training Programmes

The employment situation in the country has not been very encouraging in the past few years. On the contrary, it has been showing a declining trend. The gap between the growth rate of labour force and that of employment has been widening, thus increasing the total quantum of unemployment. The Planning Commission has come to the conclusion that the employment situation in the country should be a cause of worry (GOI, 1992a). The situation is likely to worsen further as a result of the new economic policies of liberalisation and privatisation (Mehta, 1994a).

Direct Interventions for Employment-Generation

As mentioned earlier, while discussing the functioning of agricultural and rural development programmes, direct interventions like IRDP and JRY, initiated specifically for generating employment in rural areas, have also not created the intended impact. In fact, despite clear guidelines and instructions of the Department of Rural Development for functioning of the JRY, local managers of the scheme seem to succeed in distorting the policy in implementation and diverting benefits to the richer sections of society, including themselves. As a result, such schemes have not been able to create any significant assets and capability in the targetted rural poor.

The experience of the functioning of these rural development and employment generation programmes serves to illustrate the fact that it is not so much the policy or the political announcement which accompany such policies, that are so crucial, as the actual implementation of the given programme on the ground. Socio-economically powerful sections of the society, which also tend to come from upper castes and the traditionally exploiting-groups, manage to divert the benefits of such programmes to themselves, thus further strengthening their economic hold over the poor. One of the inevitable results of such implementation is the continuation of unabated atrocities on the marginalised people as well as inhuman and illegal practices of forced child and bonded labour. Assertion on the part of the poor results in violent suppression of their aspirations by the influential section, often in connivance with the state apparatus, as has happened in several parts of the country.[17]

Representation in Public Services

One important aspect of the functioning of public systems is the representation of the marginalised people and vulnerable sections like SCs/STs and other backward sections in public services. As the studies conducted by various agencies including the Commissioner for SCs/STs and the Planning Commission indicate, the percentage representation of Scheduled Castes in Central Services for the period 1960–84 has been rather very small, particularly in Class I, II and Class III services. Such representation has increased only in the category of Class IV services. Thus, the proportion of Scheduled Castes in the population as a whole was 14.7 per cent in 1960 but their representation in central services in Class I, II and Class III respectively was then only 1.2 per cent, 2.5 per cent and 7.2 per cent. Interestingly, this was 17.2 per cent in Class IV Central Government employment. Some 25 years later, i.e., in 1984, the SCs accounted for 15.8 per cent of the population in the country. Their corresponding representation then in Class I, Class II, Class III and Class IV central services was respectively 6.9 per cent, 10.4 per cent, 14.0 per cent and 20.2 per cent.[18]

Such data speak volumes about the implementation of various Constitutional provisions for promoting and safeguarding the representation of socio-economically exploited categories of people like SCs in central services. The Commissioner/Commission for SCs/STs have been entrusted with the task of monitoring the implementation of such safeguards. However, they find it difficult even to get proper information from the concerned state agencies. The Commissioner for SCs/STs, remarked thus, 'Our Constitution is a beautiful document of human rights. No other system in the world is more comprehensive and liberal. But these unparalleled merits of our Constitution have not been given due attention. They have not only remained unseen, but have been violated' (Commissioner for SCs/STs, 1990:46).

It is thus clear that despite various Constitutional safeguards and policies, the marginalised people have not been able to get the required and adequate representation in public services. Such an imbalance in the state apparatus in favour of the socially and economically powerful groups may also have contributed to distorting, and, at times, slowing down of various programmes of human development.

III

Systemic and Behavioural Tendencies

The foregoing case studies of the functioning of our public programmes bring out inadequacies in our public policies and, more particularly, in the functioning of our public systems which are responsible for the related interventions. The ground level reality shows that the concerned state agencies have not been very effective in discharging their various Constitutional responsibilities. As we are more concerned here with programme implementation, it would be appropriate to discuss some factors which seem to retard their functioning and performance. The foregoing analysis of some programmes and other research studies suggest the presence of some inherent tendencies and orientations which seem to contribute to their slow and distorted progress. Discussion of such systemic tendencies and behavioural factors could help in planning interventions for improving public systems for more effective social development programmes. Let us first take a look at some systemic characteristics as revealed in review studies of social development programmes and in related research.[19]

Systemic Tendencies in Programme-Management

Number and Target Syndrome

Various development programmes stress the need for qualitative monitoring for possible mid-course corrections in a given programme. For example, the National Literacy Mission (GOI, 1988a) puts stress on such efforts for achieving the specific objectives. However, in practice, programmes invariably tend to deviate from such a strategy. Officials, both in government and non-government organisations, tend to monitor the programme in terms of numerical targets, and not in terms of quality in performance. This tendency is also seen in over-emphasis on quantitative and 'budget' reporting and in filling periodical performas. In such cases, expenditure and 'reporting' become ends in themselves (rather than means) both for the inspecting officials as well as for the field functionaries.

Such a tendency implies scant regard for quality and social impact of the given development programme. The functionaries show either inadequate understanding of the stated goals of the programme and/or they are over eager for routine activities and expenditure. They are more anxious to spend the budget rather than achieve the specified objectives. In the process, they not only distort implementation, but also tend to impose their own personal goals on the programme. On the whole, such a distinct tendency can be described *as number and target syndrome*. Many a time, this fondness for numbers and expenditure is at variance with the needs of the local community.

The Rentier-Dole and Dependency Syndromes

Most development programmes emphasise the need for linkages with other similar programmes and for teamwork in order to promote harmonious action towards fulfilment of common objectives such as development of skills and capability and promotion of people's participation. For instance, the National Literacy Mission and similar other programmes underline such a need (GOI, 1980b, 1988a). Similarly, the programme for polyvalent education, i.e., integrated progrhave amme for literacy and skill development, lays great stress on such a need. However, the officials tend to implement the given programme unilaterally. It is interesting to recall remarks of some senior Central Government bureaucrats in this connection. They put a counter question, 'Who is interested in coordinated management of development programmes? Nobody'. Some 53 per cent of the officials interviewed clearly perceived a lack of harmony in this respect (Mehta, 1989a:51). Moreover, the district administration is marked by intense inter-departmental rivalries and the public officials find it difficult to cooperate (Chaturvedi, 1988).

Years ago (Nehru, 1946/1982:295) had decried that the Indian Civil Service tended to reinforce caste-like exclusiveness and rigidity in India. Over the years, such a tendency has greatly increased rather than decreased as the ICS became the model for all-India services and other cadres. As the members enjoyed near complete security of service, with increase in the number of cadres and their intake, the service cadre system has further cemented such 'caste' divisions in the administration. Such a system retards teamwork and harmonious functioning and promotes the *tendency for centralisation*. They compete, not for performance, but, for seeking 'rent' from programmes. Such a system, on one hand, fosters (and thrives on) *rentier-dole syndrome* among the officials, and on the other, *dependency syndrome* among the people, on the other. Irrespective of the policy documents and manuals, such tendencies minimise the possibility of linkages and cooperation and maximise mistrust, one-upmanship and conflicts, all to the detriment of effective implementation of policies and programmes.

Tokenism: Lack of Interest in Processes and Performance

Guidelines for various development programmes, such as the National Literacy Mission, also emphasise the need for paying attention to various processes: teaching–learning process, managerial and administrative process, interaction process and the process of people's participation.[20] In actual practice, however, the officials and the field functionaries tend to ignore such processes. On the contrary, they show a lack of interest in processes involved in implementing a given programme. Lack of such process-sensitivity is thus an important correlate of the tendency to ignore qualitative monitoring and mid-course corrections. In most cases, the concerned functionaries lack skills for problem diagnosis and of understanding such process variables.

Over-attention to numerical targets, reluctance for qualitative monitoring and mid-course corrections and neglect of implementation processes highlight functionaries' lack of involvement in such programmes. They show just 'official' interest rather than getting actively involved in their implementation. Lack of performance and absence of desired social impact, therefore, do not bother them. Their *concern for tokenism* is much stronger than the concern for quality performance.

Lack of Integration with People's Needs

The guidelines of various programmes also stress the importance of integrating them with the needs and problems of the concerned people.[21] Such a strategy requires a creative and innovative approach, which is seldom tried. The tendency for numerical targets also comes handy in such cases as the real qualitative goals are replaced by numerical goals. The tendency to avoid mid-course corrections also reinforces such routine implementation. As field studies have repeatedly pointed out, the concerned people give insightful feedback about their needs as well as about specific problems relating to the given programme. However, the officials seldom listen to such feedback and are not able to understand the latent meaning in various problems posed by the people. As a result, they are unable to integrate their activities with the needs and problems of the concerned people. In the absence of such integration, the programmes tend to drift and the objectives are not really fulfilled.

Lack of attention to people's needs and problems and to the processes of implementation seem to be correlates of officials' *reluctance to promote people's participation* and involvement in implementing development programmes. Such reluctance is again at variance with the stated objectives. On the contrary, as mentioned above, instead of releasing people's initiative, they dampen it by strengthening their dependency behaviour. Lack of programme integration with the people's needs and problems and the tendency to exclude rather than involve people, have serious consequences for social change as these weaken people's capability, distort their self-concept and hamper the progress in human development.

Bureaucratisation of Development: Contradicting Development Activism

Development programmes have repeatedly been stressing the need for debureaucratisation of administration and for decentralised decision-making. The jobs involved in field work like conducting a literacy class, mass campaigns for health, education, etc., and in ousting alcoholism from homes have intrinsic motivational potential. The concerned field functionaries, therefore, feel challenged by such jobs.[22] However, the tendencies discussed earlier, hamper and prevent the growth of debureaucratised, decentralised and participative decision-making in practice. Ironically, lack of interest in processes and performance results in routine implementation of a programme, which in turn gets further centralised and bureaucratised. Such a situation contradicts functionaries' as well as people's need for challenging tasks at the ground level. The tendency toward bureaucratisation distorts field work and weakens its motivational potential which further lowers people's involvement in the programme. No wonder such tendencies succeed in achieving just the opposite of the stated objectives in a given programme.

Bureaucratisation of programme implementation and the tendency for centralised decision-making also contradict the growing activism among field level functionaries including volunteers and social workers. In programmes like adult education under the National Literacy Mission, volunteers and field level functionaries tend to be rewarded in terms of their own psychological development. They tend to acquire an activist orientation and also motivation for collective action.[23] Such a situation creates a contradiction between the administrative mechanism and the field functionaries' and volunteers' sense of activism.

The tendency towards bureaucratisation tends to spill over and get infused even into new organisations which are set up for promoting social development. As a result, contrary to the objective of debureaucratisation, as some case studies show, government departments tend to expand and proliferate into activities unrelated to their original mission. Instead of encouraging public participation in the policy-making process and in its implementation—important elements in the mission—they tend to move towards rigid bureaucratisation and acquire similar insensitivity to their constituencies (Sinha, 1979).

Paternalistic Manipulativeness

One of the interesting findings of various review studies of development programmes is that the field functionaries such as volunteers, honorary instructors, village-level workers, etc., show remarkable insights regarding problems and needs of programme implementation, similar to those laid down in various policy documents, although most of them were not even aware of such documents. For example, the adult education field functionaries including volunteers, most of them only marginally educated, came to the same conclusions about problems facing adult education, as were drawn by the National Literacy Mission after widespread analysis. They talked about various inhibiting factors such as social backwardness of the people; lack of political and administrative support; bureaucratisation and rigid rules and regulations; lack of seriousness among the project officials; lack of proper environment; absence of qualitative monitoring and attention to quality; lack of guidance and mid-course corrections; and lack of linkages with the needs and problems of people as well as with the project objectives.[24]

Interestingly, the field functionaries also perceived and suggested, more or less the same strategy as has been laid down in the National Literacy Mission document. Such an identity of perceptions suggested that the Mission was closer to the needs and problems as viewed by the field functionaries, as well as the people on the ground. However, in between (i.e., the Mission and the people), the officials responsible for implementing the programme, including non-government officials, were not able to internalise the programme objectives and strategies.

In the absence of such preparedness, the programme continued to be implemented in the usual routine manner. As a result, even after years of functioning, the programmes were faced with the same problems as were identified before they were launched and which the Mission set out to eliminate.[25] Such problems as were identified in the Mission document and which were later perceived by the field functionaries and the people, included: delay in delivery of materials; low credibility of monitoring; misreporting; poor quality of training; dull learning environment at the literacy centres; drop-out and relapse into illiteracy; and absence of post-literacy activities.

One of the root causes is that bureaucrats are more educated than the common people, and come from higher social strata and castes, they tend to think, almost instinctively, that they are more knowledgeable and have greater wisdom than the people. They think that the people are not only poor, but lazy, ignorant and good for nothing. 'After all, what do they know about education?' They thus tend to ignore the citizens' insights and ideas regarding public affairs along with their needs and problems. On the contrary, they persist in imposing their ideas and theories on the people and manipulate them in various ways, inducing them to accept their decisions without questioning. The social position of the public functionaries and their administrative power are thus used to reinforce self-doubts, sense of insecurity and negative self-image among the poor, further strengthening their dependency behaviour (Mehta, 1985). Such paternalistic attitudes and manipulative power inevitably result in distorting programme implementation. This is particularly true for programmes aimed at promoting people's capability, initiative and empowerment. These may, therefore, end up in creating disillusionment, resentment, cynicism and anger among them.

Dominant Tendencies and Slow Progress

The foregoing review of implementation of programmes and research studies, thus brings out certain dominant behavioural tendencies which have a negative bearing on programme effectiveness. These emerge as important inhibiting factors in the pace and quality of human development in the country.[26]

IV

Behavioural Inhibitions in Programme Implementation

All these systemic tendencies, manifested by public officials in implementing development programmes, suggest some entrenched values and behavioural orientations. These include: social status quo orientation;

authoritarian values; low concern for achievement and performance; low sensitivity to the people's needs and problems; low concern for goals and objectives of a given programme and their social impact; and high concern for their own status, power and self-interest. They tend to be manipulative of people rather than participative.[27]

The officials show a sense of complacency about their supposed competence and wisdom. The officials concern for centralisation and avoidance of community participation indicates their need for personal power and a desire to diffuse accountability and avoid responsibility. They thus show a low sense of moral and social responsibility and a low concern for social achievement.[28] Behaviourally and motivationally, they seem to be tied more strongly with the interest of the dominant social groups rather than with the interest of the common people (see Chapter 3).

Planned Interventions Needed

Despite these typical systemic tendencies and behavioural orientations manifested by our public officials in implementation of social development programmes, there are some officials and functionaries who show strong motivation and commitment to social change. They are innovative, creative and courageous in the discharge of their responsibilities. They show positive tendencies in processing various programmes, as opposed to the negative practices discussed earlier.

Such officials are sensitive to the needs and aspirations of the people and show a sense of moral and social responsibility in this respect. They have a concern for social achievement and readiness to assert for obtaining the social objectives of the given programme. They take the risk of defying the systemic tendencies and the entrenched social values and show entrepreneurship in helping people in various ways, thus facilitating human development and social change. Such public officials, are, however, the exception, rather than the rule. There is a need for planned interventions for restructuring the system in order to multiply such exceptions for vitalising public policies and programmes for better, quicker and more sustainable social and human development in the country (Chapter 7).

END NOTES

1. For details, see UNDP (1994) and other Human Development Reports. Also see EPW Research Foundation (1994).
2. Such social conditions tend to promote a chronic sense of inefficiency and a sense of helplessness resulting from the learning that one's action has no effect on one's environment. For related research, see Saligman (1975); Abrahamson et al. (1978).

3. The Commission for SCs/STs have been submitting annual reports to the President as required under Article 338 of the Constitution since 1951. In addition, there was also a Commissioner for SCs/STs for some years who has also published reports on the functioning of various Constitutional provisions for protection and development of Scheduled Castes and Scheduled Tribes. For a progress report, see Radhakrishnan (1991) and the reports of the Commissioner for Scheduled Castes and Scheduled Tribes for 1986–87 (1988) and 1987–89 (1990).

4. For review of analysis of various reports on atrocities on *Dalits* and on implementation of Civil Rights Protection Act, see Radhakrishnan (1991). Also see an article by Madhav Godbole, formerly Home Secretary to Government of India, entitled 'Crime and Punishment: Trying Times for Tribal People', *Times of India*, February 4, 1997. He concludes by saying that the conditions of tribals have worsened in post-independence India.

5. Following the survey of bonded labour in India, the National Labour Institute arranged follow-up discussions with senior officials of various states in 1978–79, in which the present author was also present. One senior official from Madhya Pradesh reported that there was only one bonded labourer in the state whereas the survey had identified a very large number.

6. For analysis of such data, see Radhakrishnan (1991).

7. For story and comments, see *Times of India*, October 12, 1994.

8. ibid.

9. For discussion of various Supreme Court judgements in this connection, see Singh (1994 : 165, 203-04).

10. For review of the functioning of various forest programmes and government's schemes including management of forests, see Arora (1994).

11. For details of the progress of literacy programmes with respect to SCs/STs, see a review by Radhakrishnan and Akila (1993). Also for review of the functioning of adult education programmes, see Mehta (1987, 1990, 1992a).

12. A Planning Commission review has come to the conclusion that, given the present status of the functioning of the health programmes, it would be difficult to cover the entire country by primary health centres by the year A.D. 2000 (GOI, 1994a). For achievements in health and medical care programmes, see EPW Research Foundation (1994, Table 1); and for bureaucratic functioning of health programmes, see D. Banerji (1992).

13. For story of outbreak of malaria, plague and other epidemics and for studies of public health and sanitation in the country, see a report in *India Today*, October 15, 1994; *Frontline*, November 18, 1994.

14. For health targets set from time-to-time, see report in *Times of India*, November 9, 1994.

15. See report in *Times of India*, October 18, 1994.

16. For details of under-utilisation of external assistance, see a report in *Times of India*, October 24, 1994.

17. For a report on atrocities on *Dalits* and increasing violence, see a story by Balagopal (1981) and a report by a Team of Researchers (1991).

18. Review of functioning of such legal safeguards for the protection of vulnerable groups regarding their education and employment, etc., a report by Radhakrishnan (1991).

19. This analysis is based on review studies sponsored by the Ministry of Human Resource Development for various programmes like Shramik Vidyapeeths, State Resource

Centres for Adult and Continuing Education, adult education projects in Rajasthan and a total literacy project in Uttar Pradesh; a study of agricultural extension, sponsored by the Ministry of Agriculture and a study of the scheme for organisation of rural poor, see Mehta (1987, 1988a, 1988b, 1990, 1991, 1992a). For some related recent studies, see Potter, 1986; Trivedi, 1994; Basu, 1992; Mukherjee, 1994; Bajaj and Sharma, 1995.

20. The National Literacy Mission and guidelines for implementing the Mission programmes lay stress on participatory training and other processes (GOI, 1988a : 28) and on managerial process and the process of implementing various activities such as training process, learning process, process of organised women and others and processes involved in organising various education committees, etc. (GOI, 1992e).

21. There has been a continuous stress on people's participation in development activities (for example, see GOI, 1979, 1980b). The National Literacy Mission noted that 'a Societal Mission depends on social mobilisation, active participation, above all potential beneficiaries, literacy workers and the whole community' (GOI, 1988a: 34). It also emphasises the need for decentralisation and functional autonomy and the need for debureucratisation in management and implementation of programmes (ibid.: 41).

22. During the field review of the functioning of adult education, although the field functionaries were critical about various aspects of programme implementation, they were positive about the usefulness and challenging nature of the adult education work. They thought the programme gave them an opportunity of working with their own people and helping them in various ways (Mehta, 1990). Thus, the nature of work contained considerable motivational potential.

23. The adult education field functionaries including instructors who were responsible for conducting adult literacy centres were found to show faith in people and a sense of political efficacy. They showed positive democratic orientation and a sense of activism. They were quite keen to get involved in various educational, developmental and motivational activities. In fact, this was one of the positive outcomes of the adult education programme. See Mehta (1990).

24. For example, the National Literacy Mission emphasises the need to make literacy a people's mission and to pose literacy as a challenge to the youth in order to release their energy and to secure people's participation, particularly women's participation in the programme (GOI, 1988a: 30). It visualises training and employment of youth as 'Activists for Education' (ibid.: 25). For review studies, see footnote 19.

25. Review studies in connection with the formulation of the National Literacy Mission reveal several pressing problems facing adult education programmes in the country. Such problems include: poor quality of training, lack of credibility in monitoring and reporting, inadequate learning environment at centres, irregular attendance and tendency to drop-out, inadequate attention to objectives like awareness, absence of post-literacy activities and lack of political will and administrative support (GOI, 1988a: 13).

26. For failure of the state to provide for justice and welfare to the people and to safeguard democratic rights, see Kothari (1993). He notes '...we also know that what has contributed to both the decline of the State as an instrument of equity and justice, of people's democratic rights and the current right wing attack on it has been its failure to implement the radical measures that it had accepted in principle but all along failed to carry out. This ranges from land reforms to the "right to work", from democratic decentralisation to workers' participation, from employment guarantee

to enabling the youth of the country to become the vanguards of national renaissance' (ibid.: 10).

27. For example, the Government of India has ratified the ILO Convention 141 concerning education and organisation of the rural poor as a national policy. In an interview study, 57 per cent of the senior Central Government bureaucrats were, however, not aware of this Convention. They thought that such a programme would hamper the growth of the economy as has been the case with the organised sector. According to them, trade unions were holding the country to ransom, encouraging laziness and indiscipline among the workers and employees and that organisation of rural workers would lead to more political conflicts. Even programmes like protection of minimum wages soon become a law-and-order problem. See Mehta (1989a: 41–45).

28. For some details regarding the concept of social achievement, see Mehta (1994c).

CHAPTER 3

GOVERNMENT, BUREAUCRACY AND HUMAN DEVELOPMENT

I

Some Historical Antecedents of Political Processes and Administrative Behaviour

The preceding chapters clearly indicate that our progress in various fields of human development leaves much to be desired. This is true not only in comparison with other similarly placed countries,[1] but within the country itself, where there are wide variations among different states. For instance, Kerala is at the top on HDI while Uttar Pradesh, Madhya Pradesh and Bihar are at the bottom.[2] The fact is that 50 per cent of the country's population has been forced to live under conditions non-conducive to human development (Chapter 1).

Why have our public officials been ineffective in implementing human development programmes and discharging their Constitutional obligation? Some inhibiting or restricting tendencies have already been identified, viz., quantitative evaluation and activity reporting; lack of readiness to learn and undertake mid-course corrections; insensitivity to people's needs and problems; and unwillingness to forge linkages among related programmes (Chapter 2).[3] These tendencies are merely the tip of the problem. There are other latent, deep-rooted and powerful social, structural, systemic and ideological factors on the one hand and motivational factors, on the other, affecting and influencing the functioning of the state, the underlying political processes and administrative behaviour. A brief look at some of them will give us a clearer picture of the problem as a whole.

1. Public functionaries show a strong preference for hierarchy and status, thus distancing their subordinates in the organisation and also alienating the citizens from developmental tasks.

2. This stands in stark contrast to countries like South Korea where the government functionaries have played a major role in enabling the common man to participate in economic growth processes (Drèze and Sen, 1989:189–97). The functionaries of India's 'socialist' state shrug away their inaction in the name of 'professional neutrality' or 'law-and-order' problems (Mehta, 1989a:42–46).[4]

3. There is an underlying fear of people's awakening and capability in public officials which makes them reluctant to support programmes for the betterment of the common man. They feel threatened by social changes which do not match their value system.[5]

4. The pursuit of self-interest, including caste and class interest leading even to abuse of official power, is a stronger motivating factor than public interest or social goals, hence the low priority accorded to improvement of the quality of life of the common man. Thus plans and programmes are distorted in implementation, creating a continuing split between policy and practice, promises and deeds.[6]

Considering that even after nearly 50 years of Independence, we have not been able to fulfill the basic Constitutional directives for a better life for our citizens, these hindering values, attitudes and motives must indeed have very strong social and systemic roots. Since administrative values and motives are learnt in society and grounded in the given social and administrative structures, it is important that we examine these roots closely and develop a connection between political and development processes, on the one hand, and related bureaucratic behaviours and tendencies, on the other. Only then will a true understanding of the same emerge and enable us to move towards achievement of goals of human development. To this end, let us briefly look at some aspects of the administrative system in Section II and its historical antecedents in Section III ahead.

II

The Administrative System

The Indian system of administration is characterised by certain typical tendencies as summarised in Table 3.1. Some of these like centralisation, secretiveness, paternalistic manipulativeness and caste-like rigidity, have been inherited from the British colonial rule along with the system itself. For a proper understanding of the functioning of our public bureaucracy, it is necessary to decode this legacy and examine the consequences of its continuation after Independence.

Table 3.1
*Systemic Tendencies at Play in the Functioning of Indian Administration**

Characteristics

1. Caste-like rigidity: Service cadre and status consciousness.
2. Centralisation: Reluctance to team and forge linkages.
3. Number and target syndrome: Neglect of quality and social impact.
4. Lack of community participation: Impersonal; avoidance of accountability.
5. Rentier-dole syndrome: Corruption; diversion of public funds.
6. Tokenism: Lack of interest and involvement.
7. Secretiveness: Reluctance to share information.
8. Paternalistic manipulativeness: Nurturing dependency in people.

*For discussion, see Chapter 2.

Legacy of the ICS

As is well known, the British established a central authority in the form of bureaucracy headed by the Indian Civil Service (ICS) to serve their various policies and to protect their interest in India. One of the principal goals of the colonial regime was to contain and control the population. They, therefore, promoted a kind of 'caste' system in civil administration and a sense of exclusiveness in the ICS and nourished a need in them for distance from the common people. The civil servants were socialised and trained not as servants of people but as 'higher caste' feudal masters.[7] No wonder the ICS became a symbol of the British imperialism and its lackeys in India.

The Indian freedom movement, therefore, kept a safe distance from civil servants, particularly those belonging to the ICS. In his autobiography, written during the freedom struggle, Jawaharlal Nehru emphasised the need for demolishing the ICS and its values. He wrote, 'no new order can be built in India so long as the spirit of the ICS pervades our administration and public service' (Nehru, 1953:282). Thus, the Indian people and the national movement greatly decried the attitudes, values and the administrative tendencies ingrained in the ICS and perceived them as impediments to national freedom and development.

Gandhi's Dictum for Public Servants

The freedom movement not only rejected the value system embodied in the ICS but also projected alternative values and motives for public servants. In keeping with the ethos of the national movement, they were expected to help build a new India. Gandhiji sought to bridge the gap between them and the people. He gave a dictum in this respect to guide and set the tone of public behaviour. He laid down his famous ground test for the public services as follows:

'I will give you a talisman, whenever you are in doubt or when the self becomes too much with you, apply the following test. Recall the face of the poorest and the weakest man whom you may have seen, and ask yourself, if the step you contemplate is going to be of any use to him. Will he gain anything by it? Will it restore his control over his own life and destiny? In other words, will it lead to Swaraja for the hungry and spiritually starving millions? Then you will find your doubt and your-self melting away' (Quoted in Haldipur, 1984:98).

Gandhiji thus sought to make the public services accountable to the people. He called upon the civil servants and others to become sensitive and responsive to the needs of the poorest of the poor. It was an attempt to inculcate a sense of inclusiveness in them and to socialise them to serve the common man.

Continuation of the ICS Frame

However, despite its strong denunciation by the national leaders, particularly Jawaharlal Nehru, the ICS continued to exist after Independence and the last of its members retired only in 1980. Not only did the ICS continue, but its successor, the Indian Administrative Service (IAS), was formed soon after Independence. Gradually, state administrative services and several other all India, central and state civil services came into existence. The IAS took over the functions of the ICS. The values associated with the 'steel-frame' continued to inform the functioning of the Indian bureaucracy. The ICS, with its administrative traditions and values, survived because its continuation did not pose any threat to the dominant classes at that time. With the political support of the ruling party, the system could block all radical administrative reforms. It could do so also because of the power which it exercised from within through members of the ICS and IAS (Potter, 1986:125–127).

People's Discontent with Bureaucracy

An interesting and dialectical aspect of the continuation of the ICS-like system and mentality was that the political leaders were also aware all along that these were not serving the interest of the public. For instance, during the first split of the Congress party towards the end of the 1960s, the role of the bureaucracy came under sharp focus and criticism. It was then mentioned that the bureaucracy, under the orthodox and conservative leadership of the ICS with its prejudices, could hardly be expected to meet the requirements of social and economic changes along the socialist line. From time-to-time, prominent leaders of the ruling party have been demanding a review of the situation and creation of an administrative cadre committed to development objectives and responsive to people's needs. They thought it was an urgent necessity.[8]

Along with some radical economic issues, reforms in bureaucracy were also posed as important themes by the ruling party at the 1971 Lok Sabha elections, which yielded them rich electoral dividend. The electoral behaviour clearly suggested these as the felt needs of the people who wanted not only radical economic and social policies but also reforms in administration (Mehta, 1975). Issues pertaining to the functioning of various policies and programmes and administrative behaviour of government officials along with the conduct of political functionaries have not only continued to sway the electoral mind and voting but now tend to cause significant difference in the structure of Parliament and the government. This was indicated by the results of the Assembly elections held in 1994 and 1995, first in the two southern States of Andhra Pradesh and Karnataka and later in some other States and by the Lok Sabha elections held in 1996.[9]

Supremacy of the IAS

The people's felt needs and their discontent with government functioning expressed from election to election, have not led to any perceptible change in the structure of administration. Despite the political rhetoric of the elite in this respect from time to time, the ICS-like bureaucratic set-up has not only continued, but has got further strengthened as seen in the manifold growth of government departments. The number of secretariat departments was 18 in 1947 which increased to 25 in 1957, 51 in 1953 and 71 in 1985 (Third Pay Commission, 1973:86).

The Central Secretariat of the Government of India was manned by 878 officers of the rank of Deputy Secretary and above in 1984. Of these, 378 or 43 per cent belonged to the IAS. The remaining posts were held by members belonging to several other services including Indian Audit and Accounts Service (IA&AS), Indian Revenue Service (IRS), Indian Police Service (IPS), Indian Railway Accounts Service (IRAS), Central Secretariat Service (CSS) and others. The post of Joint Secretary is the lowest level of the senior management cadre. The Joint Secretary in charge of a particular wing is expected to function more or less as Secretary, submitting papers directly to the Minister from whom the orders emanate. The Secretary is generally responsible for the functioning of the Ministry as a whole. The importance of the IAS can be understood by the fact that, out of the total of 192 Joint Secretaries in 1984, 135 (i.e., 70.3 per cent) belonged to the IAS. There were 61 Secretaries and 66 Additional Secretaries of whom 36 (or 59 per cent) and 27 (or 41 per cent) respectively belonged to the IAS (Fourth Central Pay Commission, 1986:114).

Shaping of Bureaucratic Ethos

Continuing the legacy of the ICS, the IAS now occupies a pre-eminent and powerful position in civil services at all levels and in all parts of the country. For example, in 1983, 27 per cent of members of the IAS were posted in district administration, 40 per cent in state governments, 13 per cent with state or central public enterprises, 14 per cent with the Government of India and 6 per cent elsewhere. Such a dispersal of their positions give them a wide network of power and influence over the entire Indian administrative set-up. They occupy most of the Secretaryships, not only in the Central Government departments, but also in the states. Their political power is reflected in the crucial position which the District Collector occupies, a post which is invariably occupied by an IAS member. The Collector's post gives them direct link with political activities and manipulation at the district level (Potter, 1986:212–217, 229).

The IAS has thus, emerged at the apex of the civil services. Members of the IAS occupied most, i.e., 62 per cent, of the senior management posts at the headquarters of the Government of India in 1984. Moreover, roughly 75 per cent of the IAS officers work in various states and the rest on deputation to other posts including those in the Government of India. From their powerful position in the organisation of civil services, they shape and set the tone of bureaucratic ethos and functioning of the public systems in the country (Mehta, 1989a).

The Social Background of Bureaucracy

As may be expected, the Indian members of the ICS of the British regime came from the urban intelligentsia, *zamindar* and other dominant groups, particularly those who were the early recipients of western education with the benefit of knowledge of English. Their social position and *zamindari* background eminently suited the requirements of British rule. Like their forerunners, most of the IAS officers also come from dominant social groups having access to English-medium education, with stress on respect for authority and discipline, character-building, leadership qualities and good manners. During the 1980s, members of the IAS came largely from the highly educated service class. During 1980–81, 71 per cent were recruited from this class, 19 per cent from agriculture and the rest from other categories (S.N. Singh, 1982). They were, therefore, not representative of the wider society as the middle class was not even 10 per cent of the India's workforce.

The Hierarchical Structure

The ICS tradition makes it easier for civil servants to talk about concepts like 'unity', 'stability' and 'neutrality' and 'law and order' rather than to face problems requiring innovativeness, specialised expertise and responsiveness to local demands (Potter, 1986). No wonder they tend to show a strong tendency to justify their performance, a sense of complacency and a lack of sensitiveness to people. Their social background contributes to promoting a thought pattern in support of the social status quo and the privileged section of the society, thus creating a sense of discontent among the common people. Such an allegiance, however, serves their self-interest and helps satisfy their need for status. The centralised and hierarchical structure of administration creates a 'caste' hierarchy and consciousness of 'cadres' in the organisation of the civil services, concentrating powers at the top and taking away initiative from the field officials.

III

Some Historical and Social Antecedents of Systemic Behaviour

The British system of administration was set up, and it functioned, not in a vacuum, but in the context of social organisation then prevailing in the country and in pursuit of colonial power and interests. In this respect, they borrowed and adapted some social and administrative practices from the earlier regimes, notably the Mughal period. As the British established themselves in India, first as merchants and then as colonial rulers, they were historically confronted by the then dominant social, political and administrative classes. Such interactions contributed to their system of administration in various ways. It would, therefore, be useful to identify some such historical antecedents in this regard. It would help us to understand the meaning of the persistence of the ICS-like administrative system, (despite people's discontent) and the contemporary political-cum-bureaucratic behaviours, administrative tendencies and practices as manifested in state functioning.

The British policy of permanent settlement in Bengal, the *ryotwari* system in the presidencies of Madras and Bombay and other related policies created seething discontent among the people and turbulence both in rural and urban areas. The emergence of new cities like Calcutta, Bombay and Madras created a wealthy industrial and commercial class, a small middle class and a large industrial working class. The professional middle class of lawyers, doctors, etc., provided volatile material for political movements in the late 19th and 20th centuries. The emerging protest against the British was partly rooted in the system of land control and revenue administration which they inherited from the Mughal period and partly in the growing urban industrial and middle classes.

Zamindar-Dominated Administration under the Mughal Empire

Prior to the arrival of British colonial rule in India, i.e., during the Mughal period, the administrative and political superstructure was based on the system of land control at the local level. Studies undertaken in this connection, in different parts of India, have revealed as to who controlled the land and who appropriated what portion of the agricultural produce. The various types of landed interests and the system of administration which then existed, evolved over centuries. By the 7th century, all officers, high or low, came to be remunerated by allotment of revenue of land. Such arrangements tended to become hereditary and set permanently over particular territories. The *bhogikas* (administrative officers) have been represented as exacting unpaid labour from peasants including women. The official, thus, appears as having land of his own and enjoying semi-feudal rights over the peasantry. By the 12th century, a pyramidal structure in agrarian relations had already evolved. During the period of the Delhi Sultanate (1206–1526), agrarian exploitation was further intensified with intense concentration of resources (Habib, 1974 : 264–84).

This process was further accelerated during the Mughal period when several categories of *zamindars* came into existence. Though these categories were not exclusive, they served varying functions and enjoyed different rights and privileges. Thus there were autonomous chieftains who functioned under various imperial regulations and controlled large areas of land. They helped the empire in promoting peace, trade, commerce, and industry and in maintaining security.

There were intermediary *zamindars* who formed the backbone of the land revenue and law-and-order administration. In return, they enjoyed revenue-free land, commissions, share in revenue, etc. This category of administrative officials included *chaudharies, desmukhs, desais, despandes*, certain types of *mugaddhams, kanungos, ijaradars* and *talukdars*. The entire country was practically under some kind of intermediary *zamindar*-cum-administrative officials who were supposed to realise land revenue, help develop agriculture and assist in maintaining law and order. However, in actual practice, they were constantly struggling to enhance their own privileges and to appropriate to themselves a greater and greater share of the revenue (Hasan, 1969/1979:24–27).

Below chieftains and the intermediary *zamindars* were the primary *zamindars* who held proprietary rights over land. They were peasant proprietors who cultivated land themselves as well as with the help of hired labour. They were sandwitched between the bigger *zamindars* and the state, on the one hand, and the peasantry, on the other. On many occasions, they led revolts of the peasantry against the growing exactions of the state, often utilising the caste and clan appeal (ibid.: 27–28).

The intermediary village *zamindars* came from higher castes enjoying higher social status. They were Brahmins or *Bhumihars* or *Rajputs* or *Pathans* who controlled land and paid dues to the state. The primary *zamindars* or proprietary peasants came from the cultivating castes like *Jats* in north India who owned land on a modest scale. Most cultivation was, however, left to the socially lowly placed labouring castes of *Kurmies, Ahirs* or *Chamars*. The various categories of people engaged in agriculture were thus linked with the ties of subordination and superordination and the *varna–jati* scheme (Hasan, 1973). The *zamindars*, on the one hand, tried a variety of methods to reduce their dues to the state and, on the other, subjected the lowly placed villagers to the most gross forms of exploitation (Kumar, 1986:67–86).

Inner Contradictions: Manipulative Politics and Protest

The *zamindars*-cum-administrative officials and the imperial government were, therefore, partners in economic exploitation of the labouring people. However, they were also in constant struggle with each other because of their inner contradictions. The *zamindars* engineered revolts against the 'state' from time to time. Such revolts were motivated largely by self-interest, i.e., their need to retain and improve their own wealth, power and status. Thus the administrative officials, responsible for revenue collection and maintenance of order for the state, were themselves involved, at the same time, in protest and in manipulative politics against the state.

Along with the protests of the village *zamindars*, the cultivating classes, like *Jats* and *Kunbis* also revolted against the state from time-to-time, particularly during the later Mughal period. Though the Mughal empire offered greater stability, the property relationship gave rise to a number of contradictions which were the real source of the political crises of the Mughal empire (Habib, 1974:315). Apart from political mismanagement of the later emperors and crisis in the *jagirdari* system, peasant uprisings led by *Jats* and *Kunbis* played an important role in the breakdown of the Mughal empire (Habib, 1963). It should, however, be noted that although there was a difference in the popular content, there was no difference in the ideological orientation in the protest of the village *zamindars* and those led by the cultivating castes/classes (Kumar, 1986:78). Both the groups were motivated by a desire to retain and expand their power vis-à-vis the state and over the labouring people.

Zamindars and the British

The *zamindars* continued to sway the village society during the British regime. During the early period of this regime, *zamindars*, whether new or old, appeared to have been exercising greater authority than under the Mughals. The pivot of this was the new regime's large revenue demand (Habib, 1974.:316). However, here also, the main cause of their conflict with the government was the same—revenue. They were habituated to using various methods to get their revenue burden reduced. At times, some of them were declared defaulters as they failed to pay their public revenue. In such cases, their estates were auctioned off to the highest bidder who got the *zamindari* rights and also the obligation to pay the government revenue. However, the 'dispossessed' *rajas* and *zamindars* who 'lost' their land between 1795 and 1885 'retained their position economically, politically and socially, within the local areas in which they had held rights as *zamindars*' (Cohn, 1969/1979:89). For example, most of the *Rajputs*, whose *zamindari* rights were sold, continued to live as they lived before in their villages and *talukas*, dominating the lower caste cultivators and offering sustained and, at times, effective opposition to auction purchases. It did not seem important to the lower caste cultivators or landless workers whether the traditionally dominant *Rajput* was a *zamindar* or an ex-*zamindar* or a tenant. A popular adage, as put by a person of a lower caste—which held good both in the 19th and 20th centuries—runs thus: 'Living in a village with *Rajputs* is like living under a thorn bush' (ibid.: 112). This expresses the uneasy power relationship between the lower labouring castes and the dominant higher caste *zamindars*-cum-administrative officials throughout these centuries. It underlines that the labouring classes and castes, such as the *Chamars*, were very unhappy with the exploitative, manipulative and coercive acts of *zamindars*/officials. They were, however, not able to articulate such feelings, subjected as they were to the principle of subordination and superordination.

Due to their traditionally higher social status, the *zamindars* retained their social power even when they were dispossessed of the *zamindari* rights. However, because of the inner contradictions in the system, the *zamindars* as well as the cultivating classes, including the administrative officials, came in conflict with the centralised power (whether the Mughals or the British), from time to time, on issues primarily related to revenue collection.

Traditional Methods of Village and People-Management

The foregoing discussion shows that land relations in India were an integral part of the power play in society. It has therefore, been suggested that 'the Indian view of land was political' (Neale, 1969/1979:7). In addition to the structural dimension of this power play, the land-related and *zamindar* dominated administrative system was marked by a notable behavioural characteristic, i.e., the manipulation of people. The *zamindars* were not so much interested in raising agricultural production, as in managing the village, i.e., managing people by manipulating the rules of hierarchy (ibid.: 12).

Record Keeping; Falsification of Information: Management by Deceit and Cunning

The various administrative functionaries, as mentioned before, thus played a crucial role in political management. *Patwaries* in north India and *Karnams* in south India, for example, came to occupy strategic positions in such a manipulative political system. They were responsible for keeping land records for the purpose of land revenue, etc. This function was vitally important in the lives of cultivators, tenants and the labouring people. Such officials were, however, notorious in keeping unreliable and false records. In the game of politics, such corruption became a powerful instrument in the ongoing system of village management (Neale, 1969/ 1979:15). Falsification of records and village accounts, cunning and such other methods of deceit were important elements in political manage-ment which characterised the behaviour of the officials on the ground, during the pre-British as well as the British periods.

Subversion: The Political Behaviour of
Zamindars-cum-Officials

It is interesting to note here that the officials combined in themselves multiple roles. They were the traditional village leaders because of their higher castes or higher social status; economic and political leaders be-cause of their control over land; and administrative leaders because of their official positions. Playing their roles skillfully, they were able to influence and/or distort the decisions of the imperial power. Under their leadership, the dominant local agrarian forces were able to enrich them-selves at the cost of the centralised imperial structure. The political method of such local powerful groups was almost like the corrosive 'white ant' which could subvert and undermine the strength of the imperial structure from within (Frykenberg, 1969/1979b).

Administrative Processes of Power

Thus, the power of *zamindar*-cum-administrative class flowed primarily from their control over land. Such control over land had, however, to be managed by weakening the 'centralised' regime or the state, on the one hand, and by controlling and ruling the labouring people, on the other. For such tasks, they used the administrative processes of Manipulation, Information Control, Corruption and Subversion to constantly enhance their own income and power. They used these processes to divert public revenue to themselves as well as to fleece the labouring classes.

Local Power and Influence Upwards:
Monopolising Skills and Knowledge

Another feature of the above administrative processes and political beha-viour, which is important for the present discussion, is that the locally powerful *zamindars* and the administrative officials, i.e., those entrenched at the village and *kasba* (district) levels, were able to exercise immense influence upwards in the centralist imperial machinery. As the case studies of traditional processes of power in south India during the pre-British and early British periods show, such political behaviour was also primarily administrative in character. Some dominant castes came to acquire knowledge of village finances and skills of maintaining land records and village accounts which they guarded like sacred secrets and strictly preserved their monopoly in this respect. With the emergence of the British, a dominant Brahmin caste came to acquire monopoly over knowledge of English language. They had family links with *zamindars* within the district (Guntur in Andhra Pradesh) and similar Brahmin families throughout south India. They thus dominated the administration, resisted government policies, corrupted successive British officers and used every trick of deception to enrich themselves. The corrupting influence of villages spread into the hierarchy of power (Frykenberg, 1969/1979a: 218–225, 228).

Impact of Administrative Process on Labouring People: The Beggared Population

In addition to using administrative processes, as mentioned above, the ruling class came to use all kinds of oppressive means to extract more and more revenue from land and from people engaged in other occupations, but more particularly from land, as it was the main source of income and wealth. Thus, during the late 18th century, the hunger for revenue assumed pathological proportions resulting in perpetual military action against and robbery of the beggared population who were treated as conquered hostiles with no rights whatsoever. Peasants were oppressed for porterage and for unpaid camp labour (Kosambi, 1956/1975: 386–87).

As a result of such coercively manipulative administrative processes, the plight of the labouring classes deteriorated. Kosambi has quoted George A Grierson (from his Notes on the district of Gaya, 1893) as reporting that 'all persons of the labouring classes and 10 per cent of the cultivating and artisan classes may be considered as insufficiently clothed or insufficiently fed or both. This would make about 45 per cent of the population of the district or to use round numbers, a million people. The poorest classes cannot indulge in a (full) meal, even in the most prosperous localities and seasons, more than once or twice a week' (Kosambi, 1956/1975: 388).

Kosambi remarks in this connection, 'the people described in the Gaya district at the end of the 19th century, were not worse off than for several centuries preceding. The British had fixed land tenure and taxes by permanent settlements, perpetuating the misery' (Kosambi, 1956/1975: 388).

The dominant classes, including *zamindars* and the administrative officials, constantly used a variety of methods to enrich and empower themselves mostly at the cost of the labouring people who became poorer and poorer and more and more disempowered. Thus, the gap between the officials and the population—economic and social—and the psychological distance between the two tended to increase more and more. The latter were distanced at the receiving end with the former behaving like masters.

The King's Bureaucracy: The Political Nature of Administrative Processes

For our discussion of political and administrative behaviour in India since Independence, it is important to understand that, traditionally, those associated with state governance, political and administrative personnel, formed an integral part of the ruling class rather than merely being a tool of the class. The highly developed Brahminical ideological framework served to legitimise the hierarchical social order and the powers of the kings and the officials. Thus the administrative officials were conditioned, over time, to 'lord' over the labouring people. Their attitudes and values got ingrained in the ongoing socio-political culture. 'The king's bureaucracy' as Habib (1974:287) has remarked, 'thereby became the principal exploiting class in the society'.

An important characteristic of this bureaucracy was the political nature of their various administrative processes and methods, as summarised in Table 3.2. These were designed to manipulate and manage villages and to collect revenue for the state and for themselves. Their main motivation was, however, personal power and self-aggrandisement and to enhance their influence over the local people and upwards in the ruling hierarchy. Towards such goals, as discussed above, they used a variety of methods, (ideological and psychological) such as: manipulation of people, control over information, corruption and subversion of the system and coercion. They were very manipulative and secretive about their skills in order to maintain their monopoly over knowledge.

The Power of Social Learning

Force and other coercive methods were not enough, in some cases not even functional, to keep the common working people under control. Ideas governing the rules of hierarchy, roles of subordination and superordination, the rules of purity and pollution were equally, if not more powerful

Table 3.2
The King's Bureaucracy: Administrative Processes and Methods of People-Management

Tasks	Motivation	Administrative/Political Processes and Methods
Revenue collection	Power (self-aggrandisement, exploit, control and rule labouring people)	Manipulation; deceipt
Village and People-management	Influence upwards	Information control (falsification of accounts); corruption and subversion; secretive and monopolistic about skills and knowledge; coercion, forced labour; invoking rules of hierarchy

in this respect. Such principles were, however, patently unequal and their acceptance and enforcement required some sort of ideological socialisation of the parties concerned. Such socialisation promoted social learning of the desired self-images and self-concepts. An understanding of such processes of social learning is important for discussion of human development, particularly for the inculcation of capability, self-esteem and self-efficacy, i.e., a positive self-concept. Let us, therefore, take a brief look at some aspects of historical background of such social theorising and learning.

IV

Social Theorising and Learning of Images and Self-Concepts

Self-Image: An Intervening Variable

The civil services in independent India, as discussed in Section II, have not only inherited the legacy of the Indian Civil Service, but have also kept up the image of 'steel frame' of the colonial rulers. Recruited largely, as they tend to be, from the urban intelligentsia, and to some extent from landed-interest groups, they have imbibed values of the ruling class. The various motivational tendencies, seem to be associated with a pattern of thoughts and self-image as rulers.[10] Such a self-concept in public functionaries tends to come down to them as part of the administrative culture—nurtured and reinforced by processes of socialisation, including family rearing, education, training and the structure and culture of their cadre and service itself.[11] As a part of this inheritance, they seem to have been culturally conditioned by values, needs, administrative processes and methods, as discussed in Section III and summarised in Table 3.2. The administrative tendencies and managerial behaviour could, thus be described as dependent variables with various historical, social and structural factors as independent variables. In between, public functionaries' self-image along with values and motivation (Section I) work as intervening variables, activating various behaviours and tendencies.

However, state officials' self-image as 'rulers' can remain functional only, when the dominated classes, at the same time, acquire and internalise self-image as 'ruled', i.e., an inferior, subordinate self-image. Such a relationship between the 'dominators' and the 'dominated' between *raja* (state officials) and *praja* (the people), i.e., the *mai-baap* (paternal) political culture, remains alive only till the latter remain under the sway of the ideological framework of the dominant social groups. Social motivation and roles are not innate but are socially learned and acquired. These can, therefore, be weakened, strengthened, trained and manipulated. This explains the importance of planned efforts at, and socialisation for, inculcating the desired values, images and self-concepts.

The Interlocking Roles of Subordination and Superordination

A look at society in India from the late Vedic period to the middle of first millennium A.D., as brought to us by the scholarly perceptions and the historians of the time, shows the importance of social theorising informing the roles of subordination and superordination. With the growth of the iron industry, agriculture became the dominant economic activity which, in turn, shaped the social and political institutions of the then society. The surplus generated by agriculture sustained the dominant social groups who were otherwise not directly involved in cultivation. This led to the consolidation of two orders of society, the Brahmins and *Kshatriyas*, on the one hand, and the *Vis* and other labouring classes, on the other. The *Kshatriyas* established control over the *Vis* and the Brahmins upheld the political authority of the former. This brought into being the human relationship of subordination and superordination between different classes. Simultaneously, the religious ideology of *dharma*, a subtle principle, maintained order in the moral and material world. The concept of *dharma* was reinforced by the post-Vedic notion of transmigration of soul based on the doctrines of *karma* and of the cycle of birth and rebirth consisting of *sansar*. Thus, the three principles of *dharma, karma* and *sansar* determined the moral and material parameters of human existence according to the classical Indian philosophy.

The above parameters of human existence can be understood only in the context of social, economic and political organisation of contemporary society. There was a close relationship between the social reality and intellectual beliefs which established the right of the *Kshatriya* and the Brahmin to appropriate the surplus produced by the cultivators. There was a brutal frankness in the literature of the period. For example, 'nobility is the feeder and the people are the food', states the *Satpatha Brahmana*.

Thus the social organisation in ancient India was based on social differentiation between the rulers and the ruled. The theory of *karma* rationalised it and the concept of *dharma* contained social frustration and tamed social rebelliousness by tying each member of the society. The doctrine promotes the notion that the society and the entire universe 'rested upon the complementary and inter-locking roles of different social orders sanctioned and sanctified by *dharma*' (Kumar, 1986: 117–131, 125, 126).

Law-Makers' Interest in Philosophical Matters

It is interesting here to note the excessive interest of the law-makers in philosophical matters pertaining to social learning, i.e., toward learning of self-concepts as 'subordinates', 'ruled', 'inferior', and 'impure', among the labouring people. This is one of the peculiarities of the Indian cultural situation that philosophical subjects were brought into the daily lives of the common people. This was because the law-makers realised the importance of an ideological weapon for policing the state. This is akin to putting external brute force into the minds of men in order to control them internally and mentally. Plato in his *Republic*, while discussing the problems of keeping the working masses under control, has recommended free use of what he called the 'beneficial falsehood' or 'noble lies'. Plato admired such cultural, philosophical and superstitious devices which enabled the rulers to keep the masses under control. Similarly, discussing the policing function of Indian philosophical thought, Chattopadhyaya remarks, 'the law-makers realised that it was not enough to enforce on the people their basic behaviour pattern with the age-old provision of police and prison, the task became comparatively easier if moreover was enforced a definite thinking pattern on them' (Chattopadhyaya, 1989: 120). The law-makers, therefore, decreed that transgression of the *Vedas* was a punishable offence and they prohibited logic, uninhibited reasoning and argumentation. People were not allowed to raise inconvenient questions as these would make them rebellious. Manu decreed, 'one must not even speak with the heretics (*nastika-s*), the transgressors of caste discipline, the hypocrites, the logicians (*haituka-s*), the double dealers' (ibid.: 117–118, 120, 121). The law-makers' decrees were, thus, loud and clear: no questioning, no thinking, just do your duty, i.e., your *dharma*. Your *karma* has destined you to a life of a low caste.[12]

Inducing Inferior Self-Concept

Along with the social theorisation, the dominant classes initiated several other measures in ancient India to socially and psychologically downgrade the image of the labouring classes such as *Shudras*, craftsmen and other categories of common people, and all women. For example, *Shudras* and women were prohibited from reading the *Vedas*. The law books decreed that the social status of women was equivalent to that of *Shudras*. *Manusmriti* defines the duties of the wife as follows: 'She should do nothing independently even in her own house. In her childhood subject to her father, in youth to her husband and when husband is dead, to her sons. She should not ever enjoy independence' (Basham, 1990 : 104). Such decrees promoted extreme gender discrimination against women. Its disastrous consequences can be seen even today as indicated by higher infant mortality rate among girl children and very low rate of literacy among women in general and among the labouring people belonging to Scheduled Castes and Scheduled Tribes in particular.

Discrimination in Social and Commercial Life

The law books further institutionalised discrimination against *Shudras* in day-to-day commercial and economic life. For example, the *Manusmriti* stipulated differential rates of interest for different categories of borrowers according to the order of their caste. Thus, a Brahmin could be charged 24 per cent rate of interest, a *Kshatriya* 36 per cent, *Vaisya* 48 per cent and the *Shudra* 60 per cent. Kosambi makes a telling remark in this connection, 'not the risk of venture (as in *Arthashastra*) but the birth-status of debtor could determine the rate of interest. This meant in particular, a specially heavy load upon the poorest cultivators, every time the harvest failed to yield enough for the whole year. When compound interest crept into the picture, this led to creation of a perpetually indebted working class, which substituted for the classical slave and feudal-serf of Europe' (Kosambi, 1956/1975:254–55).

Contempt for Physical Labour and Craft Skills: The Impure Occupations

The traditional law codes also showed explicit contempt for physical labour. Manu commanded that even when compelled to follow the profession of *Vaisya* (third class), the Brahmin and *Kshatriya* must avoid agriculture as it was considered slavish (*paradhina*). This concept changed later as material conditions changed when Brahmins allowed themselves to engage in agriculture. However, *Manusmriti* clearly projects the contempt of the higher castes for those engaged in manual occupations. It is significant for our discussion of administrative behaviour and human development to note that 'numerous names of low castes arise from the occupation they followed. For example, there are *Ayaskara* (blacksmith); *Kumbhakara* (potter); *Charmkara* (leather worker); *Taksan* (mason); *Talika* (oil worker); *Nata* (dancer); *Rathkara* (cart maker); *Vena* (worker on reeds) etc.' (Chattopadhyaya, 1990:101). All such occupations were labelled as socially inferior. Such attitudes of the dominant classes down-graded the social status of crafts, directly contributing to formation of the assigned negative self-image among the labouring people.[13]

Pure and Polluted Occupations

The labouring people—the producing classes—were expected to multiply social goods because the ruling classes thrived only on the fruits of the former's labour. The rulers were, however, not willing to contribute in any manner to the actual process of production. With the coming of agriculture, land became very important and a new social theorisation became necessary. The Brahmin authors justified the theory of royal ownership of land, on the one hand, and on the other, launched efforts to legitimise forced unpaid labour and to delegitimise all essential physical labour as 'impure' occupation. This made exploitation of the polluted peasants and craftsmen easier by the 'pure' landlords (Nandi, 1986:15–17). These twin principles (i.e., the concepts of royal ownership of land and 'impure' occupation) and the related social processes further down-graded the social image and status of the labouring people, and at the same time enhanced the image of the dominant classes, thus reinforcing the acquisition of the respective reciprocal self-concepts.[14]

Manusmriti *and the Epics: Mass Internalisation of Subordination*

The epics *Mahabharata* and *Ramayana* have great popularity and mass appeal even today in the Indian subcontinent. They convey the message of the ultimate victory of good over evil. They, however, convey other messages too, as these contain several direct quotations from *Manusmriti* and numerous instructions similar to those found in the law books (Basham, 1990:102). One of the important features of the *Bhagavad Gita* is its sturdy defence of the four classes. 'It is better', says Krishna, 'to perform one's own duty, however badly, than to do another's well. It is better to die engaged in one's own duty, the duty of other men is dangerous' (ibid.). The word for duty is *dharam* and the poet has in mind the respective *dharmas* of four classes. This verse is repeated with variations elsewhere in the *Bhagavad Gita* and in *dharamashastras*, literature of a somewhat later time (ibid.: 94).

These epics have been, and are, even now, immensely powerful. Besides being great means of mass education and entertainment, these have worked as very effective means of socialising people for various social roles informed by principles of hierarchy, subordination and superordination. Because of their mass appeal, these epics also serve to reinforce and further strengthen various social beliefs, images and rituals.[15]

Feudal 'Blindness' to Crafts and Technical Skills

The dominant classes' self-image as 'rulers' and 'pure' and the assigned negative image of the labouring classes as 'inferior' and 'impure' have produced disastrous effects on scientific and technical development in the country. This was manifested in the feudal society which failed to use available technical skills. As craftsmanship was essential for the very survival of society, it continued to exist along with, and despite, the contempt of the ruling classes. Such craftsmanship was available in plenty in medieval India, as several contemporary commentators have testified, but the ruling classes were too contemptuous to see that their own advantage lay in development of such skills. For example, 'plastic surgery began with the camp barbers in India who could make a new nose by making viable graft out of the skin of the forehead; potters set bones in hard earthern casts; the forerunner of modern plaster casts but the modern doctors went on studying the books of Avicenna and Vagbhata' (Kosambi, 1956/1975: 398). Such feudal attitudes toward craftsmen and their creative work have resulted in far-reaching adverse consequences not only for social development and quality of life of the craftsmen but also for development of technical capability and scientific temper in the country.

People's Negative Self-Image: The 'Colonisers' and the 'Colonised'

The self-image of administrative officials as 'rulers' and superior and that of the labouring people as 'subjects' and inferior created a continuing social and psychological distance between the dominant classes and the common working people. Such social conditions were utilised by the British to further strengthen such images in order to impose and induce people to internalise the 'colonial' self-image. Nehru notes in this connection: 'the feudal landlords and their kind who came from England to rule over India, had the landlord's view of the world.... The British Government of India then became the landlords (or landlords' agents).... The millions of people who lived in India were some kind of landlords' tenants who had to pay their rents and cesses and to keep their place in the natural feudal order' (Nehru, 1946/1982:292).

The British could not have ruled India without the 'acquiescence of a large majority and active support of atleast a sizeable and influential minority of their subjects'. They used 'force, cunning, a subtle exploitation and creation of divisions among Indians....' Above all, they used 'a powerful and plausible ideological legitimation of their rule'. They took a pedagogical approach to India and acted not as 'masters but as head-masters'; 'Indians were not their subjects but pupils'. They sought to educate the Indian people (Parekh, 1989:25–26).

The people were, thus, persuaded to believe that 'nothing about us is commendable.... We are beginning to believe it because we hear it everyday...' (Bankim Chatterjee quoted in Parekh, 1989:28). Indians' 'self-esteem came to be integrally tied up with their historical performance as a people or race'. They were called upon to justify themselves and their achievements were judged by the rulers against the criteria drawn from their civilisation. 'They often did not satisfy such alien criteria and developed self-pity, self-hatred and excessive, even morbid, spirit of self-criticism' (ibid.: 29).

Due to inner contradictions of colonialism, the British could not sustain their rationalism. After 1857, they propped up feudal kingdoms and landed interests, supported their legitimising ideology and culture, promoted *dharamashastras* almost as civic code and gave *Pandits* unusual amount of power. Thus, 'the colonial bureaucracy and the Brahmins struck up a sinister and complementary relationship'. (Parekh, 1989:31).

Many Indian leaders including some Presidents of the Indian National Congress in the late 19th century, also thought of the British encounter in pedagogical terms. Thus, they thought of the British rule as 'an opportunity to turn the corner', and the 'greatest gift of providence to India'. Like their rulers, they also thought that 'Indians needed to improve themselves', 'sit at the feet of their rulers' and 'learn' skills and virtues necessary for their regeneration. The British were perceived as 'wise gurus' and 'good teachers', giving them useful 'political training'. (Parekh, 1989:44–57).

Thus the British used not only the sword but also an ideology to supplement it. They brainwashed Indians to think that they were inferior to their rulers. Their active cooptation of the various feudal classes and the landed interests and support to their legitimising ideology created layers of tormentors and exploiters for the population. Their economic and social life greatly worsened under such conditions. Discussing helplessness of people and nationalism versus imperialism, Nehru wrote, 'We seemed to be helpless in the grip of some all-powerful monster; our limbs were paralysed; our minds deadened'. He describes the psychological climate then prevailing in the country in the following terms: 'The dominant impulse in India under the British rule was that of fear—pervasive, oppressing, strangling fear; fear of army, the police, the widespread secret service; fear of the official class; fear of laws meant to suppress and of prison; fear of the landlord's agent; fear of money-lender; fear of unemployment and starvation, which was always on the threshold' (Nehru, 1946/1982:357–358). Thus, the image of colonisers as 'superior' and that of the colonised as 'inferior', 'lazy', 'pupils' were sought to be formed rather doggedly. Ideology and force went hand-in-hand to impose and induce people to learn and internalise a negative self-image.[16]

Gandhiji's Movement: Liberating the Mind from Fear

The freedom movement, under Gandhiji's magnetic leadership, sought to break Indians' negative self-image of helpless and 'conquered' people. The appeal of the nationalist movement was so strong and pervasive and the anger against the alien rule so intense that millions of people were drawn to the freedom struggle, as never before. Gandhiji provided, as Nehru put it, 'a powerful current of fresh air that made us stretch and take deep breaths'. He was 'like a whirlwind that upset many things, but most of all the working of people's minds' (Nehru, 1946/1982:358).

During the freedom movement, efforts were also initiated to articulate demands of the poor and to mobilise both urban and rural workers under the leadership of All India Trade Union Congress and the All India Kisan Sabha and other similar organisations. Various political groups and parties started raising voice against exploitation and for equality. A radical leadership arose in the Indian National Congress itself to speak and struggle for the under-privileged people. Such struggles were part of the national movement which gave a new identity and a sense of self-esteem to the under-privileged people. The vast masses of people, including educated middle class, industrial workers, landless agricultural labourers, craftsmen and small peasants, thus inculcated a vision of an independent India. Gandhiji nourished this vision of new life and of *Swaraja* for the hungry and spiritually starving millions. The movement thus gave a new meaning to the dominated people and contributed toward development of positive and hopeful sense of self-confidence.

Internal Subjugation Vs Internal Capability

Thus the ruling classes in the medieval and Mughal periods, and closer to our times in the British period, used various methods from time to time to internally subjugate the labouring people and the 'colonised' people as a whole. Such a social process is always reciprocal as, on the one hand, it seeks to promote a self-image as 'superior' among the dominant classes and, on the other, a negative self-image as 'inferior' among the rest of the society, particularly among the socio-economically weaker sections. Social theorising and philosophical and pedagogical methods are used to justify and legitimise the superior image of the dominant classes and to inculcate feelings of inferiority and a sense of helplessness among the people.

Development of internal capability, i.e., a sense of self-esteem, self-efficacy and self-worth, are dialectically antithetical to the theorising for internal subjugation. Therefore, as suggested by Sen (1992b), capability is the right thing to look at when judging how well a person's life is going. Social equality is important for capability development and for development of self-esteem (Sen, 1992a). However, there are situations where inequality of esteem is sustained by explicitly inegalitarian ideology which assigns people to different categories of quality or being (Cohen, 1993:2159). We are not talking here about inequality of esteem associated with differentials in achievements, not even about inequality of esteem derived from differences of income and wealth. Instead, we are talking about planned inequality of esteem, associated with self-concepts and self-images as discussed above. The Indian Constitution seeks to remove such an inequality by outlawing untouchability, by promoting affirmative action and by directing the state to provide suitable environment for social and human development. And, it is precisely this that our public functionaries including civil servants have not been able to achieve in full, not even in substantial measure.

V

Impact of Historical Factors and Political Culture on Functioning of Administration

As discussed already, there are powerful historical antecedents which seem to contribute to promoting political processes, administrative tendencies and bureaucratic behaviours, on the one hand, and dependency behaviours among the people, on the other. The principle of superordination and subordination and self-image as 'rulers' seems to have thus, been infused into our public systems.

Administrative Values and Attitudes: Land Reforms as the Test

As control of land has played a crucial role in the formation of political and administrative processes, the current status of land reforms can be used as a test of the strength of the socio-historical and systemic factors and their impact on the present administrative values and tendencies. Implementation of land reforms also serves to illustrate the strength of the interaction of the traditional social organisation with our administrative system in this regard. The Parliament and the government had initiated a number of policies including land reforms, soon after Independence to bring about qualitative transformation of the social relations in our rural areas. As is well known, such policies and programmes have not been functioning well. A report on 'The Cause and Nature of Current Agrarian Tensions' by the Ministry of Home Affairs confirms the inadequacy and low performance in this respect. After reviewing several studies, it concludes that the existing social conditions compel the discontented elements to organise themselves, leading to an 'explosion'. It makes an interesting comment on the functioning of administration in this connection. It says, 'the administration of tenancy legislation has been left to civil servants who often lack both the qualifications and the *integrity neces-sary for the job* and are overburdened with responsibilities' (emphasis added; Ministry of Home Affairs, 1986:39). It concludes that 'inequalities in land holdings have persisted because of the failure to implement ceiling laws. As for the sharecropper and the landless labourers, they have been, more often than not, left out in the cold' (ibid.: 40).

Society, which was in turbulence during the late Mughal as well as the British periods, is thus, once again in turmoil. There is a qualitative and ideological difference, though, in the nature and content of the rural people's protests then and now. In the earlier periods, such protests were articulated and led, many a time, by the *zamindars*, who were angered by the coercive policies of the British rule and were motivated by their de-sire to reduce and /or all together eliminate their revenue burden. Thus, *zamindars* and cultivators responded positively to Gandhiji's call for *satya-grahas* during the freedom struggle. For example, moneylenders, business-men and landlords took the initiative and actively participated in the *Champaran Satyagraha*. Similarly, at Bardoli in Surat district of Gujarat, *patidars* —the dominant cultivating class, actively and successfully parti-cipated in the no tax campaign and the *satyagraha* there. Such struggles did very little to alleviate the suffering of the labouring class, for example, the lowly *Kaliparaj* at Bardoli (Kumar, 1986:81–85). Such protests have con-tinued since Independence where rich peasants and landed interests have been demanding various benefits from the state from time to time.

Agricultural workers, small farmers and other labouring classes have been now protesting against their conditions of life and the treatment meted out to them by the rich peasants, the *zamindar* class and the state. Such people, who happen to come mostly from the traditionally exploited lower castes and from the exploited section of Muslim and other commu-nities, tend now to protest, more frequently and stridently, against their masters, the landlords and/or rich peasants, who control land as well as the political power. Such rural struggles are motivated by day-to-day hard-ships, social indignities and by a desire for a equitable and just society.[17]

The need for land reforms for enabling the tenants/tillers to gain con-trol over their lives, has been repeatedly emphasised both before and after Independence. The failure of egalitarian land reforms shows not only the lack of political will but also bureaucracy's indifference, reluctance and connivance in this regard. On the contrary, they perceive and define people's struggle for land and for their unity and organisation, in this respect, as law-and-order problems. They thus tend to work in favour of the entrenched landed interest.[18]

The administration of land reforms also mirrors the importance of socio-historical and systemic factors and, the intervening variables of values and motivation. Taken together, the political processes, administrative tendencies and bureaucratic behaviours tend to suggest an interesting psychological profile of our public functionaries. Let us briefly summarise such a profile which could help us to plan measures for redesigning and revitalising our public systems for humane and people-centred development.

Psychological Profile of Public Functionaries

Various research studies reveal, generally, a sense of dissatisfaction and indifference among officials toward social development work. Such indifference is visible more at the lower and middle levels of bureaucracy. However, more interesting for our present discussion of administrative behaviour is the nature of their political orientation. They tend to show a significant sense of political efficacy as well as readiness to accept the prevailing political culture. Thus, at the workplace, they may feel like 'outsiders', as far as implementation of human development programmes like education and public health are concerned, but in the wider socio-political culture, they feel more like 'insiders'.

The same officials also show, as mentioned above, a strong tendency to justify functioning and poor performance in poverty alleviation, health, education and such other programmes. It is not their posting as such but the prevailing politico-administrative structure which seems to shape such values and behaviour. Their political behaviour reflects the prevailing political environment and functioning of our administration, particularly at the implementation level. Interestingly, for understanding of both politics and administration, the greater the tendency to identify with the prevailing political culture, greater is the tendency to accept poor 'development' performance as satisfactory.

Not only were such civil servants not bothered by the poor quality of performance, they also considered themselves as sufficiently trained, competent and equipped for handling various social development jobs. Their feeling of being active 'insiders' in the ruling political culture instilled a sense of complacency in them. Their incentives seemed to come not from helping people and from such performance, but from the rent-seeking wider socio-political system, i.e., the reigning regime. Thus, the motivation for people-welfare was the lowest when and where it was needed the most (Mehta, 1989a: 133–150).

Psychological Expression of Political Culture

The foregoing profile is exemplified by district administration which was conceived by the British Government as the strongest unit of their administrative design. From time to time, political and government leaders have been voicing their concern about such a system of administration. Various government committees (for example, GOI, 1985) have been stressing the need to reorganise the administrative structure with radical departure from the feudal and colonial structure. The district-level administrators are not only unable to cooperate with each other (Chaturvedi, 1988) but are known for their traditional paternalistic attitude for the citizens (Panandikar and Kshirsagar, 1978) and for their ineffectiveness and corrupt practices (Mukherjee, 1985, 1993).

For our discussion of administrative behaviour, it is important to note that these tendencies of civil servants are essentially political in nature. The historical factor of their being members of the ruling class not only continues to hold, but is quite visible at the district and block levels. Also at these levels, their behaviour more clearly (than at higher levels) reflects the values and norms of the prevailing political functioning. They are not interested so much in improving development performance as in collaborating with the entrenched dominant classes in manipulating and 'ruling' the local population. Their caste-like rigidity; their tendency to exclude people from programmes; tendency to justify poor performance; sense of complacency and unwillingness to learn and apply corrections; their number and target syndrome and unwillingness to work for quality and social impact; the rentier-dole syndrome; their secretiveness and manipulativeness, are all correlates of the prevailing 'feudal' type political and administrative culture.

Since our present system of administration has inherited several dimensions of the systems prevailing during the Mughal and British periods, and as the same or similar administrative culture has continued, it is not surprising that the present day civil servants behave not as servants of the people but as their rulers. Gandhiji's talisman of 'Swaraja for the hungry and spiritually starving millions' has long been forgotten and the oppressive and authoritarian culture of the revenue-extracting and maintenance departments seem to have become universal. Their day-to-day behaviour and tendencies only reinforce the argument that the administrative class is more a ruling class than a serving class. This is strikingly illustrated by continuation of the practice of untouchability and by the fact that the state functionaries have not been able to enforce the related social laws effectively (Chapter 2).

Another interesting correlate of the fact that the civil servants behave not only as agents but as members of the ruling class is that the dominant classes who control industrial production and agriculture themselves behave rather cautiously with the bureaucracy. They try to get their work done through *pyravee* or through social and cultural links or through bribes or threats. Corruption has thus emerged as an integral part of our administrative and political culture (Hargopal, 1994).

Human Development and Administrative System: A Dialectical Situation

There is a negative correlation between the political will of the state for implementing social and human development programmes and its readiness to impose its will and policies on the turbulent people. Such law-and-order tasks require the continuation of a centralised administrative system, hence the political support for maintaining the powerful position of the IAS and for continuation of the ICS mentality. Social development programmes, therefore, present a dialectical situation before the public functionaries. They are required to implement programmes whose effectiveness lies in disturbing the entrenched social order. However, their psychological profile, as evolved over the years, pull them toward the contrary. The objective (material) as well as subjective (power, status) incentives, that are built into the social and administrative systems thus motivate them to distort and/or slow down human development policies and programmes.

The functioning and structure of bureaucracy and behaviours of political and administrative functionaries, are all interrelated. Given such a centralised, hierarchical and feudal-like system, and the accompanying social values, motivation and tendencies, it is no wonder that the state has not been able to fulfill the Constitutional directives for a dignified and healthy environment for capability development and empowerment of the long deprived people, who constitute the majority of the Indian population. We need to understand and deal with the powerful legacy of our socio-cultural and historical antecedents and the systemic factors along with the dependent psychological profile of our public functionaries in order to promote effective and more sustainable social and human development in the country (Chapter 7).

END NOTES

1. See UNDP (1994:108, 129–131). Also see UNDP (1990, 1992, 1993, 1995, 1996); EPW Research Foundation (1994).
2. Various state governments have pursued human development strategies with varying intensity. For some related data, see Prabhu (1994). Similarly, school drop-out rate is much higher in some states, such as in Hindi-speaking states than some other States. In this connection, the CAG has expressed serious concern about implementation of Operation Blackboard and non-formal education schemes as well as about functioning of the District Institutes of Education and Training (DIETs); for a report, see *Times of India*, April 2, 1995.
3. Such behavioural and administrative tendencies are revealed in reviews of the functioning of several social development programmes. Similarly, reviewing development planning and experience in several countries, in a wider and somewhat different context, a United Nations Committee came to the conclusion that plan-implementation depends on requisite capabilities and motivation, which were not present in many cases, and not just on economic factors (Wasterston, 1965).
4. Comparative method of analysing performance in various development fields helps us to understand the history of a specific country. As Moore (1967) has remarked, 'In the effort to understand the history of a specific country a comparative perspective can lead to asking very useful and sometimes new questions. There are further advantages. Comparisons can serve as rough negative check on accepted historical explanations. And a comparative approach can lead to new historical explanation.' (p. xiii); Chenery and Syrqruin (1975) after analysing pattern of development over 1950–70 period has noted that 'Inter country comparisons play an essential part in understanding the processes of economic and social development. To generalise from historical experience of a single country, we must compare it in same way to that of other countries. Through such comparisons, uniform features of development can be identified and alternative hypotheses as to their causes tested' (p. 3).
5. Increasing education, awareness and assertion among the traditionally marginalised *dalits* threaten age-old hegemony of the dominant castes. Such awareness is perceived as an audacity and angers them who feel greatly insecure. In such emerging conflicts, religious leaders tend to side with the dominant caste. For a paradigm of conflict between human development of *dalits* and the economically and politically powerful dominant caste-class, see a case study by Pinto (1995).
6. Several scholars have commented on the administrative behaviour in this connection. La Palombara (1963) has commented that the public order in India, steeped in the tradition of the ICS, may be less useful as developmental entrepreneurs than those who are not so rigidly tied to notions of bureaucratic status, hierarchy, and impartiality' (p. 12). See also Trilok Singh (1963); Braibanti (1966); Higginbotham (1975).
7. MacMillan (1986) has narrated several interesting experiences and made insightful comments about the social situation prevailing during the Raj. She has described how, in everyday situations arising out of a caste society during colonial rule, the British 'picked up' the notion that number of servants was a measure of status. The British housewives were expected to control and supervise servants. The presence of servants made it easy for them to be formal while the need to uphold dignity of the Raj made it desirable (p. 146).

8. For example, two young 'turk' leaders of the ruling Congress party, namely, Chandra Shekhar and Mohan Dharia submitted a note on basic economic issues to the All India Congress Committee. In this note, they remarked that 'the present bureaucracy under the orthodox and conservative leadership of the ICS with its class prejudice can hardly be expected to meet the requirements of social and economic change along the socialist lines. Creation of administrative cadre committed to national objectives and responsive to our needs, is an urgent necessity' (*Hindustan Times*, 1 December, 1969). Later in his address as Congress President, Jagjivan Ram also referred to the lack of commitment in bureaucracy in India. (*Hindustan Times*, 31 December, 1969). Also see Pranjape for discussion of this bureaucratic inheritance (Pranjape, 1966).

9. For analysis of issues at elections in various States including Andhra Pradesh, Karnataka and Bihar, held in late 1994 and early 1995, see a cover story in *Frontline*, December 30, 1994; another story in *Frontline*, 21 April, 1995; and cover story in *India Today*, April 30, 1995; also a piece titled 'Ways of Neglect: Economics of Congress Defeat' by Praful Bidwai, *Times of India*, New Delhi, 24 March, 1995. Never before so many farmers, backward class and State leaders found place in the Lok Sabha as in the 1996 general elections. See a cover story on the 'Changing Face of Parliament', *India Today*, July 15, 1996, 37–39.

10. Mandelbaum (1972) has suggested that, in addition to other characteristics of a dominant caste, 'self-image as rulers' is an important attribute (p. 359).

11. Motivation is acquired socially through child-rearing, socialisation and other practices. Achievement and influence motives can, therefore, be developed by planned education and training programmes. For theory of motive acquisition see McClelland (1965) and for experimental motivation training programme in industry, see McClelland and Winter (1969) and in education, see Mehta (1969, 1976).

12. Illich (1981) has made an interesting comment in this regard. 'Labelling people keeps them in their place, decreases social mobility and increases social control. Tribal people who hardly have any needs will turn into "beggars" who begin to expect some thing because they are poor' (p. 70).

13. Elias and Scotson (1965) have drawn our attention to the learning process of the inculcation of negative self-image. Definition of oneself held by the adversary is taken over as the self-image. Self-doubts, based on a realistic assessment of the power of adversaries, contribute to this learning process. Doubts about oneself and low self-esteem are thus internalised.

14. De remarks, 'Such a situation was merely the base to rearing an elaborate superstructural ideology of the hierarchy of ritual purity, kinship regulation, occupational rigidities, discriminatory inequalities relating to housing in the village outskirts, job opportunities, the lowered status of artisans vis-à-vis traders and of traders vis-à-vis clerics and warriors, all of which adds up to false consciousness of the caste system....' (De, 1978 : 491).

15. Commenting on the strength of magical rites and rituals, Chattopadhyaya (1978 : 240–41) has remarked that these cannot have a direct effect on nature, but these can and do have an appreciable effect on the performers themselves. Inspired by the belief that it will bring into being the desired reality, the performers proceed to the task with greater confidence and with greater energy. It changes their subjective attitude to reality and so indirectly it changes reality. Originally, rituals were connected with man's struggle with nature, but on being uprooted from their original context, these became tools and a technique in man's struggle against man.

16. Based on library work and study of the images of the Malayas, Filipino and Javanese from the 16th to 20th century, Alatas (1977) exposes the myth of the lazy native. Such descriptions serve the ideology of colonial capitalism.
17. For stories of such agrarian struggles, see T.K. Banerjee; NLI Report; Kala et al.; Sengupta; Sengupta et al.; Iyer and Maharaj; Breman; Krishnaji; Mies; Kashtakari Sangathan; Talib; Iyer and Vidyasagar; Singh; Banerji; Mitter; and Sarkar—all in Desai (1986). Also see Chapter 6 here for further discussion.
18. For analysis of attitudes of senior bureaucrats towards people's struggle for land reforms and for workers' organisation, see Mehta (1989a: 39–46). For attitude toward violence perpetrated by the dominant classes on the labouring classes, see reports by Team of Researcher (1991); Balagopal (1991).

CHAPTER 4

GOALS OF HUMAN DEVELOPMENT: NEED FOR STRUCTURAL AND BEHAVIOURAL CHANGES

One of the primary goals of human development is to promote capability in people for various socio-political and economic affairs (Chapter 1). A citizen's feeling that he is competent to follow the functioning of government, politics and other civic affairs shows his/her sense of subjective competence. Such a psychological resource is a significant facilitating factor in people's efforts for improving their well-being and in their organisation and collective action in this regard. Such feelings of being competent and capable, weaken the traditional negative self-concept and dependency behaviour (Chapter 3). Such a sense of efficacy, therefore, forms an important element in the process of people's empowerment. Thus, the state and its various agencies were and are obliged to create a suitable and healthy socio-economic environment to enable all citizens to enlarge their capabilities and to put these to best use in various fields—economic, social, cultural and political.

I

Under-Achievement

Ground Realities: Need for Acceleration

It is now 50 years since the nation made a tryst with destiny and its leaders made promises for a better life for long deprived people. It is glaringly clear that the actual performance has been much below the expectations and that people's hopes have been rudely belied. For instance, though the population's life-expectancy at birth has increased since Independence, the status of nutrition continues to show an alarming situation. The availability of foodgrains through public distribution system (PDS) has decreased significantly over the years, particularly in the case of pulses. As a result, the nutritional status of the people in the country is amongst the lowest in the world. For want of proper drinking water, sanitary conditions, nutrition and such other basic necessities, two million children out of every 22 million children born every year die before they reach the age of one (Chapter 1).[1]

The country has long been suffering from chronic unemployment. A large number of people, particularly in the agricultural and rural sector, languish almost permanently without any dignified work. In recent years, the growth of employment in the organised sector has also slowed down, accompanied by increasing casualisation of labour. The official unemployment data hide invisible unemployment and under-employment which force the people to take up any kind of work, even forced and bonded labour, just in order to survive. This has fuelled increasing incidence of child labour, including bonded and mortgaged child labour. It is the country's utmost shame that even after 50 years of Independence, four out of every ten people, if not more, are forced to exist below the official poverty line (Chapter 1).

Failure in the field of primary education with high school drop-out rates has kept the rate of literacy lagging behind the rate of growth in population. Like the people themselves, thousands of schools also lack basic amenities like classrooms, drinking water, toilets, blackboards and even teachers. Till recently, about 27 per cent primary schools were forced to function in open space (GOI, 1990b). Female literacy has tended to persistently lag behind male literacy in all Plan periods by about 25 percentage points. In addition to gender disparity, the rural–urban disparity in literacy has not only continued but has tended to persist around 30 percentage points. The quality of the country's vast human resources obviously leaves much to be desired.

This dismal progress of social development, clearly brings out the fact that the state in India has failed not only to provide universal elementary education but even a basic socio-economic environment for its citizens. These low social achievements become more glaring in comparison with achievements of similarly placed other developing countries. In fact, countries like China, Malaysia, Sri Lanka, South Korea and Cuba had succeeded in attaining a much higher literacy rate as far back as in 1970 than the level attained by us by 1992. By this time, India was able to provide only an average of 2.4 years of schooling to its citizens against the benchmark laid down by Article 45 of the Constitution for free and universal education for all children up to the age of 14 years. This goal should have been achieved by early January 1960. The grimness of this colossal failure can be easily understood when we find that by this time, i.e., 1992, South Korea was able to provide 9.3, Malaysia 5.6, China 8.0 and Sri Lanka 9.2 mean years of schooling for their respective people (Chapters 1 and 2).

Though the quality of human development is important per se, it is also a very significant facilitating factor in economic development, as evidenced by purchasing power of the people. This is shown by the economic progress achieved by South Korea, China, Malaysia and Sri Lanka which were more or less at the same level of people's purchasing power as India in 1960. In the next 30 years, these countries were, however, able to improve it drama-tically. For example, South Korea's real GDP per capita (PPP$) of 690 (in 1960) increased to 8,320 by 1991; Malaysia jumped from 1983 to 7,400; Sri Lanka from 1,389 to 2,650 and China from 723 to 2,496. During the same period, India's real GDP per capita improved from 617 to just 1,150 (UNDP, 1994 : 90–92, 108–109, Appendix Table 4).

The inescapable conclusion is that the state in India, represented by the government at the centre, its political and bureaucratic leadership and its various organs and agencies, entrusted with the task of ensuring welfare of its people, has not discharged its duties adequately and effectively. The nature and amount of budgetary provisions accorded to primary educa-tion, health and other areas of human development are indicative of the values and priorities of the state. However, in our case, it is not only the inadequacy of funds per se, but, more importantly, the manner in which the programmes have been carried out, that has played a crucial role in inhibiting human development in the country (Chapter 2).[2]

The prevailing development scenario thus underlines the urgent need, on the one hand, for much more vigorous and meaningful state interventions (Chapter 5), and on the other, for social mobilisation of people in order to pressurise and activise the state towards the desired goals (Chapter 6). Such interventions, either by the state organisations or by the people's organisations, to be meaningful and fruitful, need to be designed properly, be goal-directed, and be implemented faithfully. It is necessary, in this connection, to spell out goals of human development in our specific socio-historical and political situation (Chapter 3) and to understand the dynamics and processes of people empowerment (Section II). In this connection, it is also necessary to recall some entrenched inhibiting forces that have persistently impeded such efforts in the past and still continue to thwart adequate and faster progress and achievements in this regard (Section III). Finally, we shall take a look at some important structural, institutional and behavioural changes required to counteract the negative forces in order to facilitate and energise both, the governance and human development performance in the country.

II

Goals of Human Development

We are considering here the need for activising the state as well as other agencies for effective intervention for attaining the desired goals of social and human development. It would be useful in this connection to briefly recall such goals. Attainment of such goals could also, in turn, contribute to releasing further energy for faster and sustainable development. These goals have been broadly discussed in Chapters 2 and 3. Let us summarise and reformulate them as follows:

Building capability among the vulnerable people: 'This can extend from such elementary capabilities as the ability to avoid under-nourishment and related morbidity and mortality to more sophisticated social capabilities such as taking part in life of the community and achieving self-respect.' (Drèze and Sen, 1989: 12).

Inculcating positive self-concepts: Human development should enable 'a person to value his/her capability and to be socially useful and influential' (Drèze and Sen, 1989: 12). Human development programmes should, therefore, inculcate a sense of self-esteem and a sense of efficacy, particularly important in India in the context of socio-historical antecedents (Chapter 3).

Developing confidence in the public: Our people have been long subjected and conditioned to a strong dependency behaviour syndrome. They have been driven to acquire not only a negative self-image but also a role of being a 'pawn' to whom things are caused to happen by others. Development programmes in general, and human development in particular should therefore aim at developing the opposite of such a behaviour and enable persons to move away from being merely recipients of favours and dole, clients of patrons and being 'objects' to being actors and subjects in their various life situations.

Promoting action by the public: Human development programmes should seek to developing a sense of unity and solidarity among people and their active participation in social and development action. There is a close relationship between public understanding and awareness, on the one hand, and the nature, forms and vigour of state action in pursuit of public goals, on the other.

Processes of Empowerment

Human development is thus a process of capability development and empowerment of people. It is necessary to understand some important behavioural dimensions of such a process in order, on the one hand, to weaken the historically conditioned social learning (Chapter 3) and, on the other, to help the vulnerable people to acquire/strengthen a positive self-concept and the related social skills.[3] Some such behavioural dimensions of empowerment are summarised in Table 4.1 and discussed next.

Table 4.1
Processes and Goals of Empowerment

Sense of Powerlessness	Sense of Personal Efficacy
Fear of freedom, dependence	Autonomy, initiative
Fear of failure	Hope of success (expectation)
Conformity: problem avoiding	Confronting reality, problem solving
Unable to take risk (security)	Moderate, calculated risk, innovativeness
Pawns: Submerged into reality	Actors: act, reflect and act; praxis, transcending self
Self-Depreciation	Self-esteem
'Being for others'	'Being for themselves'
Physically stimulated to work, to labour	Challenged by job for quality performance, creativity

Dependency Vs Autonomy

One of the important dimensions of the desired empowerment is weakening of the people's traditional dependency syndrome and enhancement of their initiative. Weak people are generally afraid of freedom and tend to depend on prescriptions given by their dominators. These prescriptions represent the imposition of one man upon another and emerge as a basic element in their mutual relationship. Thus, as Freire has remarked, 'the behaviour of oppressed is a prescribed behaviour following, as it does, guidelines of the oppressor' (Freire, 1972: 31). Some of our development programmes, including anti-poverty programmes, tend to reinforce such dependency behaviour. The social as well as work relations also tend to reinforce such dependency of workers on their managers and supervisors and of the rural people on government officials and others. Initiative and self-action, as has been demonstrated by various participatory development projects (Mehta, 1994b; 1995:162–80), weaken dependency and enhance efficacious behaviour. Such capability also promotes a process of new learning including, for example, eagerness for literacy, demand for access to health service, new vocational skills and readiness for participation in organised collective action.

Fear Vs Hope

The dependency syndrome renders people to fear even small things. They may be afraid of moneylenders, policemen, landlords, petty government officials, and even of each other, as was found in a participatory development project (Mehta, 1995:165–66). In their fear-stricken conditions of life, such people indulge in petty theft, drinking and fuddling and take a holiday from all domestic and work responsibilities. Any petty official, such as a peon, could walk into a village, lay himself cosily on a *charpai* (cot) and order them to make arrangements for his feast of rice and chicken. The villagers would arrange these things without a word. They dare not even enter into a government office nor venture to write any application. Human development seeks to help such people overcome their fear of failure and a sense of powerlessness and enable them to acquire hope of success expecting respect, dignity and a better life.

Problem-Avoiding Vs Problem-Solving

Another important correlate of a sense of powerlessness is readiness to conform to and adjust with the entrenched social system. Dependent people prefer the security of conformity. They learn to survive by avoiding or hiding their problems. They learn to live with them. Empowerment in such a situation consists in helping people learn to confront their reality and move towards solving problems. The same people who were not only afraid of taking risks but were afraid of practically everything, when enabled (Mehta, 1995:152–62), showed an active problem-solving approach. They not only talked about their social problems like drinking and wasteful expenditure on marriages and other social occasions, but initiated action for enforcing norms against such social evils. They initiated action for providing education for their children and for themselves. They were able to confront government officials and unjust traders in various ways. They were able to even get their bribe payments back from such officials. They were, thus, able to take collective action for dealing with their day-to-day problems and also for initiating projects for future. Human development should, thus, promote a problem-solving approach in people and enhance their readiness to assert themselves in various social and economic spheres. As people learn to assert themselves for solving problems, they kindle their hope of success and strengthen their sense of self-esteem.

Risk-Taking and Innovativeness

Craving for excessive security is another important correlate of powerlessness. This motivates people to avoid risks and play safe for survival. Such people, therefore, need to be helped to develop readiness for risk-taking as well as for handling their affairs creatively and innovatively. Such qualities are necessary not only for daily problem-solving but also for agricultural and small business development and for participation in organisation and in collective action.

Repetitive Vs Reflective Behaviour

Another important behavioural dimension of powerlessness is that people, 'submerged into reality', are not able to see and read their own social conditions. Empowerment consists in helping people undertake a critical discovery of conditions and causes of their dehumanisation (Freire, 1972:33–38). It thus involves helping people to reflect on their experience, learn from such experience and to acquire readiness to act to change their conditions of life.[4] Without the ability to reflect, people tend to repeat the same experience over and over again and cease to learn.

Pawn Vs Actor Behaviour

As dependency behaviour gets weakened, as people acquire new awareness about their role and a sense of self-esteem, and as they learn to reflect on their conditions of life, they learn to take an active role in various socio-economic situations. As studies show, (Mehta, 1995:163–80), the same people, who were afraid of even talking to any government employee and moneylenders, were able to assert themselves in pursuit of various decisions of their village council. They could not only go to government offices and talk over various matters, but were able to get things done on their own. As vulnerable people succeed in such activities, their ability to take initiative and to assert is reinforced. They are thus, able to transcend their self, emerge from their reality and act on their environment. This is an important goal of human development in our country where people have been conditioned to depend on powerful others and wait for things to happen to them as favours and patronage.

Self-Depreciation Vs Self-Esteem

Dominant social forces, knowingly or unknowingly, work to condition working people to a sense of self-depreciation, i.e., a negative self-concept. Such people behave as if they exist for their exploiters rather than for themselves. Empowerment thus, consists in enhancing people's sense of self-esteem and in helping them to learn to move away from 'being for others' to 'being for themselves'. Powerlessness instills a sense of self-depreciation in working people who learn to think that they are unproductive and poor because they are lazy and drunk. The programme of empowerment should, therefore, weaken such feelings about self and enhance self-esteem and a positive self-concept. This would help motivate people for collective action for social achievement (Mehta, 1994b).

Survival Vs Quality

The sense of powerlessness drives people to physical labour in their work situation. They labour in order to just survive. This is a correlate of dehumanised behaviour. Empowerment negates such a situation and helps vulnerable people learn to seek challenge for improving quality both in life and in work. They thus, like to work not just for some money (or being 'bonded' or forced to work for just survival as happens very often under poverty), but for the challenge inherent in the social worth of work and related organisational and development activities. Human development thus seeks to reverse such dehumanisation and develop in people a desire for seeking challenge in labour and various other social activities. The ability to seek satisfaction from higher social purposes at work as well as in society is essential for promoting unity, solidarity and collective action for sustainable social achievement.

Self-Assertiveness

The aforementioned goals of human development suggest the need not only for people's participation in development efforts but also for promoting in them an adversarial role for demanding and asserting for such goals. Besides political and social awareness about the existing economic, social and legal inequalities and about the possibility of radical change in this respect, it involves public readiness to act, to sacrifice, to demand and to reject unjust treatment meted out to them. Human development programmes should, therefore, aim at inculcating in vulnerable people collective action orientation, pro-active orientation, a sense of vigilance, strength and hope in order to motivate them for social achievement (Mehta, 1994b; 1994c:58–76).

III

The Inhibiting Forces

Certain strong inhibiting forces have tended to impede the fulfilment of the Constitutional directives for universal education and health. Such forces need to be properly understood and identified so that appropriate interventions can be launched to minimise or neutralise their power. Such forces have not only tended to thwart the attainment of goals discussed earlier, but also these drive the state towards the negative poles, i.e., towards reinforcing the traditional dependency behaviour and negative self-concepts among the weaker sections of the society.

The Social Organisation

Our Value System

The unequal social organisation and the traditional value system motivate the elite to protect the entrenched status quo more than to change it by implementing programmes like universal education and health care services. They are not bothered about the poor human development performance, or by the fact that they are not faithful to the spirit and the directives of the Constitution. Thus, the traditional values seem to be more powerful than the values of equality and social justice enshrined in the Constitution.

The inhibiting power of the traditional value system is shown by the widespread endemic deprivation and malnutrition among children and women and in the widespread illiteracy in the country. It is ironic that though the state agencies have been able to prevent famine deaths, slow deaths due to nutritional deprivation have persisted. Even the adversarial triggering mechanism, constituted by political parties, social activists, NGOs and the press, who succeed in activising the state for preventing famine deaths, are not equally sensitive to preventing chronic malnutrition. It seems that the ruling elite have been taking such long-standing deprivation for granted. It does not bother their conscience at all.

Ideological Barriers

A comparative analysis of human development performance further highlights this inhibiting power of traditional ideology. The pro-people ideology in China (and also in Sri Lanka and our own State of Kerala) has helped them to achieve faster social development. The cases of China and Jamaica illustrate the importance of socialist ideology in effective implementation of education, health, nutrition, literacy and such other programmes, particularly during the pre-reform period. In India, Kerala shows the important role played by the left-oriented environment in achieving remarkable social development there, unlike most other States of the country where no such social transformation has taken place (Chapter 6). The long-standing hierarchical caste-ridden social organisation informed by the principle of superordination and subordination and other related values, thus continues to constitute a very powerful inhibiting force retarding human development in most parts of the country (Chapter 3).[5]

The Politico-Administrative System

The centralised system of administration symbolised by the Indian Civil Service (ICS) has not only continued but has got further expanded and entrenched since Independence. With the outside political support and the inside organised strength of the IAS, the system has been able to successfully resist all attempts of reforms (Potter, 1986). The state agencies have thus, continued to be ideologically dominated by the ICS kind of elitism and distance from the people. Because of the domination of one service, i.e., the IAS, in the system, functionaries belonging to other services have tended to feel alienated. No wonder, not only are the various government agencies and departments not able to collaborate with each other, they are also, generally, not able to use insights of the lower level field functionaries in improving development performance.[6]

Feudal Political Culture

The political processes and administrative tendencies informed by deep-seated historical antecedents condition the public functionaries' self-image as rulers, i.e., masters. Along with such a self-image, the system as a whole has inherited some typical methods of people-management such as manipulation; control of information including falsification of records; subversion of policies and corrupt practices; secretiveness and monopolistic control over skills and knowledge (Chapter 3). Such practices along with the newly acquired systemic tendencies were and are political in nature. This is more clearly visible at the district level where such political culture of managing people dominate. Thus, the various manipulative and coercive practices designed to exploit and exclude people from governance and from 'development' along with the tendency to justify even poor performance and the rentier-dole syndrome are all characteristics of the entrenched ruling fuedal type political culture (Chapter 3).

The system and nature of governance, ingrained as it is with hierarchical and inegalitarian social values and ideology, is thus itself a strong structural barrier to sustainable human development in the country.

Structural Adjustment and Transnational Corporations

The policies of economic liberalisation and structural adjustment need to be understood in the context of the entrenched socio-economic system. The market forces and the entry of TNCs are likely to further widen the already wide income disparities, curtail the meagre social security and enhance imitative consumer culture in the country.[7] As the corporate sectors' competitive behaviour of 'heads I win, tails you lose' is strengthened in the country, the civil society is likely to be afflicted by its various negative fall outs.[8] Such 'competitive' policies permit corporations to exploit national resources and to manipulate markets for unbridled profits. These, therefore, cannot but weaken the society's moral fibre and impede the process of human flourishing (Weiner 1992).

The theory of trickle down of social security could work as an ideological tool to weaken anti-poverty development and welfare programmes in the country. The public functionaries already show a strong tendency to distort such programmes on the ground. Policies of unplanned economic liberalisation and opulence could further strengthen the entrenched rent-seeking tendency at the cost of public welfare. Such economic policies could, therefore, pose a serious threat to the much needed sustainable and equalitarian human development in the country (Chapter 5).

IV

Obtaining Human Development Goals

It is necessary for quick attainment of the goals of human development that, the power of the inhibiting forces is eliminated and/or minimised. Such impeding forces tend to arise mostly from the entrenched social organisation, administrative system and the nature of governance and from certain economic policies. There is an urgent need, therefore, to bring about certain structural and institutional changes, in order to strengthen and release positive forces towards better development performance in the country.

Need for Structural Changes

The most pressing need and by far the most difficult to achieve, is: change in values, attitudes and motivation of public institutions concerning the welfare of the vulnerable people who also happen to belong to lower castes and other deprived sections of our society. Further, there is a need for greater political commitment in government for providing direct public support for social security and human development. Such values and commitment have greatly contributed to better human development performance in several developing countries. It is now well documented that economic growth and expenditure per se are not as crucial for social success as the government's determination and egalitarian belief system (Chapter 5).

Decentralisation and Self-Governance

The present system of governance has tended to become more and more centralised and rigid as it has moved away from the public which it is supposed to serve. Centralised administration is not only not able to reach people effectively, it also tends to alienate regions and people living in remote areas and at the periphery in our vast subcontinent. The recent Constitutional amendments seeking to vitalise *panchayati raj* institutions (PRIs) and local bodies is a welcome step toward decentralisation of governance. Fulfilment of some of the major goals of human development, requires active involvement of people themselves in formulating and implementing various policies and programmes.[9] Effective decentralisation of governance will, however, come about only when the *panchayati raj* institutions are promoted as the third stratum of governance (i.e., in addition to the centre and States). Such a radical structural change (i.e., to help promote PRIs as centres of self-governance) would be in consonance with Article 40 of the Constitution.[10]

Such a change is also likely to create a powerful dent in the hierarchical social order. Effective involvement of people in their own governance and development could also contribute to the required changes in values and belief system of both, the people and the public institutions. In turn, this would create conditions for speedy and adequate human development in the country (Chapter 7).

Egalitarian Land Reforms

Effective land reforms in favour of vast masses of marginal farmers and landless agricultural workers can also help to remove structural barriers to development. Land reforms are likely to boost the morale and motivation of the people and release their productive energy and collective creativity for sustainable, faster and participatory agricultural, industrial and human development as well as for democratisation of governance. Such reforms are also likely to facilitate the process of change in the values and beliefs of our public institutions.[11]

Restructuring Government Organisations

Along with certain basic structural changes, there is a need for radical change in the functioning of the government organisations and other state agencies which tend to function more as an inhibiting rather than as a facilitating force as far as equalitarian and people-oriented governance and development are concerned. A new vision needs to be infused in the government and in various public institutions of education and health. The state agencies need to move from mere 'tokenism' to active pursuit of social objectives and goals.

These are in no way easy tasks. Resistance to such changes is bound to come not only from within the administrative system but from the vested interests outside that the system has been serving for a long time. Strategic efforts are, therefore, needed at all levels to overcome such resistance and to reward and strengthen the positive forces for change. We briefly discuss below some areas where efforts are needed to promote new practices, norms and structures of institutional functioning:

Shared Objectives for Teamwork

It is imperative that public systems involved in implementing various human development programmes appreciate their common social objectives. Currently such organisations seem to think in terms of their piecemeal individual activities. This tendency for fragmentation and 'departmentalisation' contributes to rigid centralisation of decision-making which prevents inter-organisation, even inter-departmental cooperation and teamwork. Such systems (e.g., health) promote thinking within narrow grooves where the concerned officials try to grab more and more resources and power for themselves. Each system evaluates itself and its employees in terms of number of activities (e.g., number of vasectomies or sterilisations performed). The tone of such systemic behaviour is set at the apex level. Such a tendency tends to become autistic and gradually pervades the nature and manner of government functioning throughout the country. It is no wonder, therefore, that the performance of individual employees is appraised (and rewarded) in terms of the number of such activities conducted by them and for the degree of their conformity rather than creativity (Chapter 2).

In industry, where a similar tendency exists in managers, it has been described as one of the management's deadly diseases as it favours practices which reward mostly individual performance. In large public systems like education and health, such a tendency for individual performance in terms of numbers and fixed targets could assume an epidemic form and destroy an entire national programme with disastrous consequences.[12] This also contributes to promoting (besides departmentalisation and the 'empire building' tendency), inter-departmental and inter-cadre rivalries and mutual bitterness. This further erodes the quality of overall performance and diffuses public accountability.

In policy documents, such as for literacy and health, the need for inter-departmental and inter-programme linkages and cooperation has repeatedly been stressed. This, is however, seldom put into practice (Chapter 2). The experience suggests that such cooperative functioning is not possible unless the system is restructured so as to reward shared and socially relevant performance as informed by a *vision* of universal education and health for all. Perceptions of administrative personnel and functionaries also need to be enlarged so as to include the vulnerable—the long deprived people—in their thinking and definition. Such a vision of all, along with socially meaningful functioning and teamwork, needs to be infused in our public institutions for better performance.

Pro-Active Institutions

The various systemic tendencies also show that our public institutions are more reactive than pro-active. A reactive attitude is dysfunctional for human development programmes such as health and elementary education and in the fight against untouchability and such other social evils. Instead of waiting for problems to occur, there is a need to plan action in advance in order not only to prevent problems before they take root but also to achieve results in a positive direction. A plan of action is also needed to promote and reward pro-active interventions in various fields such as maintenance of communal peace and harmony, and prevention of civic rights violations, school drop-out, chronic malnutrition, and infant mortality and occurrence of deadly diseases. Pro-active institutions can make a difference in all such matters.[13]

Institutional Vigilance

Along with pro-active orientation, there is a need for inculcating a sense of vigilance in our public institutions and government organisations which tend to show a considerable sense of complacency (Mehta, 1989a: 78–81). This lowers their preparedness for development tasks, nurtures the tendency to justify even poor performance and creates hazards for the security of the country. There is thus a need for an effective institutional mechanism, not only to punish complacency but more importantly, to reward and promote a greater sense of alertness and vigilance for timely mid-course as well as pre-emptive action.[14]

A Conducive Social Environment

The socio-political environment plays an important part in inhibiting or fostering an activist orientation in public institutions and government organisations. Its importance can be seen in inter-state disparities in human development. Take the case of Kerala (Chapters 2 and 6) which has shown remarkable progress in literacy and in reducing infant mortality and overall death rates. In terms of nutritional well-being, Kerala remains firmly ahead of other Indian States. Public support to literacy in Kerala goes back to the early 19th century. In 1817, the ruler of Travancore, Rani (queen) Gouri Parvathi Bai had issued a rescript commanding that 'the state should defray the entire cost of education of its people so that there might be no backwardness in the spread of enlightenment among them; that by diffusion of education they might become better subjects and that the reputation of the State might be advanced thereby' (quoted in *Census of India*, 1931, Vol. xxviii, Trivandrum, 1932:301). The Rani was right.

Historically, the wide educational base in Kerala seems to have created a major impact on other public policies including medical care and food policy as well as in encouraging intelligent health practices at the family level (Drèze and Sen, 1989 : 223). Such historical factors have greatly contributed to inculcating a conducive social environment in the State towards motivating public institutions for enacting various social legislations and for effectively implementing social and human development programmes. Some other States like Rajasthan provide a contrasting picture in this respect where the 'feudal' type social environment still seems to persist and which tends to influence governmental functioning and public institutions in various ways (Chapter 6).[15]

The need for inculcating a conducive social environment for faster and sustainable human development thus, cannot be over-emphasised. Both, the state (Chapter 5) and the public (Chapter 6) have an important role to play in this respect. Such an environment, in turn, could energise the state agencies for shared social functioning and contributes to creating vigilant and pro-active institutions.

A Conducive Physical Environment

Along with a conducive socio-political environment, there is an urgent need for improving the quality of the physical infrastructure in various public services such as primary schools, primary health centres, public hospitals, drinking water facilities, public sanitation and housing. Such a need has been repeatedly pointed out by various government committees and commissions and by numerous review studies of programmes like literacy, primary education, primary health services and women and child care. There is an urgent need to provide basic infrastructure such as teachers, toilets, safe drinking water, classrooms, blackboards, libraries, seating arrangements, lighting and mid-day meals, for universalising education and for eliminating the chronic problem of school drop-out.[16] Similarly, the recent resurgence of epidemics and deadly diseases like tuberculosis, malaria, etc., underlies the urgent need for providing safe drinking water, public sanitation, medicines, trained personnel and other preventive public health facilities in the country. It has long been a matter of public knowledge that the primary health service in most parts of the country has fallen into disuse and decay because of lack of even basic infrastructure including medical personnel. Lack of proper physical environment at literacy centres has been similarly identified as one of the persisting causes of poor performance in adult literacy (Chapter 2).

Besides adequate budgetary provisions for creating the necessary physical infrastructure, it is important to sensitise the government and non-government organisations and public institutions in this regard. Sometimes, even the existing provisions for such basic needs are not utilised or mis-utilised as shown, for example, by several case studies of anti-poverty programmes. In addition to leakages, there is a tendency to divert funds to non-essential items on personal and other considerations (Chapter 2). There is thus a need, not only for greater budgetary outlays for education, health, etc., which is of course essential, but, at the same time, to enhance institutional sensitivity and concern for basic physical infrastructure for proper functioning of public services.[17]

Transforming Opportunities into Achievements

In addition to social concern and sensitivity, there is a need for developing institutional capability for transforming existing opportunities into concrete achievements. We hear from time-to-time, that even the meagre funds for primary education have not been utilised and/or that projects have overrun without any concrete results. The concerned public functionaries and departments seem to lack capability for utilising the resources optimally for meaningful programmes. Such a need cannot be over-emphasised in a country like India with limited financial resources. These need to be utilised with utmost care, commitment and in pursuance with the desired social objectives.

Entrepreneurship and Accountability

Administrative tendencies manifested in implementing social development programmes; low readiness for pursuing shared objectives; low orientation for quality and social achievement—all these are symptomatic of a weak and indifferent work culture obtaining in our public institutions and government organisations. Excessive attachment with one's own cadre, tendency of building an 'empire' within the system and lack of respect for vulnerable people further decimates the work-culture. There is, thus, a need for inculcating a democratic and achievement-oriented work-culture where teamwork, collective achievement and readiness to own responsibility are valued.

Our government organisations and public systems tend to play safe and work 'by rule' as the system expects them to show compliance with instructions rather than creative functioning. Institutions, therefore, need to be empowered to provide an entrepreneurial, creative and innovative response to various social situations, in policy-making, and more importantly, in implementing programmes. Centralised departmental functioning through commands and manuals cannot deliver goods under diverse regional and social conditions such as ours. They need to take their own decisions, and be responsible and accountable for their actions. Such institutional development does not happen automatically.[18] It requires a series of planned efforts designed to promote and sustain entrepreneurial motivation and capability in government functioning and in our schools and health systems.

Public Ability to Command

There is thus, a need for various structural and institutional changes in order to prepare and motivate state agencies and government functionaries for pursuing and obtaining social objectives of development programmes. In addition to such changes, it is necessary to activise the public themselves to command better services and performance. For instance, we know that it is not just the availability of food, but people's power to command such essential items that is crucial in fighting malnutrition. This includes their capability to demand and obtain access to services and facilities for food, education, health, water, sanitation, employment, etc. Such public activism can be instrumental in energising the state agencies and public functionaries for more egalitarian policies and for proper functioning of such services and programmes.[19]

Public 'Stake' in Public Services

Public pressures for social achievement can also play a crucial role towards the desired institutional development. Such pressures are, however, activised only when people perceive a stake and meaning in public programmes and articulate their needs and demands. Public pressures help in weakening the strength of entrenched inhibiting forces and in bringing social issues at the centre of public policies and programmes. Thus, public 'demand' for education, health care, etc., could work as a moving force for obtaining democratic and socially more responsive public systems and institutions (Chapter 6).[20]

The Need for Behavioural Change and Leadership Development

While structural changes and institutional development would help create and shape new values and attitudes in public functionaries, concurrent efforts designed to strengthen new modes of behaviour will also help in boosting such systemic changes. Functionaries themselves could be motivated to resist and overcome the various inhibiting forces. Though they are influenced by the system under which they work, functionaries also act on the system and reshape it. There is thus, also a need for planned behavioural changes and leadership development. Specifically designed training could be of great help in this respect. We briefly recall training needs in this respect.

A Democratic Self-Image

Public functionaries' sensitivity to the needs, problems and aspirations of population, particularly the vulnerable people, is hampered by their self-image as rulers (Chapter 3). People's dependency behaviour has a reciprocal relationship with such an image. Effective public activism however, requires inculcation of a more democratic and more assertive self-concept in people. It demands a greater concern for social achievement in the public functionaries. It involves a change in their self-image and strengthening of pro-active and collective action orientations, sense of vigilance, social awareness, faith in people's strength and hope of success in efforts for obtaining the various stated goals of human development (Mehta, 1994c). Inculcation of such motivation is likely to release activism for faster and better human development in the country.[21]

Attention to Process of Development

Greater sensitivity to public needs and demands requires the public officials to pay greater attention to the processes of development and implementation of programmes. For instance, they need to listen to feedback, understand the latent meanings in the manifested people behaviours and be able to convert such experience into learning, for mid-course corrections in programmes and for better performance. It therefore, requires new people-oriented leadership styles—less prescriptive and dependency inducing and more facilitating, empowering and initiative-releasing.[22] Structural and institutional changes could also be facilitated by such leadership behaviour.

In addition to these changes required for the attainment of human development goals, the Directive Principles of State Policy also enjoin the public officials to play a facilitative role for developing a conducive socio-economic environment for all people, particularly for the weaker sections of our society. Such an environment is essential for flourishing of human potentialities. The functionaries' behaviour on the ground, plays a crucial role in the inculcation (or inhibition) of such an environment. Their leadership styles, therefore, assume great importance in obtaining the various goals of human development (see Table 4.1). Certain leadership styles are dysfunctional and, therefore, barriers to obtaining the desired goals (Chapter 2). Efforts are required to help develop more positive and facilitative styles (Table 4.2), as discussed later, in this connection.

Table 4.2
Leadership Required for People Empowerment

Direct Dominative Approach	Indirect Integrative Approach
Prescriptive	Dialoguing; Facilitative
Explaining; Directing	Enable people to transcend themselves via action and reflection
Shaping climate where people are objects of control and domination	Climate of critical discovery; Awareness of humanising and dehumanising conditions
Developing by narration; by banking; by depositing	Communication; Coding and decoding; understanding
Work for and/or against people	Working with people
Extracting; Stimulating labour, production	Challenging jobs; higher goals; Total vision, and parts as elements in the whole.

Prescriptive Vs Facilitative Leadership

The actual functioning of various development programmes and governance shows (Chapter 2) that our public functionaries on the whole, tend to be more directive, prescriptive and, many a times, dominative in dealing with the people. Decision-making in such situations is mostly top-down, leaving little scope for the people to get involved. Such leadership styles have both unintended and intended social implications. They tend to develop and/or reinforce dependency, fear of failure and conformity behaviours among the people to the detriment of the goals of human development.

There is thus, a need for the functionaries to develop facilitative skills for promoting a dialogue with people.

Explanation Vs Reflection

One of the important goals of human development is to help people develop capability for action and reflection on their ongoing socio-economic reality. The functionaries, therefore, need to behave and act accordingly. Merely explaining programmes to them (which is also often not done, as people generally lack even basic information about the various programmes and policies) and directing them to accept government decisions only reinforces their cynicism and /or dependency behaviour. Therefore, it is essential that public officials develop a reflective and enabling leadership style in this connection. This would, of course, require a radical change in their value system and motivation.

Domination Vs Discovery

Human development also seeks to help people confront the reality of their life and to acquire a problem-solving approach. To this end, it is necessary for the functionaries, whether government or non-government, to motivate people and involve them in critical discovery of their dehumanising conditions of life. For example, the National Literacy Mission calls for development of awareness among the people about causes of their deprivation and to help them in amelioration of their conditions (GOI, 1988a: 14). Similarly, Health-for-All programme envisages the need for making people aware of the ill-effects of insanitary conditions. Such goals cannot be achieved without creating a climate for learning, reasoning, questioning and critical discovery. It is, therefore, necessary that the state agencies and public functionaries are helped to unlearn their old attitudes and styles and to learn dialogue skills in order to promote a climate of critical discovery.

Working with People

This brings us to the core of the desired leadership behaviour, i.e., readiness and capability to work for and with people. This amounts to a radical departure from the current practices and tendencies (Chapter 2), and would therefore require almost a total change in the mind set of state functionaries. They have long been conditioned to either work against the interest of the common people or to work for them, i.e., to reinforce their dependency behaviour. For attainment of human development goals, it is necessary to help the public functionaries to develop readiness and capability of working jointly with people in order to release their active involvement in various socio-economic affairs and development programmes. They need to develop respect for rather than distance from people. Such a value system is essential for effective policies and programmes, for example, for the elimination of school drop-out, improvement of quality of education and for universal education, for elimination of child labour and for health, public sanitation and other related programmes of human development.

Working with people also involves helping them develop an orientation for self-action. For instance, political and social activists seeking to act on the system for social achievement help inculcate collective assertion and a sense of social efficacy in the people themselves. People are thus, not only enabled to develop a sense of efficacy, but also 'outcome expectation' (Bandura, 1977; 1982), i.e., a sense that the given behaviour would lead to a certain outcome. A sense of efficacy is the belief that one can successfully perform the behaviour required to produce the outcome. The combination of these two, i.e., efficacy expectation and outcome expectation is likely to motivate the people for social activism either within the system or outside the system to achieve social achievement goals. Social activists and public functionaries, therefore, need to be helped to learn to work with people in order to develop their competence and capability and to facilitate the release of such expectations, initiative and assertion in them.

Compliance Vs Challenge

Public functionaries are also conditioned to manipulate people in order to extract compliance from them. Such a behaviour, for example, is often observed at the workplace where managers use various techniques of physical stimulation to extract more work in order to increase production and profits. Such techniques fail to motivate workers for higher goals and for a total vision of work. Such leadership styles at the workplace, therefore, hamper capability of people and lower their morale (Mehta, 1994a). Such a tendency is also observed in our development programmes where public functionaries including some NGO functionaries, dole out inputs to buy people's traditional loyalty. As is well known, such actions hardly develop people's capability. For this, the functionaries need to challenge the concerned people with a vision of higher goals involved in improving the quality of life, individually and collectively. A sense of challenge is essential to motivate them to stretch mentally in order to develop capability and morale among the people.

Facilitative leadership enables people not only in setting challenging goals but also in achieving significant results. For instance, tribals in a remote village in Bihar were helped to set up a village-level organisation and initiate some significant social and economic projects. The same 'docile' and 'timid' tribals were thus, able to set challenging goals for themselves and to actively pursue and achieve worthwhile results. It is possible to motivate people by challenging goals involved in development tasks such as: drought control, tree protection, preservation of forests and wildlife, water and irrigation facilities, land and soil management and health care. Such success experience illustrates the importance of facilitative leadership in helping people undertake challenging and socially worthwhile tasks (Mehta, 1994b)

Narration Vs Communication

Most development programmes stress the need for two-way communication instead of narration, i.e., top-down communication. It has been observed in various review studies that officials, both in government and non-government organisations, are unable to understand the latent meaning of the feedback which people provide in meetings, discussions, etc. In the absence of readiness to listen and because of their fondness for lecturing and ordering, officials continue to 'narrate' their tailor-made priorities.[23] Effective communication requires skills of coding and decoding of messages and for probing and interpreting the latent meaning in the manifested behaviour.

Another important aspect of effective communication is the leaders (in this case the government and non-government functionaries) expectation of the common people. For instance, it has been widely observed that teachers' expectations from their pupils help shape their self-image. When teachers (i.e., classroom leaders) think that their pupils are intelligent and expect high performance from them, they treat them with respect, pay more attention to their achievement and motivate them for success by providing positive reinforcement (Rosenthal and Jacobson, 1968). Experimental studies, designed to arouse a sense of competence among pupils in low-performing rural primary schools by using indirect integrative classroom communication, resulted in helping both the teachers as well as the pupils. Teachers showed greater initiative, creativity and readiness to learn.

The teachers' expectation of pupils, and his/her classroom communication helped shape a conducive classroom climate. This motivated the children to significantly boost their personal efficacy as well as their scholastic performance (Mehta, 1976). When public officials only lecture as to what people should do and should not do, they in fact convey the message that they do not consider the people competent to act on their own. Thus, both the methods and content of communication are equally important and it is necessary that the officials show skills in communicating with people in order to help and motivate them to take up the challenge of getting involved in various development tasks.

V

Social Mobilisation and State Interventions: Minimising the Inhibiting and Maximising the Facilitative Forces

As we have seen, the task of energising human development performance in the country and the task of eliminating/minimising the power of the entrenched inhibiting forces are highly interrelated. These are, in fact, two poles of the same reality. As human development is strengthened, the inhibiting forces are likely to be weakened. As vulnerable people acquire a positive self-concept and an actor-role, the political and civil functionaries' self-image as rulers and 'masters' is bound to be dented. The suggested structural, institutional and behavioural changes are directed towards such ends. Such changes are however, not likely to occur on their own. Powerful resistance is inbuilt in the situation. These and other similar changes require active state interventions (Chapter 5). As the state agencies and the nature of governance themselves are indifferent, it is necessary to pressure them to change their direction. This is possible only by vigorous and organised social and political mobilisation. Public activism is thus needed for activising the state. People's movements are required for neutralising the inhibiting forces and for releasing positive forces for change (Chapter 6).

To sum up, faster and sustainable human development in the country requires a symbiosis of public activism, on the one hand, and active state interventions, on the other. We discuss some issues pertaining to: state interventions in Chapter 5, social mobilisation and public activism in Chapter 6 and a suggested alternative development strategy in Chapter 7.

END NOTES

1. There have been very disturbing reports in newspapers and other mass media from time-to-time regarding poor conditions of public health in the country. In the absence of effective public health programmes, malaria, tuberculosis and other such diseases have been raising their heads in a very serious way involving millions of people in the country. See Chapter 1. According to UNICEF (1993) studies, avoidable infections due to malnutrition and unsafe drinking water result in infant mortality rate. In the worst reported disaster in which hundreds of people including a large number of children were burnt alive at Dabwali in Haryana in December, 1995, lack of hospital facilities and timely medical aid aggravated the problem. See editorial comments in *Times of India*, December 26, 1995.

2. There are several instances where economically poorer countries have been able to achieve faster social progress. For crucial importance of political commitment and belief system in promoting social security and human development, see Drèze and Sen (1989); UNDP (1994).

3. In this connection an attempt was made some time ago to conduct participatory adult education designed to promote psychological empowerment, see Mehta (1995: 120–136).

4. One of the objectives of the National Literacy Mission is to increase awareness and help people get organised and act to ameliorate their conditions of life. See, GOI (1988a: 23).

5. The inhibiting and facilitating force of values and ideology in human development performance is seen in the wide gaps in such achievements in India and China. See Drèze and Sen (1995: 61–67). Contestation of Brahminical values seems to have played an important role in what is known as Sri Lanka–Kerala Model of Development. See Casinader (1995).

6. Serious inter-cadre and inter-service rivalries and bitterness have been reported from time-to-time in newspapers and other reports. This came out dramatically in connection with the Pay Commissions appointed by the Government of India periodically. For instance, non-IAS services have articulated their bitterness at the preferential treatment shown to the IAS in various ways and have expressed their humiliation in this respect. See Chapter 5.

7. The markets in India have traditionally been narrow in their social base, catering only to the wealthy sections of the society. A large number of people who are practically resourceless and do not have the necessary purchasing power, therefore, are left out of such market operation. See, Vyas (1994); Patnaik & Chandrasekhar (1995).

8. For discussion of the impact of structural adjustment and TNC culture on the workplace and the society, see Mehta (1994a); UNRISD (1994).

9. The need for people's participation and qualitative performance has been emphasised repeatedly in various policy documents regarding literacy, elementary education, health, etc. See GOI (1988a: 24–25).

10. The Constitution was amended (73rd and 74th Amendments) to provide for more effective structure, functions and powers for *panchayats* and municipalities. *Panchayats* have been empowered subject to the provisions of the Constitution, the legislature of the State to enable them to function as institutions of self-governance. For discussion about requirements for the evolution of effective third stratum of government, see Mukherjee (1993); Krishnaswamy (1993).

11. For effect of land reforms on morale and motivation of the rural poor in West Bengal, see Das Gupta (1987) (cited in Rao, 1992) and for contribution of such reforms to faster social development in various countries such as China, South Korea, Malaysia, Sri Lanka, see Drèze and Sen (1989 : 177–225; 1995 : 41–42).

12. The population planning programme under the Ministry of Health and Family Welfare has been suffering from such a number-target syndrome. It has been decided now to give up the target approach and develop a new reproductive health approach. In the meantime, the population has continued to explode. See CRRID (1996) and Mehta (1996).

13. There are instances where even under emotionally surchaged conditions, pro-active and vigilant people were able to prevent communal riots. See, for instance IPHRC (1993 : 124–25). The rising mortality due to the dengue fever (92 deaths were reported till October 8, 1996 in Delhi alone) has forced the Delhi High Court to ask the concerned State authorities to explain why action should not be taken against them for 'slackness and indifference'. Justice Mehra of the High Court observed, 'It is obvious there has been a collapse of civic amenities leading to the spread of the epidemic'. *Times of India*, October 9, 1996.

14. A glaring example of lack of vigilance on the part of the concerned public agencies is the case of illegal air-dropping of arms by mercenary aircraft hired by international smugglers. See, a report in *India Today*, January 31, 1996 : 58–61.

15. Social environment, evolved in Kerala over the years, can be contrasted with lack of such environment in some northern Indian States such as Rajasthan where instead of promoting education, the rulers were actively engaged in preventing and even punishing social workers engaged in spreading education. Consequently, a negative or an indifferent social environment seems to have evolved there with very adverse impact on public health and education, particularly of females. For a comparative analysis regarding female literacy, sex ratio, infant mortality rate, etc., in Rajasthan, see Drèze and Sen (1995 : Table A.3). The Barmer district in the State has the dismal distinction of having just 8 per cent female literacy rate in 1991—the lowest in the country. See (ibid.: Table 3, p.30).

16. The Operation Blackboard project seeks to correct some of the glaring deficiencies in physical environment in schools. See GOI (1993a). The Common Minimum Programme of the United Front also mentions the need for improving the school infrastructure and the physical environment, see UF (1996). People at the grassroots level, have been, however, articulating such needs and problems in various ways for a long time. See Mehta (1990, 1992a). The National Literacy Mission policy documents also expressly discuss the need for inculcating conducive physical environment at the literacy centres. See, GOI (1988a).

17. In the absence of such social sensitivity, functionaries whether in government or in non-government organisations are unable to appreciate the needs at the grassroots level. This is a common phenomenon in implementation of literacy, primary education, health care, public distribution services. See Chapter 2.

18. For example, the National Literacy Mission stresses the need for decentralisation, debureaucratisation and for social mobilisation and participation of all the current and potential beneficiaries, literacy workers and the whole commitment in decision-making and implementation of programmes. See GOI (1988a : 34, 41). Such institutional development for literacy programmes has however, not taken place. See Chapter 2.

19. For case studies of role of public activism in sustainable development, see Mehta (1994b) and for discussion of the role of activism in obtaining social security in several countries, see Drèze and Sen, 1989.

20. For instance, policy documents concerning the National Literacy Mission stress on the role of public demand for literacy and education. See GOI (1988a). However, it has not been possible to generate such a demand in and absence of public pressures, as found in several review studies of the functioning of literacy programmes. See Mehta (1990, 1991, 1992a).

21. The case studies from several countries indicate such a concern as an important ingredient in motivation of public agencies which plays an important role in promotion of social security. See Drèze and Sen, (1989 : 13).

22. For instance, the National Literacy Mission policy documents require the various field functionaries to pay attention to processes of implementation as well as social process. see GOI (1988a). However, as field reviews revealed, they were not able to show such sensitivity in programmes and continue to implement them as usual. See Chapter 2. Programmes conducted some years ago to boost primary education, children's personality and scholastic development underlined the crucial importance of the teachers' integrative and empowering leadership behaviour. See Mehta (1976) and other contributions cited there.

23. In a case study of a total literacy programme under a non-government organisation, the organisers were unable to listen to the real meaning of people's feedback, including their silence, and kept on insisting on their vocational training programme for women. See Mehta (1992a). On the other hand, several NGOs with greater social sensitivity to the ideas of people and to their needs and problems have been able to achieve significant developmental results. See Mehta (1994b).

CHAPTER 5

ACCELERATING HUMAN DEVELOPMENT: THE NEED FOR ACTIVE STATE INTERVENTIONS

I

Dysfunctional Administration and Citizens' Alienation

Our state functioning and management of human development programmes show several dysfunctional administrative tendencies (Chapter 2 and Table 3.1). Such tendencies seem to be rooted, on the one hand, in some deep-seated social, systemic and ideological factors and, on the other, in some entrenched cultural and motivational factors (Chapter 3). The state, on the whole, has been rather unwilling to show respect for the need to develop people's capability and reluctant to act and support human development programmes. Contrary to the values and leadership required for human development (Chapter 4), the public functionaries have tended to show a strong need for hierarchy and status power and to deliver benefits more to themselves and to the affluent than the poor even in poverty alleviation programmes (Chapter 2).

Government Response to Citizen's Alienation: Attempts at Administrative Reforms

The Government of India, however, has not been unaware of the citizen's alienation from their policies and governance. They have been trying to 'manage' people from time-to-time. They have also been aware of the citizens' disillusionment and their growing anger, particularly with certain socio-economic policies and functioning of programmes on the ground. For instance, as far back as in 1963, the mid-term appraisal of the Third Five Year Plan identified administrative malfunctioning as an important inhibiting factor in shortfalls in economic and social achievements. The government's malfunctioning, therefore, has not been for want of feedback from the people. Instead of addressing the people's needs and problems, their response, however, has been typically bureaucratic. A new Department of Administrative Reforms was created in 1964 and the Bureau of Public Enterprises was set up in 1965. In the same vein, the growing dissatisfaction with the functioning of administration led to the setting up of the Administrative Reforms Commission (ARC) in 1966.

The ARC was specifically asked to suggest ways and means of ensuring high standards of efficiency and integrity in public services, making them an instrument of economic and social development and more responsive to the needs of the people. It submitted 20 reports, containing 537 recommendations, in the period 1966 to 1970. Following such recommendations, some changes were effected in the administrative set-up such as: creation of a central department of personnel; redefinition of the role of the Department of Administrative Reforms; introduction of performance budgeting; and delegation of financial powers. Reviews undertaken in the 1980s of the functioning of such new practices further found the need for a new work-culture. Such suggested measures were once again stressed in 1985 by Rajiv Gandhi, the then Prime Minister, who announced a new package of administrative reforms including decentralisation of decision-making; enforcement of accountability; simplification of rules and regulations; promotion of courteous service to citizens; and an effective machinery for redressal of public grievances.

Some further suggested measures reiterated the need for accountability following the recommendation of the Jha Commission in 1983. It was suggested that, stress should be laid on performance and results rather than on mere rules and procedures. The Fazal Committee (1980–82) also suggested the need for accountability in terms of the goals and objectives of the organisation, appropriate mechanism for performance appraisal in public enterprises in terms of achievements and reward for achievements, inter-departmental consultation and appropriate monitoring of performance. Following such recommendations, the Government of India introduced the concept of an annual action plan and the concept of management by objectives in implementation of programmes. By 1989, the DAR had completed as many as 469 studies including some on the need for: improvement in work environment; innovative measures such as work improvement teams (WITs); introduction of quality circles; participation of people at grassroots level; improvement in employee morale; and improvement in productivity and the need for reducing costs.[1]

The suggested reforms recognised the need for energising administration and governance in the country. From time-to-time various committees have suggested the introduction of a variety of managerial concepts and practices such as: accountability, goal-clarity, performance appraisal in terms of achievements, inter-departmental linkages and cooperation, qualitative monitoring, people's participation, employees' own participation and involvement in decision-making at the workplace, teamwork, quality circles, annual action plan and creation of a conducive work environment. However, as we have seen, such measures were either not put into practice or have not succeeded in improving the administrative behaviour for implementation and management of development programmes (Chapter 2). The practice of action plan, for instance, has largely become an annual ritual without promoting the desired improvement in the functioning of administration and in implementation of various programmes (Trivedi, 1994). Such suggested practices also indicated a limited managerial response to an essentially socio-political situation. Such attempts did not address the heart of the matter, i.e., the structure and the values ingrained in the social system as well as in the system of administration and the dynamics involved in achievement of social goals of development programmes.

The suggested reforms thus, failed to make any appreciable difference in the functioning of the administration as far as social and human development programmes were concerned. The performance of the various States and the country as a whole in 1991 as shown by some selected indicators such as life expectancy, female–male ratio, literacy rate in 7+ age group and incidence of poverty, left much to be desired. By this time, the female–male ratio was down to 927 (for 1,000 males) from 972 in 1901. The incidence of poverty in the population was 44.9 per cent in rural areas and 36.5 per cent in urban areas in 1987–88.[2]

Downhill Trend and Growing Judicial Activism

Persistence of negative systemic tendencies, despite the Directive Principles, and the continuing non-performance of the state underline the unabated strength of the deep-seated values in the social and political systems. The vested interests entrenched in politics and in the administration have thus been able to successfully thwart reforms and the restructuring of governance as it threatened their pre-eminent and dominant position (Chapter 3).

The success of the bureaucracy (in thwarting restructuring of administration) highlights its strength vis-à-vis the state and the latter's failure in discharging its responsibility to the civil society. It has brought the state as a whole, and the governments in particular, into further disrepute with the common people. The worsening situation is highlighted by recent serious executive lapses and resultant dramatic judicial actions. Such omissions and commissions on the part of the Executive have spurred, what has come to be known as, judicial activism.

During 1995, the Supreme Court of India dealt with a number of scandals involving bureaucrats, politicians, businessmen and the underworld. It swung into further action when the Executive was found to be non-responsive and non-cooperative. Several senior bureaucrats, including some IPS and IAS officers, had to be sent to jail for their disregard of the Court's directives. The Chief Justice of India directed payment of compensation of Rs 50,000 to each of the 10 innocent persons killed in the so-called 'encounter' at Pilibhit in Uttar Pradesh. The executive was thus held responsible for violating human rights of the people. A mother petitioned the Court saying that her only son was gunned down in cold blood by the police and was cremated by them as an unidentified body. The Court directed the Uttar Pradesh government to pay an interim compensation of Rs five lakh to the mother and asked the CBI to arrest the accused police officials and prosecute them. The Court called it the worst crime against the entire humanity and human rights and warned that it would not allow this to happen again.[3] The deteriorating health of the system of governance is glaringly revealed by the officials' and politicians' nexus with criminals. Its anti-people nature is clearly seen in the wide network of patronage, public corruption, bribery and liaison with anti-social and anti-national elements. This nexus has come to be symbolised dramatically by the Jain Hawala case.[4] No other scandal had rocked this nation so much before. It had created a pandemonium, sweeping across almost the entire political establishment. The Supreme Court had shown crusading zeal in this regard, generating the hope that it would help cleanse the system and bring about greater accountability.[5]

Administration: Intra-System Maladies

The Executive's non-responsiveness to the people's needs and its lack of accountability and its tendency to act more in self-interest that has resulted in increasing intra-system mistrust and bitterness. This comes out publicly and vehemently from time-to-time.This was illustrated by the anger of the officers of the Central Services who seemed to have declared a virtual war against the IAS. The All India Confederation of Central Services Officers' Association was reported to have decided to move the Supreme Court to secure justice for its members in service matters which have allegedly been thwarted by the IAS lobby.[6] A petition was also filed in the Supreme Court requesting it to decide guidelines for appointment to the post of Comptroller and Auditor General (CAG) and to fix qualifications for a person to occupy such a post. The petition was designed to prevent IAS officers from occupying the post.[7]

The people are getting disillusioned with the government for not being able to deliver development gains and welfare, its increasing nexus with criminals and its lack of cohesiveness and sense of purpose. The administration is thus discredited in the people's mind as not only inefficient and corrupt, but as one motivated more by personal interest than by commitment to public welfare.

II

Structural Adjustment and Human Development

New economic policies of structural adjustment, particularly the reforms being implemented since 1991, need to be understood in the context of the poor social development performance and the malfunctioning of the state, particularly government behaviour on the ground. Measures suggested for structural adjustment under the aegis of the World Bank and the IMF include: liberalising the financial market, unifying exchange rates at competitive levels, lowering tariffs, privatising state enterprises, opening the economy to foreign investment on a competitive basis, rationalising and reducing government regulations, cutting state budgets and ensuring property rights (Williamson, 1990:5–11). Some such measures have already been implemented in India which seek to give primacy to market forces for stimulating economic development. Some other policies such as privatisation of the public sector and changes in labour laws making for easy exit have been demanded from time-to-time by the TNCs and the leaders of business and industry in the country.[8]

Release and use of market forces accompanied by debureaucratisation and weakening of the rentier-licence-quota-permit and contractor *raj*, could play a positive role in stimulating innovative and competitive private initiative. However, for such gains to materialise, creativity, initiative and entrepreneurship need to be released among the common people, both in urban as well as rural areas. This alone can stimulate new enterprises and contribute to participatory and shared growth. Simultaneously, competition for achievements has to be released at the workplace where products are created. Workers and managers have to be motivated for excellence. For this, the workplace needs to be appropriately organised with widespread and effective participation of all, particularly the workers.

The new policies do not seem to have stimulated such changes at the workplace. If anything, workers in the organised industry, and even managers, show a growing sense of insecurity because of threatened downsizing and the job policy of reducing the size of permanent workforce by replacing them with non-regular workers at low wages. Such a situation could actually demotivate and dehumanise people at the workplace. As a result, instead of releasing competitiveness, such policies could undermine the worker morale, creativity and, in the long run, productivity itself (Mehta, 1994a).

Negative Social Consequences

The new economic policies, therefore, also need to be judged in terms of their impact at the workplace and in the civil society as a whole. As studies show, declining trends in the extent of poverty obtained in the 1980s seem to have been reversed in 1992. There was a big jump in poverty in the rural sector, from the earlier 35 per cent to 41.7 per cent of people now driven below the poverty line. After making price corrections, real wage changes showed a declining trend and even became negative for skilled labour. On the other hand, the proportion of expenditure on food in the total household expenditure showed an increase from 64.01 per cent in 1987–88 to 64.99 per cent in 1992. The per capita consumption (i.e., physical units of calories) came down both in urban and rural areas, particularly in the rural areas. There was a decline in investment growth, specially in agriculture, and fall in household savings along with increase in market price of goods in 1993–94. With increase in the price of foodgrains, the off-take through the public distribution system (PDS) also declined.[9]

Like several other developing countries, structural adjustment programmes have led to loss of jobs in India also. There is an indication that rural unemployment had increased in 1994–95, thus corroborating the findings regarding poverty. There has also been a marginal decline in urban employment growth from 1.6 per cent to 1.3 per cent per annum due to decline in public sector employment. In absolute terms, the additional unemployment created on account of stabilisation would amount to 10 million persons out of a total unemployment of around 25 million persons. The expenditure on IRDP went down from Rs 744.3 crores in 1990–91 to Rs 666.2 crores in 1992–93. Over the 8-month period of 1994 till November, the number of families actually assisted under the Integrated Rural Development Programme or IRDP went down by 9 to 10 times. TRYSEM (Training the Rural Youth for Self-Employment) also showed a decline in terms of number of youth to be trained, number of those actually trained, number of self-employed youth, and those employed on wages.[10]

Declining Expenditure in Social Sector

Public expenditure on elementary education is an indicator of the importance attached to it by the government. It is, however, not a sufficient indicator by itself because of the nature of state functioning (Chapter 2). India, ranked 82nd among 116 countries in 1990 in terms of the proportion of public expenditure on education to GNP. The proportion is even lower in terms of the proportion of education expenditure in total public spending. The proportion of government expenditure to GNP, however, started increasing in the mid-80s. These increases were entirely accounted for by sharp increases in teachers' emoluments. The period of increases, in fact, was accompanied by sharp decrease in the teacher–population ratio (i.e., an increase in teacher–pupil ratio). There was, however, no substantial improvement in the pattern of education expenditure in the 90s. If anything, this slowed down after the structural adjustment programme was introduced in 1991.[11]

There has been a significant decline in budget allocation on education in various states since the launching of economic reforms in 1991. This has been due to the lower transfer of resources from the Centre to the States. For instance, the share of education in the Central budget was 27.8 per cent of the total budget in 1989–90 which came down to 12.2 per cent in 1993–94. Similarly, in the combined State budgets, it came down from 18.6 per cent to 12.4 per cent during this period. Health and medical services also showed a significant decline in 1992–93 and 1993–94 as compared to 1989–90. The sharpest cuts occurred on some preventive diseases financed by the central government such as programmes on malaria, tuberculosis and leprosy—the diseases which strike the poor the most and who are also without medical insurance. The reduced provisioning, therefore, adversely affects them the most. The decline in total human development expenditure at the centre was from 17.3 per cent to

15.3 per cent per annum. This decline was largely for infrastructure from 15.9 per cent to 5.7 per cent before and after the reform period. The major expenditure on human development came from the states where there was a perceptible decrease from 16 per cent before to 12.4 per cent after reforms. Interestingly, human development expenditure is the only item to suffer the decline because of reduced transfer of resources from the Centre to the States which has come down from 13.9 per cent before to 7.2 per cent after reforms.[12]

The National Renewal Fund

In view of an anticipated and actual adverse social impact of 'reforms', the Government of India decided to project a 'human face' and floated some social safety measures. Apart from the Public Distribution Scheme, it created a social National Renewal Fund (NRF) in February 1992 to protect the interests of labour, enhance their welfare and equip them in all aspects. This social safety net seeks to pursue two main objectives of human development, namely: (i) creation of National Renewal Grant Fund (NRGF) to compensate workers dislocated because of down-sizing and closing down of various industrial units; (ii) Employment Generation Fund (EGF) to facilitate redeployment and retraining of entrenched workers and to ensure employment-generation in areas affected by economic reforms. Studies of the functioning of NRF show that its allocations have remained stagnant during 1992–93 and 1994–95 period and its coverage in terms of workers has really declined.[13]

Thus, the already bleak human development scenario has further been adversely affected by economic liberalisation. As discussed below, a minimum level of human development infrastructure is necessary for faster economic growth (Drèze and Sen, 1995: 1–8). However, our policies seem to be headed in the opposite direction (see Chapter 7). Not only do the budget outlays tend to show a decline, particularly in the post-reform years, even the meagre existing programmes have faulty implementation so that the benefits tend to go largely to the rich. Studies also show a large amount of leakage in such programmes such as the public distribution system (PDS). For example, less than 22 per cent of the subsidised food went to 20 per cent of the poor households at the bottom. Similarly, in JRY, 56 per cent of the employment generated went to the households above the poverty line.[14] Under such conditions, not only human development, but even the goal of economic growth itself, so stoutly expounded by the supporters of economic liberalisation is likely to suffer. All this deterioration is bound to result in further cynicism and social turmoil in the country.

Growing Resentment against Transnational Corporations

The new economic policies seem to promote easy entry of transnational corporations (TNCs) in the country. It is argued that these would play a positive role in technological upgradation and in promoting competitiveness in the local industry. However, this is possible only if their entry is regulated as per national priorities and according to some plan of technology development. Unplanned entry could bring undesirable consequences in its wake, for which TNCs are known the world over. For instance, they could widen the gap between the poor and the rich not only between countries but also within the country itself. They are known for exploiting natural resources of developing countries and have been responsible for several tragic environmental disasters, for instance, the Union Carbide tragedy at Bhopal in our own country. They have great expertise in manipulative lobbying. As Korten says, 'Tobacco companies spend millions to convince the public that there is no scientific basis for claims that smoking is harmful to their health; auto-manufacturers fight emission standards; gun manufacturers fight gun control; chemical companies illegally dump their toxic wastes; and drug companies engage in monopoly pricing' (Korten, 1995:157). The TNCs are also known for being responsible for generation of 50 per cent of the greenhouse emissions and for global warming as well as for large-scale deforestation. While there has been increasing environmental degradation, the TNCs have sky-rocketed their profits. By effecting mergers and take-overs of other, perhaps smaller companies the giant TNCs have been able to acquire control over 80 per cent of the world's land cultivating export crops, 60 per cent of the aluminium mining and 40 per cent of the world's agro-chemical products.[15]

Because of the adverse impact of TNCs on the lives of the common people and on the environment, there is a growing sense of anger and resentment against them. Several non-governmental and citizen groups have protested against unethical and other negative consequences of TNCs in many countries (Kolodner, 1994). Similar anger has been expressed from time-to-time in India against some big TNCs, particularly those which touch the very core of people's lives. Traditionally, farmers have been saving and using seed from crop to crop. Under the changed circumstances, the TNCs want the farmers to pay a royalty for using seed for commercial crops. 'This is just another way of stating', as Vandana Shiva says, 'that global monopoly over agriculture and food systems should be handed over as a right to multinational corporations' (Shiva, 1992 cited in Korten, 1995). No wonder, therefore, that people are moved to protest against the entry and control of TNCs over the means of their livelihood. There have been, therefore, strident campaigns in India, for example, against entry of TNCs into fisheries, acquaculture and agro business operations. These include Cargill Seeds India (P) Ltd. in Karnataka and its salt manufacturing plant in Gujarat, Dupont joint project with the Thapars for manufacture of nylon tyre in Goa, Nestle's infant formula as a substitute for breast feeding and Enron Corporation Power Project in Maharashtra. Similarly, there have been sustained movements against dumping of toxic waste in India.[16]

Indifference to Social Responsibilities

In addition to the TNCs' adverse effects on the livelihood of people, the ideology of economic liberalisation and structural adjustment seeks to privatise 'public' services. Such policies tend to eliminate public benefits in fields like nutrition, transport, health and education. Protesting against such negative policies, citizens in several developing countries have been involved in what is known as IMF riots. Concerned citizen groups in India and elsewhere and international agencies like the UNICEF have raised their voice from time-to-time against the negative social consequences of such policies (UNRISD, 1994; Kolodner, 1994). Such protests in India need to be further understood in the specific context of increasing unemployment, under-employment, casualisation of labour and decreasing real income.

Experience of structural adjustment programme and the TNCs in different parts of the world and our own experience thus show that, such policies tend to retard social development. Ideologically, there is almost a planned shift from state interventions to market interventions in promoting both economic growth and human development. It is justified on the basis of the trickle down theory which assumes that fruits of economic growth would gradually go to the larger masses of people. The social consequences of such policies, however, firmly negate such assumptions. On the contrary, these policies and programmes directly work, on the one hand, toward weakening of natural solidarity in the community and, on the other, toward shifting values and motivation from public interest to sectoral, individual and personal interest. The corporations seek to take over the reins of the society and use all possible means, foul or fair, to enhance their own wealth and power. Mostly, this is achieved at the cost of the society and the working people. Profit becomes the be-all and all other values take a back seat. Such policies, therefore, encourage aggressive competition for one-upmanship, whittle down social security for children, women and other vulnerable groups, and promote anti-people attitudes in the corporations and public functionaries (UNICEF, 1993b).

Such social and psychological consequences of economic liberalisation would, therefore, add another significant ideological dimension to our socio-political situation where state functionaries have already long been unhelpful in promoting human development. These policies would only reinforce the people-indifferent administrative tendencies in state functioning. Such a scenario is bound to further alienate the population from the system of governance with serious social and political implications. In fact, social responsibility is deliberately weeded out from the corporate governance when socially conscious managers are fired by the predatory system of large corporations. Investment bankers see to it that such managements are replaced by pliant ones to ward off hostile takeover bids.[17] Such corporate tendencies could work towards strengthening indifference to public welfare and social insensitivity in our business, social and political governance.

Worsening Situation for Women and Children

Economic liberalisation and the neo-philosophy of corporations cannot but make the state indifferent to female and children's welfare. This is already reflected in their worsening nutritional and health situation as found by the first National Family Health Survey (NFHS). In India's capital city, Delhi, over 40 per cent of the children surveyed were under-weight and one in every eight suffered from problems of severe malnutrition. The survey conducted in 1992–93 in 24 states and Union Territories, showed that the health objectives set for women and children are far from being achieved. Only in Kerala, the malnutrition level for children under five years was less than 30 per cent.[18] The Central Council of Health and Family Welfare has, therefore, concluded that the goal of health for all by the year A.D. 2000 was no longer possible.

The health care system has long suffered from neglect. Funds have been inadequate and even the meagre available resources have been misused. Inadequacy of primary health centres has greatly contributed to the deteriorating status of public health. Most primary health centres suffer due to shortage of trained staff and lack of essential drugs. The State governments have not been able to motivate doctors to work in rural areas. While communicable and non-communicable diseases are increasing, an enormous amount of money is being wasted in tertiary care hospitals. Equipments worth crores are purchased without the facility to handle them and in many hospitals expensive machines lie idle.[19] Economic liberalisation and the emerging commercial interest now threaten to further bring down the quality of health services in the country.

The values of market forces could thus play havoc with the country's child care system. Already there are wide disparities in child care programmes. Such disparities exist between and within States, between rural and urban areas, between males and females and between different social groups. As a result, nearly two million children die every year before reaching the age of one, almost the same number as in 1961. There are nearly 75 million malnourished children in the country, the largest number in the world, with 63 per cent of children below five years (Chapter 1).

Persistent and chronic malnutrition is a potent indicator of poor social development and failure of the state in this respect. Even when food availability, on the whole, increases, a large number households do not get access to adequate food. Some 30 per cent or more households have to spend 70 per cent or more of their family income on bare food, yet their nutritional needs are not met (Gopalan, 1995). It would be extremely cruel to think that such vulnerable households would be able to operate the market to get their needs met.

Grab-the-Money Ethic

Economic liberalisation and the related new economic policy need to be examined from yet another socio-psychological tendency, i.e., the cut-throat competition for private gains. As mentioned above, such a tendency undermines the values of cooperation, solidarity, public interest and social welfare. Pursuit of unbridled profit also releases unethical and socially undesirable tendencies into business and industry. Unregulated privatisation implemented in countries like the United Kingdom, has led to a depressing loss of idealism in the country.[20] The permanently jobless youth have taken to crime and vandalism. This has corroded the society's long cherished values and promoted the 'pernicious grab-the-money ethic'. The mad cow episode in the U.K. was not just a human tragedy but much more.[21] It represented the stifling ethos of the market in its most unadulterated form, which has been described by the American Sociologist, George Ritzer as 'McDonaldisation of society'.[22]

There already exists a deep-seated tendency among our politico-bureaucratic elite for seeking rent from society by diverting public revenue to personal accounts and also through other corrupt methods (Chapters 2 and 3). Business elites are not only not immune to such tendencies but are leaders in this regard. This has come to the fore rather dramatically in recent times in the form of a series of gigantic scams and scandals. If anything, such illegal practices of 'making a fast buck' (making money, not earning it) have increased tremendously in the last few years.[23] During the pre-economic reform regime, the state itself played a role in promoting primary accumulation of private fortune through lucrative contracts at the expense of the state exchequer. Disregard for laws of the land, especially tax laws, was an important component in primary accumulation of capital. Unregulated privatisation and unplanned race for investments, in the name of economic reforms, have now further fuelled such tendencies.[24] One of the main arguments in favour of liberalisation, namely, that it cuts down bureaucratic arbitrariness in decision-making and eliminates corruption from governance, has been rudely belied. In reality, just the contrary has happened with great increase in the level of public corruption and government arbitrariness.[25] One of the primary reasons for promotion of such ruthlessly corrupt pursuit of money is the fact that, what the new policies promote is not globalisation of production but globalisation of finance. Such policies cater largely to the requirements of international rentier interest. Corruption, cronyism and arbitrariness have always been the characteristics of finance capital (Patnaik and Chandrasekhar, 1995).

Reinforcing the Rentier-Dole Syndrome

Economic liberalisation and structural adjustment policies need thus to be evaluated for their reinforcement of elites' (whether corporate, political or bureaucratic) self-seeking and immoral tendencies and behaviour, on the one hand, and for their restriction of social opportunity for the common people, on the other. Market forces may help in releasing private initiative and competition and thus, may promote economic growth. But unplanned, unregulated and unbridled liberalisation would, at the same time, release socially undesirable and unethical tendencies. Such liberalisation would, therefore, further strengthen (instead of weakening) the entrenched rentier-dole syndrome in the unequal and oppressive system of governance. Market forces have a tendency to dampen public expenditure on human development and divert resources from society to corporations. Such policies, therefore, adversely affect the civil society in general, and vulnerable people in particular and thereby the level of social development in the country.

III

The Changing Social and Political Scene

The state governments' disappointing performance and their glaring failures and the widespread nexus of important functionaries with organised crime and contempt for common people and their welfare have provoked citizens' anger, on the one hand, and some active judicial interventions on the other. The latter has been perceived as an expression of people's aspirations, and therefore widely welcomed. The people hope that it will help in cleansing the system and make it more law-abiding and welfare oriented.

The governments at the centre and in most states were already indifferent, if not negative, to people's welfare, even in the pre-reform period (when they were supposed to implement 'socialist' policies (Chapter 2). It is not surprising that the post-reform period has been characterised by cuts in public provisions for human development. The quality of education, health, employment and social opportunity has, therefore, further deteriorated.[26] Not only have the material conditions of the common people tended to worsen, the social fibre represented by values of cooperation, unity, solidarity and common good has been systematically eroded. 'Making quick money' has been promoted as the top-most value and as an end in itself—no matter how. The ideology of liberalisation and market forces seeks to further erode the state's role in discharging its obligations to the people as reflected in the Preamble, Fundamental Rights and the Directive Principles of the Constitution. No wonder, therefore, that such policies and performance deepen the citizens' anger and disappointment. Judicial activism, stimulated by a spate of public interest litigations, clearly shows the Constitutional failures of the government.

Competitive Electoral Politics

The social organisation in India has long been dominated by the Brahminical values of superordination and subordination with the labouring castes/class facing the brunt of exploitation, discrimination and gross inequality (Chapter 3). Administrative tendencies in the system of governance in general and implementation of programmes in particular, show the impact of such values and motivation (Chapter 2). The citizens' bitter experience at the receiving end of governance, on the one hand, and their participation in competitive electoral politics and in repeated voting on the other, have contributed greatly to their education and awareness. Electoral participation facilitates inculcation of social efficacy and readiness for collective action in them and strengthens their concern for a better life (Mehta, 1981). Such concerns were dramatically reflected in the general elections of 1996.[27] The voters' response in 1996 elections was not a stray phenomenon as the Indian electorate, particularly the weaker sections— the urban and the rural poor—have, in fact, a history of responding positively to radical socio-economic themes.[28] They have repeatedly been exposed to such electoral stimuli, from election to election. It is another matter that electoral promises are implemented only rarely.

This long process of learning, bitter experience of government functioning and a variety of mass movements has gradually led to a perceptible change in the political psychology of the people. This brought about a significant change in the socio-political scene in the country in 1996[29] (Chapter 6). One very important development in this respect is that the voting arithmetic seems to have changed radically. For instance, the traditional social relationship of the superior and subordinate has been greatly dented, as has been brought out in a case study of five districts, namely, Kheda (Gujarat), Guntur (Andhra Pradesh), Madurai (Tamil Nadu), Calcutta (West Bengal) and Belgaon (Karnataka). It has been noted that 'until recently India's modern democracy rested and gained stability from a very traditional Indian society characterised by widespread acceptance of caste hierarchies and the associated patterns of socio-economic domination and subordination'. Now, the dominant castes no longer command that respect and authority which could enable them to influence the political behaviour of those beneath them. Increasing conflicts between the haves and the have-nots indicate the changing social values and the assertive behaviour of the poor in the civil society (Kohli, 1991:91, 299).

Market-oriented economic changes have further contributed to enhancing not only anger but also awareness among the people. Increasing economic (and relative) deprivation has boosted their aspirations as well as their frustration. Heightened social awareness, deepening disillusionment with government functioning and policies, and increasing readiness for collective assertion contain seeds of radical socio-political changes in the country. Such changes not only bring the traditional authority structures under severe strain but also indicate the increasing desire on the part of the dispossessed to get their due share in the governance of the country (Chapter 6).

Thus, the power of the numbers has increasingly come to be pitted against the power derived from wealth and high social status. Bihar is a good example of this emerging situation where the power of land-owning castes is deeply entrenched. The mobilisation of lower castes there has, therefore, been the product of frustration born out by scarcity (Kohli, 1991:299). The significant difference in the social situation now is that such deprived people are not only angry but that they are also ready to assert for a change in political power.[30]

Electoral Verdicts and Government's Bureaucratic Response

The changing socio-political consciousness has drawn wide media attention. Such analyses brought out, among other factors, the apathetic and inefficient governance as an important issue in the 1994 Assembly elections in the country. There was little doubt that the worsening conditions of life had created a strong resentment and anger against the ruling establishment. The ruling party at the Centre, understandably, found it difficult to accept that, although they had got the message, the people were disillusioned with economic reforms. This was shown by their rather hasty response in creating several new departments for implementing programmes of poverty alleviation with very significantly hiked budget outlays. The press rightly dubbed such a response as a bureaucratic gimmickery and as a lamentable lack of initiative and leadership at the higher level of civil services. Such public postures further suggested that government measures were reactive and half-hearted. Poverty alleviation needed, not merely increased government expenditure and much less, expansion of bureaucracy, but greater access to economic assets for the poor, land reforms, decentralisation of development administration and greater public investment in social infrastructure.[31]

Whether the then government at the centre admitted it or not, the policies of economic liberalisation hurted the common man's interest. The instinct of political survival, therefore, forced the government to take some corrective actions. This was further indicated by the rising fiscal deficit during the reform period. The government was forced not to implement this important conditionality of reform (i.e., reducing fiscal deficit by reducing government expenditure) even at the cost of Fund–Bank combine's displeasure. The combined central and state governments' deficit, as proportion of the GDP, on an average, was 9.5 per cent during 1985–90 period and 10 per cent in 1990–91. This was brought down to 7.5 per cent in 1991–92 and 7.4 per cent in 1992–93. It again increased to 9.0 per cent in 1993–94 and 8.4 per cent in 1994–95 (Patnaik and Chandrasekhar, 1995). Hike in central government expenditure could have been due to its profligacy. It was, however, also a reaction to common population's growing disenchantment with its economic policies and their adverse electoral verdict. The compulsions of democracy, thus, forced them to ignore the external pressures for curtailing government expenditure. The fact that the government's response was evoked as a reaction to the voters' adversary behaviour underlines the importance of democratic politics in development policies. Their response was however, merely in the nature of fire-fighting and damage-control rather than a pro-active genuine policy change and a concern for people's welfare (see Chapter 4).

Safety-Net Projects: A Public Relations Exercise

Another evidence of the growing resentment of common people and their anger against policies of structural adjustment and pressures from below, is that governments in various countries have been forced to introduce some social security measures such as the National Renewal Fund in India, social safety nets and similar other projects. Their efforts to project a 'human face' once again highlight the significance of democratic politics in development policies. It is a different matter that such measures, as discussed above, are hardly effective as these tend to maximise 'numbers' rather than the quality of social security (Vivian, 1994). Our public functionaries have already been suffering from a 'number and target syndrome'. They tend to neglect the desired quality and social impact in programme implementation (Chapter 2). Safety-net projects, therefore, are likely to reinforce such a tendency and thus hamper social progress and capability development.

Social safety nets and such other projects, like some anti-poverty programmes tend to become a big exercise in public relations. Such social funds, rather than promoting a human face, represent a 'face saving device' in structural adjustment programmes. Fruits of such projects hardly reach the poorest. This may, therefore, further worsen their conditions of life and prevent them from participating in economic development. Such unshared and inequitable development and social safety projects end up in strengthening the existing power equation (Gayie, 1994 : 33). Such projects are, therefore, political in nature, which seek to promote the impression of being beneficial to all people by publishing the number of benefits available and the number of people covered in various projects. In fact, such quantitative evaluation is the weakest feature of social safety net projects (ibid.: 1994).

Reinforcing the Entrenched Elite

There is yet another political aspect of social safety nets and other similar projects for which funds come from international agencies. These seek to create an impression that the donors are pro-people, and, like the affected people, are also against the 'apathetic' state. They use this argument and try to strengthen NGOs against the government and weaken public support policies (Mackintosh, 1994). As experience in several countries shows, such foreign-funded projects talk of participatory efforts but in fact reinforce the powerfully entrenched elite. They tend to increase participation of people in consumption rather than in efforts for social restructuring, thus providing lucrative opportunity to local powerful elements to use new ways of exploiting the poor (Wolfe, 1981 : 287). In a society like ours with pervasive inequality and unmet needs, such projects in the name of promoting greater participation can, in fact, act as a fig leaf to cover the powerlessness of the poor (Dooyal and Gough, 1991 : 308).

Social safety net and other such projects, thus, tend to empower the 'giver' and to shift the attention of the common people to obligation of the giver (Vandergeest, 1991 : 439). Such a situation permits a shift from people's struggle for their basic welfare rights to welfare gifts. Such projects therefore, provide an opportunity to the state and its bureaucracy to acquire (or atleast seek to acquire) a benevolent (patron) image vis-à-vis the (client) recipients. This could reinforce the age-old dependency behaviour among the population, on the one hand, and the self-image as rulers in the dominant elites including the bureaucracy, on the other. Such safety nets, working as adjuncts to structural adjustment, by publicising and projecting a 'human face', seek to pacify the anger of the dispossessed and the deprived against the dominant elites in a sharply divided inegalitarian society. These, therefore, may help boost the sagging authority of the traditionally entrenched power centres in our society.

IV

Ideological Assault on the State's Democratic and Developmental Role

Because of the growing anger of the people, the Bank–Fund supported structural adjustment seeks ways and means of strengthening the ruling elite against the working people. Such a political message becomes clear when their theorists discuss the role of state in implementing development policies. Massive protest of common people against such policies in several parts of the world has forced them, instead of respecting the democratic aspirations of the people, to turn their attention to identifying political conditions and institutions under which adjustment can best be carried out. One influential school of thought in this connection, described as 'neo-liberal statism' (Vieux and Petras, 1996: PE23), is very pertinent for our present discussion of state interventions for sustainable human development. It stresses the need for state bureaucracy to acquire a high level of technical and administrative capacity in order to wrest autonomy from the society. The theorists of this approach argue that the state has to get this autonomy from the interested groups and what they call, 'rent-seeking' social forces. They consider this as essential for successful implementation of structural adjustment programmes (ibid.: PE23). Such theorists argue that since there are no significant social forces which will be willing to support adjustment, the state acts as a kind of substitute which can press for adjustment. Clearly, such an analysis is an 'appalling obfuscation', as it obscures the true social damage inflicted under structural adjustment upon the ordinary people. It also hides the fact of substantial support for adjustment among the upper classes stemming from the relative certainty that they will derive large and concentrated gains from such policies.[32]

All Power to the Bureaucracy: No Role for People in Structural Adjustment

Thus, the sponsors of structural adjustment may talk of a 'human face', social safety and people's participation, but their theorists see no role of people in implementation of such programmes. As we have seen (Chapter 2), the bureaucracy in India, with its dysfunctional tendencies and behaviour on the ground, has played an unhelpful, if not negative, role as far as implementation of human development programmes is concerned. Similarly, the over-fondness for rules and regulations and rigid bureaucratisation have been unhelpful to economic development including management of public enterprises. It is interesting, therefore, that the theorists (of structural adjustment) see bureaucracy as their main supporter and talk, not for weakening and removing its stranglehold over the society, but for strengthening it. And for what? Not to serve the common population but to wrest autonomy from the civil society and to insulate the state against the pulls and pressures from below so that adjustment programmes could be carried out smoothly.

It is noteworthy that the theorists of structural adjustment, do not think in terms of ameliorating the quality of life, but of insulating the state from social pressures from the disadvantaged and suggest ways and means to disorganise the opposition. In other words, the prescription of the theorists of structural adjustment is: enhance the capacity and power of the bure-aucracy to implement the reforms and to contain, manage and repress the protest which is bound to come from vast sections of the population. This is, therefore, a conceptual recipe to provide strength to the dominant and entrenched power groups at the cost of the vulnerable and the poor—the vast majority of the population. Structural adjustment, if implemented in the manner suggested by its theorists, would not only reinforce the existing inegalitarian social and political organisation but further narrow down its social base. Such policies would, thus, on the one hand, further alienate the state from its population, and on the other, greatly enhance the power of the private corporations, mostly the TNCs, in collaboration with the local elite over the society and the country.[33]

Widening the Social Divide

As we have seen above, civil society in India has been experiencing a deep stirring from within as marginalised people, living at the periphery of society for a long time, are no longer prepared to accept the political authority of traditional structure of power. Policies of globalisation and liberalisation would, therefore, aggravate such conflicts in the civil society as the neglected population assert for participatory development, for a share in economic growth, and in the system of governance itself. There has been increasing assertion from *dalits* and OBCs and pressures from below for government jobs and other rights, which in turn have brought hostile and violent reaction from the upper class bureaucracy and middle class parents, resulting in what has been described as Mandal and Masjid Explosion. Economic liberalisation threatens to further dismantle state interventions which could curtail even the meagre mobility which was available through education, training and other social development programmes. Increasing assertion of the marginalised people for mobility, on the one hand, and the shrinking of opportunities and public support in this regard, on the other, would only aggravate the socio-economic divide and make the situation more explosive.[34]

Political Processes of Structural Adjustment

There is thus not much place for democracy in political theorisation of structural adjustment, as it seeks to insulate the state and empower the bureaucracy against its own people. Under such conceptualisation, there is no room for respect for the ordinary citizens' needs and aspirations. The literature on adjustment is, in fact, pervaded with contempt for the common people, advocating that such people should be manipulated to support reforms. The theorists openly support the use of Machiavellianism saying that 'loss of benefits to various constituents should not be made clear. The higher the potential of political and economic costs of adjustment, the greater the premium of obfuscation' (Waterbury, 1989:54). Some other authors have recommended the use of mixture of packaging, manipulation and stone-walling for the urban masses (see for example, Haggard and Kauffman, 1992:29). Democracy is considered dangerous by such theorists as democratic pressures are likely to derail the programme of structural adjustment.

There is, thus, a striking resemblance between the political processes of people-management as advocated by structural adjustment, on the one hand, and the historically conditioned political processes of the 'king's bureaucracy' in the country, on the other (Chapter 3, Table 3.1). The current politico-administrative culture of the dominant elite in the country is already characterised by tendencies motivated by their contempt for ordinary people and social distance from them. The system is marked by use of deception, cunning, manipulation, falsification, secrecy and coercion in order to 'manage' and to seek rent and personal profit from various programmes. Given such administrative tendencies and motivation (Chapter 2), the country's performance in socio-economic fields has already been rather dismal (Chapters 1 and 4). No wonder, therefore, that the underlying processes of structural adjustment and economic liberalisation tend to further widen the gap between the haves and have-nots and to strengthen centralisation of power to the detriment of public services and human development.

The Washington Consensus: Ignoring Local Realities

Political theories underlying the measures under Bank–Fund structural adjustment have come to be known as the 'Washington Consensus'. The latter seeks to weaken the state's role and enhance the role of market forces in economic development. Such universal recipes and theories violate the local social and cultural realities. The basic educational and health levels are so low in India that withdrawal of the state from such programmes is bound to further dissipate the country's social progress.

Unemployment and under-employment situation enables the corporate sector to introduce flexible use of workforce and to reduce formal employment and worker-benefits and weaken their collective bargaining power—all resulting in a downward trend in real wages (Mehta, 1994a). The civil society as a whole is adversely affected in various ways, as livelihood of people is jeopardised. Increasing job insecurity and economic hardships and the state's weakened role in social security result in fragmented identities. This further cripples the capacity of society to provide an appropriate and minimal framework for stability and justice within which people can interact productively. The framework of structural adjustment, therefore, contradicts the social goals enshrined in the Constitution and the objectives of equitable and sustainable development. Increasing joblessness and decreasing social security is nothing but withdrawal of the state from one of its fundamental responsibilities to its citizens. Such a situation is bound to further slow down the pace of human development of the vulnerable people.[35]

The slowing down of human development can be illustrated by the Chinese example where the rate of improvement in life expectancy and the fall in infant mortality rate have suffered a decline in the post-reform period of 1981–91. During this period, its decline in IMR was only 16 percentage points against India's 27, South Korea's 30 and Sri Lanka's 40 percentage points. Similarly, the progress in improvement in life expectancy at birth also slowed down during this decade in China. It improved by only 1.6 years as against 5.3 years in India, four years in South Korea and by two years in Sri Lanka. One reason could be that longevity was already high in China in 1981—67.7 years—which improved to 69.3 years by 1991. However, in Kerala (in India) also, it was 66.9 years in 1981 which improved to 71.5 years by 1991, and the IMR declined there by 57 percentage points during the same period. Such data, therefore, suggest that the pace of human development got slowed down in China after it opened up its economy to 'reforms' (Drèze and Sen, 1995 : Table 4.3). This has an important lesson for India.

V

Lessons from the East Asian Tigers

The supporters of economic liberalisation and market forces often cite the example of rapid and high economic growth of the East Asian 'tigers', particularly South Korea. They argue that by releasing market forces via a new economic policy, India would also be able to achieve similar faster growth. It is conveniently forgotten however that, in these countries, known as High Performing Asian Economies (HPAEs) (South Korea, Taiwan, Thailand and Hong Kong) education, health care, land reforms, distribution of income and similar other human development measures have made very significant contribution to promoting faster economic growth. Basic education, literacy and cognitive skills were much higher in these countries (than many other developing countries) which made it possible for them to upgrade the skills of workers for mastering the new technology (World Bank, 1993:349). For instance, as late as in 1992, India's literacy rate of 50 per cent was much lower than the rates already achieved in these countries by 1960: South Korea (71 per cent), Hong Kong (70 per cent) and Thailand (68 per cent) (Drèze and Sen, 1995: Table 3.2). If anything, the experience of these high-performing Asian economies illustrates the importance of human capability as an essential facilitating factor in promoting participatory economic development and even for the very success of market economic policies.[36]

Pre-Reform Social Progress and Rapid Economic Growth in Post-Reform China

The Chinese experience presents yet another instructive case about the importance of human development in ushering in rapid and participatory economic development in newly industrialising countries. Its post-reform economic growth has been greatly facilitated by its outstanding educational expansion and egalitarian social progress obtained during its pre-reform period. For example, it had already attained an adult literacy rate of 69 per cent (as against India's 36 per cent) by 1980 when economic reforms were launched there. By 1992, they were able to achieve a literacy rate as high as 96 per cent for males and 85 per cent for females in the age group of 15–19 years. Similarly, pre-reform China had achieved remarkable progress in land reforms which was an important factor in its post-reform rapid economic development (World Bank, 1993; Wade, 1990). On the contrary, in India, the progress in adult literacy of young people, health services and in land reforms, has been very dismal. The lesson from China, therefore, is that it is not only the elimination of controls and opening up of the economy to market forces, which have helped them to achieve faster economic growth, but also the creation and release of widespread social opportunities brought about by determined and persistent state interventions. Post-reform China had, thus inherited social opportunities released by its pre-reform transformation which have greatly facilitated its economic growth.

Market Mechanism as Means and Not as Ideology

Another important lesson for India from China is that it is possible to accelerate economic development without losing one's political orientation. Their goal is faster and greater economic growth for which the market mechanism is being used as a means for creating operational channels of social and economic opportunities. In other words, their approach to market economy is instrumental and pragmatic, not ideological. Contrary to the conditionalities usually associated with Fund-Bank type liberalisation, China has been able to provide adequate basic social security for its population (Hussain, 1993, 1994 and literature cited there). Similarly, in pursuance of their social policies, they have also succeeded in raising income levels of their people and in reducing income disparities even while implementing market reforms.

China's experience, therefore, suggests that it is possible to adhere to values of equality and expansion of opportunities for all while implementing market economic policies, provided these are accompanied by appropriate social policies. It is possible to use market forces for accelerating participatory and egalitarian economic development provided the state and its organs and functionaries, show greater commitment to social welfare, i.e. public good (than their own private interest). The China's experience also shows that market 'reforms' may help in achieving faster economic growth but not necessarily faster social progress as shown by the fact that the real incomes there have increased much rapidly while improvements in life expectancies have slowed down. Such results serve to confirm the proposition that faster economic growth does not automatically translate into human development. The fact that, despite political commitment, social progress is somewhat hampered by the forces released by market mechanisms further underlines the importance of state interventions for human development in India.

State Vs Market: Government's Active Role

The foregoing discussion shows that the ideology of elimination of state's active role in promoting economic development, is bound to hamper not only human development and egalitarian social progress but also economic development itself in countries like India. Market forces may be useful for promoting competitive economic development in some areas by releasing private enterprise and a drive for improving quality. Such competitive excellence, however, does not happen because of market forces only. The competition for achievement of quality and excellence has to be designed, released and obtained both at the societal level as well as at the workplace where the production process is conducted. Without the involvement and motivation of working people, it may be possible to obtain profits but not innovative excellence. On the other hand, such profit-seeking endeavour (without caring for excellence) may demoralise workers, in the long run, depress productivity and quality. Workers' capability plays an important role in achieving competitive excellence, not only at the micro enterprise level, but also at the macro societal level. Human and social factors have greatly contributed to promoting faster economic growth in the HPAEs. In these countries, such advantages made it easier for them to upgrade the skills of workers for mastering the new technology (World Bank, 1993:349). This needs to be reiterated in view of the tendency of the supporters of structural adjustment in India to repeatedly cite the example of these east Asian countries while projecting the dream that India could also become another Asian 'tiger'.

The supporters of the Fund-Bank type liberalisation tend to often forget yet another important fact about the HPAEs, that the governments there played an active role not only in promoting human development but also in regulating economic development as per their own national goals, local needs and resources. Therefore, even for market-operated 'liberalised' economic growth, there are several important lessons for India from the HPAEs. These include: (i) India needs to catch up, rather very fast, in the fields of social and human development, particularly adult literacy and basic education, health services for all people and in implementing egalitarian land and agrarian reforms; (ii) The state needs to actively intervene for accelerating the process of development as per the needs and aspirations of the people and show strong political commitment in this respect.

Scope for Human Development with Low Economic Growth

The experience of some (other than the HPAEs) other newly industrialising countries such as Cuba, Vietnam, pre-reform China, Costa Rica, Jamaica and Sri Lanka shows that it is quite possible to achieve faster and adequate progress in education, health, etc., without waiting for high economic growth to take place. Even under conditions of poverty, as obtained in these countries during various periods and even now, it was possible for them to achieve remarkable progress in literacy and health services. For example, Sri Lanka has been able to achieve 85 per cent adult literacy rate for females and 94 per cent for males by 1992 against India's 39 per cent and 63.4 per cent respectively. Similarly, Sri Lanka's life expectancy at birth in the same year was 74 years for females and 70 years for males against India's 59 years for both; infant mortality rate of 18 per 1,000 live births against India's 79 and female–male ratio at 99 against India's 93. On the other hand, the per capita GDP in percentage terms during 1980–82 period was 2.6 in Sri Lanka and 3.1 in India whereas the estimated PPP per capita GNP (USA = 100) 12.2 in Sri Lanka and only 5.2 in India (see Drèze and Sen, 1995: Table A. 2). Such data suggest that, as compared to India, despite relatively lower growth, there has been much greater equality in distribution of income in Sri Lanka. Similarly, several other countries have achieved much faster social development in terms of education and health indices under similarly poor economic conditions or with even poorer conditions.

VI

Activising the State for Human Development

Not only is India lagging behind in human development than countries like Cuba, Sri Lanka and Jamaica, there is no place in the world with as high an infant mortality rate as the district of Ganjam in Orissa and as low an adult literacy rate as the Barmer district of Rajasthan. These districts fare badly even in comparison with Sub-Saharan Africa despite the fact that, unlike the latter, India has been relatively much more peaceful. Yet, it has failed to take advantage of these favourable circumstances. The dominant elite have shown no or little interest in human development of vulnerable people. They have been quite active in promoting higher education facilities for themselves and at the same time neglecting elementary basic education for common people for all these years (Drèze and Sen, 1995:27–56).

The Imperative Need for Active State Interventions

The state, in India, which has already been rather indifferent, is now being further threatened by the 'Washington Consensus', seeking to make it still more inactive vis-à-vis welfare of the vulnerable people. Yet, without the active interventions of the state, we can neither have faster social progress nor shared and participatory economic development in the country. Such ideological efforts and pressures accompanying economic liberalisation and globalisation are motivated by the interest of the international finance capital and those of the TNCs. People's welfare and the quality of their life are their least concern. If the state yields to such pressures, the economic development would not make any meaning to the vast masses of people in the country. Such international mechanisms have, therefore, to be stoutly resisted and attempts made at the same time to activising the various state organs for promoting and regulating social and economic opportunities in the country.

The Common Minimum Programme

The Common Minimum Programme (CMP) of the UF Government did verbalise the need for reactivating the state agencies for the welfare of the people. It promised representative and responsive governance at the Centre, states and local levels for obtaining higher standards of living and a better life for people. It also promised the right to information and stressed the need for public functionaries' accountability to people. It talked of empowerment of deprived sections and women and promised to launch programmes for enhancing their skills and capability. It also promised to make education a Fundamental Right under the law and to provide budgetary provision of 6 per cent of the GDP for this purpose, of which 50 per cent was proposed to be spent on primary education. They promised to take active steps to meet the basic needs of the people like providing drinking water, health, housing, education, literacy, employment and skill development. They had promised higher investment in public sector and protection of environment and other natural resources. Interestingly, they also talked of better implementation of programmes and promoting participation and involvement of all citizens, i.e., the civil society in development efforts. On the whole, the UF Government at the Centre, had promised to activise the state for people's welfare and development and to build a just and humane society (UF, 1996).

The Need for Planned Action

The crucial question, however, is: how can the state which has been indifferent, if not hostile, to obtaining even the basic needs of the common people for such a long time, be activised now for these vital tasks? The task becomes still more difficult because the government continues to be wedded to the policies of economic liberalisation, which ideologically, threaten to further curtail the state's role in development. It is quite clear that, despite promises made in the Common Minimum Programme, the state in India would not be so easily and automatically motivated to promote the goals of human development, i.e., capability development of the vulnerable people and their empowerment (Chapter 4). It is indeed a stupendous task and would require planned efforts. Studies and experience, as discussed above, suggest some insights which could be used to plan and launch social and other interventions designed to activise the state in the desired pro-people direction. We summarise some suggested action hypotheses in this regard.

1. **Contesting the Ideology of Market Forces:** Economic liberalisation policies tend to reinforce the already entrenched political processes of administration. These further bring about a motivational shift in the public functionaries from public interest to personal and sectoral interest. Such policies help the system to rationalise the cognitive dissonance created by the gap between promises and practices. Now, their ground behaviour vis-à-vis the promises and the performance can be conceptually justified by the ideology of market forces. Concerted efforts are, therefore, required to contest this ideology and to reassert the need for direct public support for human development. Adversary political groups, press and other mass media, trade unions and other people's organisations have a crucial role in this respect.
2. **Strengthening the Concern for the Lives of Vulnerable People:** There is some scepticism that a poor country like India cannot afford to make large-scale public provisioning for public services and human development and that without huge funds, such goals cannot be achieved. The experience of countries like China, Sri Lanka and Jamaica shows that this is a misleading diagnosis, as the main cause of their success is not merely higher expenditure but involvement and political commitment

of their public functionaries. Efforts are, therefore, needed to strengthen their concern for the lives of common people in order to motivate them for effective public services of health care, education, drinking water, public sanitation, employment generation, etc.

3. **Inculcating a Sense of Stake in the Public Mind for Effective Public Services:** Planned efforts are needed to gear the public functionaries to give up their patronising role and to develop an enabling role in order to facilitate inculcation of a sense of stake in the public mind for the functioning of public services like education and health. It is necessary for promoting fruitful people's participation in translating promises and policies into concrete programmes on the ground and for converting opportunities into achievements.

4. **Enhancing Readiness to Learn and Effect Mid-course Corrections:** Planned efforts are needed to help public functionaries enhance their readiness: to learn from people, to use feedback for effecting mid-course corrections in programmes, to be flexible and creative, and to take moderate risk and innovate in order to achieve social objectives of sustainable human development programmes. Such administrative capability could make a crucial difference in programme implementation and generate success experience in this regard. Which would, in turn, further reinforce their readiness to learn and be creative in working with people.

5. **Promoting Social and Gender Sensitivity:** Economic liberalisation and structural adjustment programme could reinforce the already entrenched gender discrimination and retard caring for children. Specifically planned efforts are needed, not only to contest such policy consequences but also to promote women empowerment via employment, literacy, elementary education, health care and for eliminating child labour. It is necessary to help the public functionaries to develop the required social and gender sensitivity and to gear up for implementing the related programmes.

6. **Creating a History of Pressures and Success:** A history of empty promises enhances the sense of public cynicism about government programmes. This hinders the functioning of state agencies and distorts and weakens programme implementation. Planned efforts are, therefore, needed to force the ruling party to implement their electoral and other promises made from time-to-time. Adversary and competitive electoral politics and other mass organisations play an important role in this respect. There is a need to create an alternative history of public pressures and success in this respect.

Such action hypotheses call for sustained people's movements and social mobilisation for changing direction and character of the state and its political behaviour. Only then will the country truly move towards the goal of human development with steady, concrete steps. We discuss some related issues in this respect in the next chapter.

END NOTES

1. For a brief history of administrative reforms and the suggested new practices, see Basu (1992) and government reports, studies and other contributions cited there.

2. For performance in human development and availability of social opportunities, see Drèze and Sen (1995:27–56 and 140–178, particularly Tables 3.3 and 7.1). The resurgence of diseases is another glaring example of the failure of the state on the health front. See a special report entitled, 'We are a Sick Nation' by Sanghmitra Chakravarthy in *Times of India*, November 10, 1996. The state failure is also indicated by another startling fact that the year 1996 was marked by a phenomenal growth in child labour in illegal fire cracker manufacturing units mushrooming in North India. This led to a landmark judgment of the Supreme Court directing the employers of child labour in hazardous industries to set up a corpus fund for their rehabilitation. See *Times of India*, December 26, 1996.

3. For details of such trials and scandals, see a report entitled 'Year Marked by Trials and Scandals' by Rakesh Bhatnagar in *Times of India*, December 25, 1995. For scandals detected during 1996, see a report in *Times of India*, December 26, 1996.

4. The Jain Hawala case has drawn very wide media coverage, indicating the deep interest it created in the country. 'Hawala', meaning illegal transaction of foreign exchange, was used as a conduit for financing anti-national activities of the militants in the Punjab and Jammu & Kashmir and also for paying bribes and commissions to politicians, bureaucrats and others. See reports in *India Today*, February 15, 1996:28–56; *Frontline*, February 23, 1996:4–19.

5. There have been wide media comments on the growing judicial activism and on its possible positive consequences for cleansing the politico-administrative system and for making it more transparent and accountable to the people. See cover story in *India Today*, March 15, 1996 and other related stories and also an interview with Justice J.S. Verma, heading three-judge-bench of the Supreme Court, on the Hawala case. Justice Verma has been quoted as saying that 'a strong arm is needed to make executive work'. See the interview in the cover story, pp. 120–122.

6. See a report in *Times of India*, February 18, 1996.

7. See a report by King Shuk Nag in *Times of India*, February 19, 1996. However, subsequently an IAS officer was appointed as the CAG.

8. The organisations of private sector industry have been clamouring for privatisation of lucrative public sector undertakings. See *Times of India*, April 2, 6 and 8, 1994. It has been estimated by B.B. Bhattacharya of the Institute of Economic Growth that a sum of Rs 15,000 crore was lost through the sale of 30 blue chip stocks in public sector undertakings and nothing was done to discover who actually benefitted from the sale of public assets. He termed it as a disinvestment scam. The recent telecom bids controversy is another example of privatisation scam. See a report by Sakina Yusuf Khan along with other stories in *Times of India*, November 10, 1996. Also see

a piece by L.K. Sharma in *Times of India*, August 25, 1996 quoting two British scholars on liberalisation and new corruption. The two researchers have questioned the assumption that corruption can be reduced by rolling back the role of the state through privatisation, deregulation and competition.

9. For poverty and for poor functioning of the PDS and its low reach for the needy, see research surveys quoted in *Times of India*, April 16, 1996 and the article by Praful Bidwai in *Times of India*, August 2, 1996.

10. It has been reported that the percentage of families in rural areas living below the poverty line has risen from 33 per cent in 1987–88 to 49.16 per cent in 1995–96. The actual employment generated was 2.24 million per annum against the target of 6.26 million per annum. While the outlay for the JRY increased from Rs 3,306 crore in 1993–94 to Rs 3,855 crore in 1994–95, the man-days of employment generated declined from 10,236 to 9,515 during this period. See details in *Times of India*, February 2 and 5, 1996. An editorial in *Times of India*, December 11, 1996 said, 'The Planning Commission has rediscovered the poor living below the poverty line. If the former union finance minister, Manmohan Singh and the former Deputy Chairman, Planning Commission, Pranab Mukherjee had their way, the poor may have well disappeared by now conjured away by statistical jugglery.... According to the revised estimates of the poverty ratio... this proportion stands at 39 per cent of the population'.

11. *Human Development Report*, 1994, Tables 15, 36 and 49. For role of expenditure on education and related data see, Drèze and Sen, 1995 : 120–123 and other contributions cited there.

12. All the data cited in this section, unless otherwise indicated, are from Gupta (1995). For data on impact of economic reforms on the poor and other social consequences, also see Tendulkar and Jain, 1995; Patnaik and Chandrasekhar, 1995; and some media reports in newspapers as mentioned above.

13. See Gupta (1995).

14. See *Times of India*, February 5, 1996.

15. For such data see Greer and Singh (1996). Also see a piece by Ward Morehouse on Bhopal Tragedy: The unpaid human costs of globalisation, *Times of India*, December 12, 1996.

16. The Parliament was recently told (on August 9, 1995) that synthetic milk with urea, caustic soda and other chemicals mixed as non-fat contents are being marketed by a transnational corporation, namely, Nestle. See a report in the *Times of India*, August 10, 1995. Also see Greer and Singh (1996) and Korten (1995).

17. For discussion on cost of corporate cannibalism and strategies of takeover of companies and mergers, see Korten (1995:208–214). This discussion brings out not only the various manipulative methods used for takeover of existing companies but also consequences of such takeovers on the society at large. The latest example of such mergers is of McDonnell Doughlas (MD) with the Boeing to create a new giant in order to dominate the world's commercial aviation. This would now threaten Europe's Airbus Industry. See *Times of India*, Business Times report, December 17, 1996.

18. For details, see *Times of India*, September 1, 1995. Some three years later the UNICEF's annual report: *The State of World's Children*, 1998, found two out of every five children in India malnourished and women and girls discriminated against. For comments on this report, see *Times of India*, 18 December 1997 and items by Aditi Kapoor, *Times of India*, 1 January 1998; Rashmi Sehgal, 10 January 1998; and editorial of 12 January 1998 in the same paper.

19. See *Times of India*, November 17, 1995.
20. See a story by Walsh (1993).
21. The mad cow phenomenon in England is a good illustration of anti-social consequences of privatisation and deregulation. It was an offshoot of capitalist obsession with profits. The crisis was not just a human tragedy but much more than that. The pursuit of even cheaper food in Britain led to the use of offal in cattle feed with a view to boosting the productivity of cows with high protein diet which misfired because it was unnatural. The infected feed transferred a brain disease from sheep to cow and then to some of the humans who consumed the infected beef. The beef industry is no BCCI which was allowed to collapse. It could not be left to the market forces even by a government which believes in non-intervention. The government had to subsidise the farmers in trouble. The consumer associations hope that the government would not side with the producers' lobby all the time and would protect also the interests of consumers. See a story by L.K. Sharma in *Times of India*, March 31, 1996. Also for discussion as to how corporations and TNCs are destroying the old time liberal social values of good neighbourhood, community and solidarity in the countries of their origin, see Korten, 1995:51–103 and 227–249.
22. McDonald's, the American fast-food chain, is central to the brand image and marketability of beef in the West. It is one of the potent icons of the 'free market'. In pursuit of more and more profits, they use all kinds of techniques to increase production of beef, milk and other products, ignoring the natural side of this process. Financial analysts call it 'market correction'. All it involved was an engineered shift away from cows which produced meat of high nutritional quality to those which excelled in sheer quantity alone. The *mantra* for success was to have cattle become fat fast at low cost and high profit. At the root of the present crisis, therefore, lies the Thatcherite notion that what is good for business is good for society. See a story, 'Mad Cows: Market and McDonaldisation' by Siddhartha Varadarajan, in *Times of India*, April 8, 1996.
23. In addition to various commercial scams and scandals, the recent Chara Kand (fodder scandal) in Bihar is a glaring example of illegal transfer of state funds to private accounts. See a report in *Frontline*, March 8, 1996:30–31. The Jain Hawala case also dramatically highlights this ugly aspect of our state behaviour in which ministers and bureaucrats have been allegedly found in accepting bribes and commissions in lieu of lucrative contracts awarded to various contractors and firms. Such increasing number of cases clearly illustrates the deep-seated rentier character of the state apparatus. This characteristic has been greatly reinforced by the similar rentier character of international finance which aggressively pursues fast buck in short term gains rather than invest in long-term production processes. See Korten (1995:183–249) and various contributions cited there.
24. See Patnaik and Chandrasekhar (1995).
25. There have been several episodes of corrupt and arbitrary distribution of public property for which the Supreme Court of India have held the concerned political functionaries responsible for misusing discretionary quotas and have imposed heavy fines. The Court has laid down that damages can be awarded in cases where the state has shown disregard of the Fundamental Rights guaranteed under Articles 14, 19 or 21 of the Constitution. See a report by Rakesh Bhatnagar entitled 'Public servants will now pay for abuse of power' in *Times of India*, November 26, 1996.

26. For resurgence of diseases, see *Times of India*, October 20, 1996. In another instance of state's lethargy and, at times, connivance with violation of laws has come from Rajasthan where the State government, which has been unable to check malaria epidemic, seemed to connive with the celebration of *sati mata*. Such glorification of the practice of *sati* showed the state government's inexplicable lethargy regarding 1987 episode where a young widow burnt herself alive on her husband's pyre. See an editorial 'Burning Issue', *Times of India*, November 29, 1996.

27. See election cover story in *India Today*, May 15, 1996.

28. For a study of election campaigns and electoral response to radical themes, see a case study of 1971 general Lok Sabha elections (Mehta, 1975 and 1977).

29. *India Today*, July 15, 1996; *Frontline*, July 26, 1996.

30. Ibid.

31. The Eighth Plan outlay on rural development and poverty alleviation is expected to cross Rs 33,000 crore against the Seventh Plan outlay of merely Rs 1,000 crore. The outlay for the Fourth year of the Eighth Plan, i.e., for the year 1995–96 has touched Rs 8,000 crore and may be more to about Rs 10,500 crore. See a report in *Times of India*, February 2, 1996. Such a dramatic hike in budget outlays for poverty alleviation programmes indicates government's panicy response to growing disenchantment of the vulnerable people to its policies of economic reforms. See also an editorial comment on the subject in *Times of India*, February 5, 1996.

32. See Vieux and Petras (1996: PE26 and other contributions cited there) for discussion of the ideology of structural adjustment programme and the Washington Consensus.

33. For an exhaustive documentation and discussion of the various aspects of curtailment of the autonomy of the civil society and the sovereignty of the state and of the rise of corporate colonialism, see Korten, 1995 : 119–173. The *Fortune* magazine has recently reported that Fortune 500 companies collectively made a profit of $244 billion in 1995 as against $215.25 billion in 1994. Yet the total employment hardly budged from the previous year, rising by just 0.2 per cent. In some companies like Goodycar, the profit rose significantly although the number of workers employed by them fell. See Korten (1995) and a large number of contributions cited in the book. Also see a report in *Times of India*, April 10, 1996.

34. See Kothari (1995).

35. For discussion on jobless growth, see UNDP (1993 : 34–36) and also Korten (1995 : 171). In this connection, Korten says, 'If measured by contributions to improving the lives of people or strengthening the institutions of democratic governance, the World Bank and the IMF have been disastrous failures—imposing enormous burden on the world's poor and as a result impeding their development' (p. 117).

36. The East Asian economic miracle has been welcomed also because these countries have succeeded in achieving a certain amount of equity of income distribution and also in reducing poverty. However, over the past few years, the havenots in these countries, such as Vietnam and Thailand, have been feeling restless. In Thailand several thousand protesting poor camped for a long time outside the Prime Minister's office in Bangkok, many of whom were suffering from health problems like byssinosis, an allergic lung disease contacted during their work in textile and clothing industry, which is the most important export industry of Thailand. Economists believe that inequality is now increasing in Thailand and that by A.D. 2000, 70 per cent of

Thailand workers will have received only primary education at school. Despite improvement in longevity and decline in the infant mortality rate, most people are restless because of the increasing wealth gap in favour of the rich and powerful. See a report entitled 'Wealth gaps make East Asia's havenots restless', *The Economist*, reported in *Times of India*, April 16, 1996. In its *World Employment Report* 1996–97, the ILO has warned that growing unemployment and the spurning of the ideal of full employment would aggravate social and economic ills. They have, however, lauded the dynamic economies of east Asia for their high and sustained employment growth of more than 3 per cent per annum well in excess of the rate of increase in the labour market. See for a report, *Times of India*, November 11, 1996.

CHAPTER 6

PUBLIC ACTIVISM FOR HUMAN DEVELOPMENT

Political processes since Independence, along with the historical antecedents of such processes, have not been favourable to education, health, income generation and such other basic needs of the vulnerable people in the country.[1] As a result, the country has continued to be riddled with massive problems of illiteracy, ill-health, avoidable mortality and lack of other basic amenities like drinking water, sanitation, housing, etc. (Chapter 1).

Human development, besides being important per se, also tends to play an important role in promoting economic development including economic growth. In several countries, having high rate of basic education, improved health status and enhanced purchasing power, there has also been a relatively more shared and participatory economic development. There, the masses of educated and healthy people have been able to take advantage of opportunities for entrepreneurship. Such opportunities are hardly available to the illiterate and deprived people in India. Not only has the majority been left out of the development process, the market-oriented economic measures now tend to further boost concentration of wealth in the hands of already rich population (Chapter 5).

I

'State' Behaviour on the Ground: Public as the Prime Mover

We have seen that the current socio-economic situation is difficult for the common public, particularly the working people in the country. And yet, we have also seen (Chapter 5) that faster socio-economic progress requires release of the productive energy of the people and their active participation in such programmes and projects. The state, which has an important role to play in motivating people in this respect has, however, been largely indifferent if not hostile towards such participatory goals (Chapters 2 and 3). There is thus an urgent need to change the direction of the state and activise it in the interest of society at large, i.e., the majority of the population. This need assumes greater importance in face of the ideology of economic liberalisation and globalisation (Chapter 5). It is not an easy task, particularly in view of its entrenched and strong tendency to safeguard and promote the interests of the rich and privileged sections of the society. How can they now be persuaded to work for the under-privileged?

Kerala and Uttar Pradesh: A Study in Contrast

There is some rich experience in the country itself which could guide us about methods of energising the state agencies for better performance in human development. A comparative study of social progress in various States in the country suggests the importance of mass mobilisation and public activism in this respect. This is shown, dramatically, for example, by the contrast between Kerala, on the one hand, and Uttar Pradesh on the other. The two States are almost at a similar level of poverty, yet poles apart in human development. For instance, the child mortality rate in Uttar Pradesh was six times higher than that in Kerala. The adult literacy rate in Kerala in 1992 was 86 per cent for females and 94 per cent for males, whereas in Uttar Pradesh, it was 25 per cent and 56 per cent respectively. Similarly, the two States also present a contrast in terms of longevity, IMR, crude death rate and female–male ratio, the latter being 104 (females for 100 males) in Kerala and just 88 in Uttar Pradesh (Drèze and Sen, 1995, Table A.2). Both the States are parts of the same country and governed by the same system of administration with similar public systems and departments of education, primary health centres, public distribution system, etc. Yet, the government agencies have been relatively more socially responsive and active in Kerala than Uttar Pradesh, as the social indicators clearly suggest. The contrasting situation suggests that the public functionaries, including the bureaucracy, on the one hand, and the people themselves, on the other, in the two states have been behaving very differently, maybe in diametrically opposite directions.

In Kerala, people have been able to achieve widespread literacy and basic education, removal of rigid traditional inequalities and state provisioning for and, more importantly, reasonable functioning of basic public services. The opposite is the case with Uttar Pradesh where these vital public welfare matters have largely been neglected (see Table 6.1). The question is: why have the successive governments in Uttar Pradesh been indifferent and apathetic to human development and why have they been comparatively more active and positive in Kerala? No doubt, literacy, particularly female literacy, and general social awareness have played an important role in obtaining greater social achievements in Kerala. However, it is the social and political organisation of the deprived people, the influence of the public at large, their vigilance and political activism, in other words people's assertive behaviour, which has played a crucial role in pressurising and/or persuading the government, of whatever political party, for active state interventions including legislative action for proper functioning of public services. On the other hand, such public activism has been rather weak in Uttar Pradesh. The contrast provides evidence for the hypothesis that political organisation and processes and social environment play an important role in promoting human development. Such environment has been markedly more people-oriented and has, there-fore, played a positive role in social achievements in Kerala. On the other hand, these have been markedly more 'elite' and social status quo oriented and, therefore, have played an indifferent, if not inhibiting role, in the case of Uttar Pradesh.[2]

Table 6.1
Uttar Pradesh and Kerala: Contrast in Access to Public Services

	India	Uttar Pradesh	Kerala
Percentage of rural children aged 12–14 who have never been enrolled in a school,1986–87			
Female	51	68	1.8
Male	26	27	0.4
Proportion of children aged 12–23 months who have not received any vaccination, 1992–93 (per cent)	30	43	11
Percentage of recent births preceded by any antenatal check-up, 1992–93	49	30	97
Proportion of births taking place in medical institutions, 1991 (per cent)	24	4	92
Number of hospital beds per million persons, 1991	732	340	2,418
Proportion of villages with medical facilities, 1981 (per cent)	14	10	96
Proportion of the population receiving subsidised cereals from the public distribution system, 1986–87 (per cent)	29	3	87

Source: Drēze and Sen, 1995, Table 3.4, p. 53.

Kerala's experience shows that social development of the people can be achieved even under conditions of low level of economic growth with different forms of public activism and state interventions. This (Kerala's success story) highlights the importance of the 'actor' role of the people in their own development. Their struggles for improving their social conditions via literacy, health services, etc., and the underlying dynamics of politics stimulated by such struggles have greatly contributed to such social achievements. Public activism has also been able to activate the state, i.e., the various government agencies, to take interest in implementing the related services and programmes. Working dialectically, 'demand', from below energises the state apparatus to function towards fulfilling some basic needs of the people. Such experience, therefore, provides evidence for another hypothesis, that public behaviour acts as a prime mover of social sector development. The two, i.e., the public and the state, could work in reciprocal and/or dialectical relationship and, in turn, put pressure on public functionaries for welfare and socio-economic development efforts.

II

Some Historical Factors in the Kerala Model

The Kerala model of social development, as it has been widely designated, is thus, situated in the history of its people's struggle for a vibrant civil society with traditions of mass movements such as the library movement, people's science movement, literacy movement and various political, social and trade union movements. It would be useful for our discussion of human development, 'state' behaviour and public activism to recall some such socio-historical factors which have played a positive role in this respect.

Commonality Between Kerala and Sri Lanka

An understanding of some salient factors in Sri Lanka's success story in human development would be helpful in this respect, as there are several similarities in social indicators there and in Kerala. For example, the ages of marriage for females in Sri Lanka and Kerala are respectively about 24.4 years and 21.8 years, whereas it is 16.5 years in Bihar; the ratio of female literacy to male literacy of 100 is 88, 90 and 34 respectively in Sri Lanka, Kerala and Bihar. Similarly, the proportion of girls in total school enrollment in grades 1–5 was 49.1 per cent in Sri Lanka, 48.5 per cent in

Kerala and 29.7 per cent in Bihar and in grades 6–8, 48.5 per cent, 47.9 per cent and 21.3 per cent respectively (all data for the year 1981; see Table in Casinader, 1995). Thus, the social indicators for Sri Lanka and Kerala are strikingly similar and validate as being classified as one type of development. Another significant factor in social development in Sri Lanka and Kerala is similarities in their political history and organisation (ibid.: 3086). In addition to such similarities, there are some similarities between South West India and South East Asia. In view of such similarities, it has been proposed that 'certain aspects of the history and political organisation of Kerala are more intelligible when the area is thought of as one of the Hinduised states of South East Asia rather than as an integral part of South Asian sub-continent' (Dale, 1980:11).

Such sharing of social factors between South East Asia and South West of South Asian region include gender relations and status of women with matrilinial past. Then, Sri Lanka and Kerala, both have the common experience of radical ideology. For instance, Sri Narain Guru's teachings have greatly influenced the radicalisation of thinking and politics in Kerala. His slogan of one caste, one god, one religion was converted by radical politics into no caste, no god and no religion. Shri Narain Guru's movement itself has been described as a part of historical contestation between *Brahminism* and *Sramanism* (Thapar, 1989:211–212). Historically, the most significant contestation of Brahminism was Buddhism. As continuity of Buddhism has been maintained in Sri Lanka and as Brahminism has been absent there, such a contestation was a non-issue there. Besides contestation of Brahminism in Kerala and its absence in Sri Lanka, the two also shared anti-imperialistic attitudes in their various movements. Radicalisation of politics of trade unions together with electoral parliamentary politics have shaped social development and public behaviour in both the regions.

Shri Narain Guru's teachings and the contestation of Brahminism were conducted in Kerala, as mentioned above, in the context of radical politics. This facilitated the transformation of caste consciousness into class consciousness (Issac, 1985). The Buddhist revival movement in Sri Lanka, Shri Narain Guru's movement in Kerala, E.V. Ramaswami Naicker's movement in Tamil Nadu—though all, in some ways, expressions of resistance of Brahminical ideological hegemony in South Asia—led to varied consequences. Such a movement promoted ethnic consciousness in Sri Lanka, class consciousness in Kerala and Tamil Nationalism and non-Brahmin caste consolidation in Tamil Nadu. The Kerala model of social sector development has particularly been described as being driven by left wing politics and ideologies (Franke and Chasin, 1992).

Social Mobilisation and Human Development

The foregoing contrasting pictures underline the importance of historical factors and the nature of social consciousness in shaping motivation and, at least to some extent, attitudes of state functionaries toward formulating and implementing plans for social change and development. This is further illustrated by the example of Tamil Nadu, where there has been a long history of social movements among the socio-economically backward sections of the society. For instance, the Buddhist Sangam and Dravida Mahajana Sangam held a conference as far back as December 1881 and adopted a charter of demands which, in a way, anticipated similar demands later made elsewhere in the country. Such demands included: enactment of law to punish those who referred to the depressed classes as 'Pariahs' in order to degrade and insult them; opening of separate schools in each village for depressed classes; preference to those among the depressed classes who passed matriculation in employment as well as in higher education and that, their representatives should be appointed in villages and towns to report to the government about the grievances of depressed classes regarding employment and other matters. There were also other movements such as the movement for self-respect and the non-Brahmin movement for promoting a deep and abiding sense of Tamilness (Geetha and Rajadurai, 1993).

It is thus, not by chance, that Kerala and now, Tamil Nadu, are ahead in various fields of social sector development. They have not only achieved lowered birth and death rates but have also been successful in considerably reducing urban–rural disparities in education, literacy and health services. The people in these states, particularly in Kerala, have shown greater preparedness to confront the traditional social status quo and related values than anywhere else in the country. Given such a social environment and public activism, the state functionaries also tended to show, relatively speaking, greater readiness to work for the disadvantaged by showing, at least comparatively, greater sensitivity to the needs and aspirations of the common people. On the other hand, in most parts of the country, notably in the north, where people's social assertiveness had been rather weak, the state functionaries, barring a few notable individual exceptions, have shown a strong tendency to maintaining and reinforcing the social status quo, i.e., the traditional Brahminical social order informed by the principle of superordination and subordination with deleterious consequences for the disadvantaged masses of labouring people.

Social mobilisation and people's movements, thus, play an important role, on the one hand, in shaping the mind-set of the state agencies and, on the other, in promoting social development of vulnerable people themselves. Such movements and mobilisation and the resultant radical social consciousness strike at the root causes of disempowerment of the labouring castes/classes. This, in turn, generates 'demands' and pressures from below on the superstructure above. Such assertive behaviour on the part of the public strengthens the social environment needed for inculcating and reinforcing the facilitative behaviour on the part of state functionaries. Such confrontation between the public and the state results in effective implementation of development programmes and public services like primary health centres and primary schools. This also enhances people's access to and use of such services.

III

Emerging Mass Movements: Towards a Qualitative Psychological Change

In the last few decades, several salient issues have motivated the labouring people for mass mobilisation. Single issues have tended to spill over other interrelated issues, thus creating conditions for a qualitative change in people's thinking. In West Bengal, for instance, peasants' movement following the Tehbhaga agitation and the mobilisation of different castes and classes in rural areas in favour of redistribution of land became an important contributor to the future land reforms in the state. These in turn motivated the people for greater agricultural production even without the benefit of technological breakthrough as was available in the case of Punjab.[3] In Kerala also, several movements such as the library movement and the people's science movement paved the way for land reforms. Such movements energised the people as well as the official machinery.

There have also been several movements in various parts of the country around issues pertaining to: environment, rights of livelihood, forest rights, human rights and social justice. Such movements tend to spill over and multiply their impact on people as well as on the establishment. The anti-liquor movement in Andhra Pradesh is a good example of such spill-over and qualitative psychological change. Similar changes have also been obtained by Total Literacy Campaigns, in which millions of women have participated, as these campaigns got linked with issues of livelihood and social equality (Sengupta and Roy 1996). Movement for protection of trees, fodder, fuel and forests have got linked with and submerged into a strong movement against large dams. Anti-price movement in several States also got linked with movements for land and against the nexus of landlords, officials, contractors, politicians and moneylenders and also against 'liberalisation' and TNCs (Chapter 5).

The *Dalits*' movement against atrocities and social oppression has got evolved into a bigger movement against the caste-ridden Brahminical social order and for democratisation of the civil society (Section IV). The movements against child labour and bonded labour have tended to get linked with issues pertaining to child health, nutrition, corruption in high places and with government's mis-governance in general.[4] Smaller movements have thus tended to evolve into larger organisations such as the Kisan Adivasi Mukti Sangathan Ekta Parishad in Madhya Pradesh and the Narmada Bachao Andolan. These organisations stand for an alternative model of development and have agitated for the protection and use of indigenous seeds and other agricultural practices as also against the entry of transnationals (TNCs), particularly in agriculture. Some nationally known movements like Azadi Bachao Andolan, Himalaya Bachao Andolan, National Fish Workers Forum, Bhopal Gas Peedit Mahila Udyog Sangathana, Samajwadi Jan Parishad, Manav Vahini, Ganga Mukti Andolan, Chilka Bachao Andolan and Narmada Bachao Andolan have promoted a National Alliance of People's Movement for promoting alternative development and mobilising a cultural climate against self-defeating consumerism (Bakshi, 1996).

Emerging Women-Militancy

The anti-arrack movement, literacy campaigns in various states, the movement for protection of trees, fodder and fuel and similar other movements highlight the emergence of women-militancy in the civil society. Their cry against alcohol and for prohibition has been *Nasha Nahi, Rozgar Do*, thus, linking their anti-arrack movement with demand for adequate water, medical facilities, employment and other basic public amenities. Women tend to perceive the local shopkeepers and moneylenders as symbols and cause of their miseries. Such women-militancy has been observed in Andhra Pradesh, Karnataka, Kerala, Haryana, Uttar Pradesh, Madhya Pradesh and Maharashtra and during the Nav Nirman movement in Gujarat in 1970s.[5] The Shahada movement in Maharashtra against the local landlords also saw women in the forefront. They mobilised people from hut-to-hut against the oppressive landlords as well as against their own husbands who were forced to apologise publicly.

Women had thus, raised a banner of revolt in homes as well as against various centres of power—the state authorities, contractors and money-lenders—by using a variety of methods, unique in their own way and in the process, facing the wrath of landlords, drunk *goondas*, contractors and the police. The movement represents a remarkable convulsion in the village society suggesting a social transformation of women. The most significant feature of such a struggle was their fight on the home front, heralding transformation in their age-old mentality. This qualitative psychological change in them has been described by observers as transformation of submissive women into *Kalika-Devies (kalies)*. The change in women's attitudes and behaviour seen in the context of strong anti-caste *Dalit* movement as well as other class movements in Andhra Pradesh added a new dimension to these movements (Illaiah, 1992).

The anti-liquor movement in Andhra Pradesh, as in some other states, seems to have redefined politics and gender relations. Women demonstrated their power by calling to account the most oppressive contractor system controlling their lives. Many a time, contractors symbolise the nexus of moneylenders, criminals, officials and politicians. The anti-liquor movement, therefore, indicates the revolt of people against the corrupt administration dominated by the contractor-political culture and their assertion for a change in the ongoing socio-economic, political and administrative scenario.

Thrust for Decentralisation and Self-Governance

The Constitutional amendments (73rd and 74th amendment acts) of 1992 (GOI, 1992c, 1992d) also, in a way, came in response to the growing people's pressure from below for a share in governance of the country. There are, however, many inhibiting forces inbuilt in our social organisation and in the system of public administration, which are likely to impede the proper functioning of *panchayati raj* Institutions (PRIs), particularly the participation of vulnerable people such as SCs/STs and women. This came out clearly at the first ever held *panchayat mahasammelan* of the newly-elected chairpersons of *zila parishads* held in October, 1995. Representatives from all over the country strongly voiced their concern regarding various difficulties in the functioning of PRIs such as: lack of devolution of proper functions and powers by the state authorities; lack of cooperation from the bureaucracy; and blocks put up by the entrenched political leaders including MLAs and MPs.[6] Such assertive behaviour on their part indicated the growing pressure and 'demand' for democratic governance from the ground.

An interesting evidence of such anger and assertion from below has been reported from Madhya Pradesh. The ruling party there was reportedly bothered by their rout in the 1996 Lok Sabha elections. They thought that it was due to the failure of government vis-à-vis the *panchayati raj* system. Political executives and party leaders openly charged the bureaucrats for creating hurdles in the execution of various *panchayati raj* schemes. It was alleged that *panchs* and *sarpanchs* were 'ill-treated' by collectors and the district rural development organisations (DRDOs). What is interesting here is that the political executives recognised the importance of people's assertion at the grassroots level in electoral politics as well as in the politics of development. The political functionaries reportedly decided to curtail the power of the bureaucrats, leaving virtually no role for district collectors in the functioning of PRIs. The elected representatives were to be empowered to fully run several progammes and departments such as those for rural development, school education, agriculture, health, public health, engineering, fisheries, social welfare and child and women welfare.[7]

From Silence to Articulation

The age-old proverbial tolerance and silence of the deprived people is thus, unmistakably and increasingly, being broken. Even at places where there has been no perceptible movement or agitation, the labouring people, including the tribal people in remote villages, have been articulating their deep-felt problems and needs. For instance, way back in 1979, tribal cultivators and agricultural workers in remote villages of Rajasthan vividly articulated their problems and perceptions regarding availability of food, jobs, income, land and harassment at the hands of shopkeepers, moneylenders, police and other petty officials. Their felt-needs and hurt came out loud and clear during a field study in Rajasthan. They reported thus, '... many a times, no food to eat, sometimes forced to eat *chappati* (bread) made of grass; the average income comes to about Rs 2 a day with no regular source of income, many of us, have no land and some who have, it is mostly hilly and not fertile. Practically, there was no work or employment. Sometimes we are employed in food for work construction activity. We have to go in search of work away from our homes for 6–8 months in a year. Shopkeepers and moneylenders including cooperative credit societies fleece us in various ways. There is no irrigation facility whatsoever and also no drinking water with some wells with impure (*kacha*) water and most wells half-dug and not functioning. There was practically no hospital and medical facility. We have to carry our sick physically on our shoulders, crossing rivers and hills, to the *tehshil* hospital where also there is only one doctor who is frequently absent; not even a primary school in some villages. At some places, there are schools without buildings and teachers. Children are frequently driven out of the schools by the teachers for want of appropriate dress, etc. No facility even for adult education in our villages ...'. These widely expressed problems and needs bore close resemblance to well-documented results of various surveys and studies suggesting that such articulation was a microcosm of wider national problems and needs. They were thus, able to articulate their needs not only with great feeling but also with accuracy. Interestingly, similar themes of deprivation and needs came out in their imaginative stories written in response to pictures in a research study (Mehta, 1995; Appendix 1 and 2, and 127–132).

Literacy Campaigns

Studies of Total Literacy Campaigns, adult education and some related rural development programmes also reveal the changing self-image of the labouring rural poor. Millions of people including a large number of women have been activated into movements by such campaigns which have provided them with a new sense of identity and reinforced their sense of assertion and hope. They have been participating in various cultural activities such as *Kala Jathas* in which songs and other items are linked with basic issues of their livelihood and with the need for resisting oppression in whatever form. Such campaigns and cultural activities have thus enthused a large number of educated girls and rural youth to serve as volunteer-instructors and raised their level of political consciousness (Sengupta and Roy, 1996). Several positive psychological changes have been observed in such volunteers, even in remote districts of western Rajasthan. For instance, they were found to show increasing faith in the strength of the common people, an increasing sense of political efficacy, increasing hope in their own capability for influence and ongoing political scenario and political affairs, including the government functioning and increasing sense of dissatisfaction with the functioning of political institutions and the government. On the whole, such young instructors of adult education classes showed an increasing psychological empowerment for a better society and a better quality of life for themselves. They were also eager to help and work with their people (Mehta, 1990). Similarly, the learner–participants in a total literacy programme, including women, in a backward district of Uttar Pradesh repeatedly articulated their needs for water, irrigation, medical facilities, income generating activities, vocational and technical training and better and regular education for their children. Their instructors took the initiative and substituted themselves for the absentee government teachers, enrolled children and held their classes outside the building of non-functioning schools. It was their way of expressing anger with widespread corruption in government functioning and of forcing the teachers to return to their jobs. Interestingly, here also, women were found to be much more militant.[8]

Empowerment for Social Achievement

People's movements around different and yet interrelated issues thus play an important role in motivating and releasing their assertive behaviour and in kindling a hope for success in them. Such public action illustrates the emerging fight of common people against various everyday problems and hardships which arise because of government policies, nature of governance and the entrenched economic and social order. This has been demonstrated in several non-government and some government initiated programmes of self-action. For example, the Bhoomi Sena movement in Maharashtra shows the people's concern for self-reliance and the strength of the organisation and solidarity for success in the struggle against the vested interests. The movement succeeded in releasing collective energy of the poor and in motivating them for various achievements (De Silva, 1979). Several similar projects designed to build up countervailing power of the poor against the rich and powerful have resulted in some successful sustainable development. Such success stories include: drought control in Ralegaon Siddhi village in Ahmednagar district of Maharashtra (Agashe, 1992); protection of trees and environment such as Chipko movement in Chamoli district of Uttar Pradesh (DGSM, 1982); revival of forests and wildlife in villages in Puri district of Orissa (Behera, 1992); confrontation of bank and other officials for obtaining credit in Ghaziabad district of Uttar Pradesh (Sinha, 1992); cooperative movement of *beedi* workers in Kerala (Mohandas and Kumar, 1992); organisation and empowerment of a very poor Scheduled Caste community in Jaiselmer district of Rajasthan against malnutrition, alcohol and oppression at the hands of the dominant castes so that they could, as they said, 'live with dignity and give our children a better future' (Mitra, 1992:

40); and people's self-action for development in Singari village in Ranchi district of Bihar (Mehta, 1995:163–80).

Organised Self-Action

Mass mobilisation and organised self-action for various basic needs of life thus help in bringing about a significant, sometimes qualitative, psychological change in the participating people. They learn and enhance their sense of efficacy and readiness for collective and individual action for various socio-economic goals. Such actions, therefore, contribute to achieving some important goals of human development in terms of enhanced self-esteem, capability and empowerment (Chapter 4). They also develop: a sense of standards in evaluating performance not only of officials but also their own; higher aspirations for their children, both boys and girls; hope for a better life; a belief in unity and organisation; and greater awareness and demand for health care, education and a better community life.

One of the important outcomes of such mobilisation is that women, who have been and are being greatly discriminated against in access to education, health, employment and on other indices of human development, seem to acquire greater self-esteem and efficacy. Such psychological changes seem to have occurred more sharply among them as illustrated by anti-arrack movements, anti-price rise movements, struggle for environment and forest rights and in several other movements in different parts of the country. Such changes have also been noted in them as a result of mobilisation and their participation in self-action development projects. They tend to show positive change in their self-concept, enhanced desire for education of their children and greater concern for child and health care. As a result of such participation, they have also learnt to think in terms of new ways of dealing with problems including new ways of cultivation, and to confront erring government officials, moneylenders, contractors, police men and others (Mehta, 1995:173–74).

The Changing Political Psychology

The people's movements need to be understood in the context of the changing political situation in the country. During the 1966–77 decade, new regional powers emerged in various parts of the country which challenged the authority at the Centre. This challenge was an expression of both electoral competitive politics at one level and democratic consciousness at another.

The regional elite challenged the Congress rulers at the centre for a share in the power structure. At the same time, the rural people articulated their revolt against their concrete experience of several decades of undemocratic rule. There were inherent horizontal contradictions between the rising rural elite and the elite at the Centre and those in the regions, on the one hand, and between such elite and the democratic forces released vertically below the elite level, on the other. The period following 1977 saw adjustment in power-sharing with emergence of the BJP. However, at the same time, there has been a spurt in mass consciousness of people who are also now disillusioned with political parties. The common people are also in the web of economic policies of liberalisation, privatisation and globalisation (Chapter 5 and as discussed here).

The emerging movements are thus being caused by tension in Centre–State relations, on the one hand, and, on the other, by political experience of the common masses of the country. The ordinary people are not less oppressed by more autonomous States than the less democratic Centre. Even with the devolution of power down to *panchayats*, politically dominant elite would constantly seek to perpetuate vertical hierarchy of more or less homogeneous elite from State capital down to *Panchayats*. At the regional level, some movements like the Jharkhand movement and Nav Nirman movement led by Jai Prakash Narain have tended to take ideological or cultural character and are involved in opposing the existing struggle of power extending over several States. Such movements have tended to be motivated by social, political, economic, environmental and other such issues. At the grassroots level, inter-caste or *adivasi* and non-*adivasi* conflicts may only temporarily conceal the oppressive tendencies of middle and lower middle castes towards labour castes (*Dalits*). In the long run, such movements would be against both the upper castes as well as some of the middle caste aspirants who are trying to replace them in the name of oppressed castes (Sheth, 1996, Omvedt, 1996, H. Rao, 1995). The fact that Indira Gandhi was forced to call for new elections in 1977 following the resistance movement, showed the change in the political orientation of the common people. Such people's movements of resistance to the structure of power constitute the principal component of changing socio-political scenario in the post-1977 period. Such movements and the changing political psychology of the masses of people mark a new period in Indian politics which could work as catalyst in the formation and release of pro-democracy, i.e., pro-people, collective action. Such a psychological development indicates a qualitative change in the situation as movements do not demand or are not centred on just one issue but have taken on a general nature. For example, such movements demand accountability of those holding elective office and thus also demand democratic practices at all levels of the government. It is important to understand that such movements are motivated by a growing democratic awareness and values (Satyamurthy, 1996b; Mehta, 1994b).

IV

The Dalit and Non-Brahmin Movements: Emergence of New Political Forces

The emergence of *Dalits* and *Shudras* as crucial factors in the country's competitive electoral politics is also an important consequence as well as an indicator of growing people's movements and their increasing empowerment. This reveals the changing socio-political scenario in the country. '*Dalits*' refers to the oppressed and exploited social groups, who in common parlance are referred to as only SCs. The term is inter-changeable with terms like untouchables, depressed classes and *harijans*. The term *Shudras* is inter-changeable with the Other Backward Classes (OBCs). That the social consciousness and the mind-set of *Dalits* and *Shudras*, have been changing, rather radically, is unmistakable. This is one of the positive consequences of democratic movements since Independence and of the long history of the Dalit movement (DM) and Non-Brahmin movement (NBM) in different parts of the country.[9]

Mahatma Phule : His Political Pedagogy

Mahatma Jyotirao Phule was the earliest among the *Dalit* leaders to conduct regular mass awareness and education campaigns as early as in the middle of the 19th century. He taught the *Shudras* and *ati-Shudras* and women in general that, their miserable conditions were caused by the tyrannical Brahminical order. He relentlessly tried to make them aware of the unjust caste system which he said, had been institutionalised through priesthood, bureaucracy, moneylenders, land revenue officials, commission agents, and traders (Auti and Chousalkar, 1986: 10). In a way, he anticipated Freiri's 'pedagogy of the oppressed' (Freiri, 1972) by more than a century. Phule was not satisfied by creating just awareness. He tried to prepare the *Shudras* and the *ati-Shudras* to change their world. He sought to educate and organise them for praxis—calling upon them to annihilating the old order and for establishing a more humane, just and democratic state of workers and peasants which would implement policies to end Brahmin dominance. He further tried to prepare them strategically to forge a political alliance of various groups including the *Shudras, ati-Shudras*, or untouchables for this goal (Auti and Chousalkar, 1986: 10–14). His efforts were clearly directed at inculcating a sense of self-esteem, efficacy, assertive behaviour and a new sense of identity, thus releasing a process of their active human development (see Chapter 4).

Politicisation of the Movement

The Dalit movement leaders' thinking was politicised as the national movement got momentum in the early decades of the 20th century. At least some of the leaders were not interested in and satisified by just passive, non-violent forms of protests. For instance, Aiyankali and his followers organised agricultural workers and fought and got for the *Dalits* the right to walk on the roads in Travancore by 1900. He also organised the agricultural workers to demand the right to enroll their children into government schools (R. Rao, 1989: 14). In the next phase of the Dalit movement, the depressed classes demanded a separate electorate for themselves which witnessed the famous bitter historical controversy between Gandhi and Ambedkar. Gandhi considered untouchability a social problem, therefore, an internal matter of the Hindu community (S.K. Gupta, 1985: 169). Ambedkar, on the other hand, considered it as 'worse than slavery' and a political and economic problem. He described it as a 'gold mine' for Hindus' (Ambedkar, 1945: 196–197). Ambedkar had to make a retreat because of Gandhiji's fast unto death against the proposed separate electorates and had to sign the Poona Pact in 1931 which gave only 148 reserved seats to *Dalits* in all the legislatures. Ambedkar felt very bitter about the Pact which adversely affected the political participation of Scheduled Castes (Suresh, 1996: 362–63).

The Non-Brahmin Movement

The non-Brahmin Movement (NBM), relatively strong in the South and Maharashtra, brought together the *Shudras* and *ati-Shudras* to challenge the domination of Brahmins and higher castes. This helped the non-Brahmin castes—mostly peasants and artisans—to develop a new sense of identity, self-esteem and assertiveness (Suresh, 1996: 364–65). Such movements, as mentioned above, worked for promoting a sense of self-respect. Despite the fact that some of the leaders of NBM were themselves landlords, like the Justice Party leaders in Tamil society, who held allegiance with higher caste Hindus and favoured employers in labour disputes, it did exert a positive influence on the thinking of the various lower and middle castes and *dalit* groups. Their changing self-concept motivated them to organise and resist efforts to integrate them into movements dominated by Brahmins (chiefly the Indian National Congress) (Omvedt, 1986).

Non-Party Movements

Non-party *Dalit* political movements have been motivated chiefly by socio-economic conditions and atrocities committed by the upper caste groups, which, over the years, have tended to show an alarmingly increasing trend (Chapter 2). For instance, a total of 15,416 cases were reported in 1986 alone and a total 91,097 during the quinquennium of 1981–86. Untouchability has thus continued to affect the social relations between the *Dalits* and the upper castes (CSCST, 1988:239). The economic conditions of the *Dalits* have also been increasingly deteriorating with over 70 per cent of them living below the poverty line as compared to 48 per cent of the general population. Just seven per cent of the land was owned by them, 70 per cent of whom owned, on an average, less than 1 ha, while 82.8 per cent of the land was owned by other communities. Thus, they have remained, largely, assetless and landless. Under such conditions, it is no wonder that *Dalits'* literacy rate was only 21.38 per cent against 41.3 per cent for all communities excluding SCs/STs. The female literacy rate has stagnated at just 10.93 per cent against 29.43 per cent for other communities (ibid.: 253–54, 290–293, 320) (Chapter 2).

Such conditions of deprivation have motivated the *Dalits* to mobilise themselves on issues like those pertaining to land, resource distribution, caste discrimination in public facilities, homesteads, minimum wages, etc. Such movements have been functioning largely as pressure groups and have generally been lacking sustained political consciousness and are therefore, susceptible to cooptation by the dominant elite groups. Despite anti-caste movements, the caste has not only survived but has emerged as an important factor in contemporary Indian politics. Such politics of caste can successfully divide the ranks of the labouring people from uniting on class basis. Despite increasing assertion, such disunity could keep the *Dalits* in a state of subservience and insecurity (Suresh, 1996:383–86).

Political Gains of the Dalit Movement

Despite more than 100 years of the Dalit movement, untouchability, continues to be practised in the country. Atrocities continue to be heaped on them, maybe more because they are more conscious and, therefore, openly resist social indignities and injustice.[10] Their conditions of life have also not improved, rather, worsened further, because of economic policies of liberalisation, marketisation and globalisation (Chapter 5). Yet, perhaps because of the continuing indignities, the Movement has led to very significant political and psychological gains for the *Dalits*, particularly in terms of electoral participation. This is clearly indicated by the fact that during the preparatory period of the 1996 Lok Sabha general elections, all political parties including those on the Left and the BJP, agreed that the crucial *Dalit* votes could make or break their fortune. This was also revealed by the erstwhile Narasimha Rao Government's aborted attempt to rush through the Ordinance on reservation for Dalit Christians.[11]

Earlier, the numerical strength of *Dalit* votes was revealed in the 1993 Assembly elections in Uttar Pradesh which voted the Bahujan Samaj Party (BSP) to power in alliance with the Samajwadi Party (SP). The numerically significant Jatava (half of 21 per cent SC population in the State) played an active role in this respect. Later, the BSP fell out with the SP and it formed the first ever *Dalit* government in UP with the support of the BJP. Similar mobilisation of *Dalits* took place in Maharashtra for the 1996 elections when various groups of the Republic Party of India got united. Prior to that, when the *Dalits* got alienated from the Congress in 1980, they formed, along with Muslims, a new alliance under the numerically dominant OBCs which contributed to the Janata phenomenon of 1989.

Mobilisation of the *Dalits* and democratisation, particularly during the last half century, have thus, released new social forces for the competitive political democracy in the country. The 1996 elections revealed this rather dramatically when the *Dalits* emerged as a significant political factor which could tilt the balance of forces in three north Indian States, namely, Uttar Pradesh, Punjab and Madhya Pradesh. The BSP got 6, 3 and 2 Lok Sabha seats with 20.68, 9.64 and 8.75 per cent of votes respectively in these important States. Its performance in Uttar Pradesh was very impressive where it increased the share of vote by 11.64 percentage points between 1991 and 1996 Lok Sabha elections. The BSP, thus, raised its total Lok Sabha seats from three in 1991 to 11 in 1996 and its vote share at the national level from 1.16 per cent to 4.01 per cent.[12]

The Dalit movement right from Phule's time, has been nurtured for seeking political power. Ambedkar's statement that, 'we must become a ruling community' has been the most potent slogan of the movement. He always considered 'power' as the key to their liberation. For this, he favoured the unity of workers, *Dalits* and the Bahujan samaj (middle castes) (Ambedkar, 1979–81). Dalit Panthers—a radical element of the Dalit movement—announced that in order to eradicate injustices against *dalits*, they themselves must become rulers. They considered this as a people's democracy (Dalit Panther, 1973). Kanshi Ram's by now well known slogans: brahmin, *bania, thakur, chor, baki sab DS-4* (Brahmins, *Banias*, and *Thakurs* are thieves, the rest are with us. DS-4 refers to Dalit Shoshit Samaj Sangarsh Samiti) and *mat hamara raj tumhara nahi chalega* (no longer we vote you to rule) seek to forge unity among and between the *Dalits* and *Shudras* and create a thrust for political power for themselves, taking their destiny into their own hands rather than depending on the top-down patronage of the centralised political parties.[13]

From Submissiveness to Assertiveness

Social movements of *Dalits* and their political and electoral mobilisation over the past several decades have thus, led to the emergence of long oppressed people as a crucial factor in the country's competitive democratic system. Such political changes have been preceded and are accompanied by some significant psychological changes which have, in turn, further strengthened their political mobilisation. *Dalit* petty officials, who have themselves benefited from the country's policy of affirmative action i.e., reservation in government jobs, have been militantly helping other *Dalits* to get organised and come out and vote fearlessly for their choice. The same people were earlier timid and submissive and could be manipulated and forced to vote for candidates from dominant classes. They have now acquired a new sense of hope and new assertion. They have also set the target of motivating and organising themselves further to see that their voting percentage was enhanced to 70–80 per cent.[14]

The benefits accrued to the *Dalits* during the BSP-SP Government in Uttar Pradesh in 1993–94 and later during the BSP Government with BJP support have greatly emboldened them. The voting behaviour during the 1996 elections indicated their rising sense of political efficacy and the hope that their vote and participation could make a difference and obtain for them a share in political decision-making and in the country's governance.[15]

The poor have thus shown a significant movement away from their age-old dependency and submissive behaviour towards initiative and assertive behaviour. Political mobilisation has helped them to achieve important gains in terms of a more positive self-concept and in emerging from 'pawn' type behaviour to 'actor' and 'origin' type 'agentive' behaviour (Chapter 4). Such mobilisation, participation and the newly acquired assertive behaviour may force the various state agencies to pay at least somewhat more attention to their needs and problems.

The emergence of the *Dalit* and *Shudra* phenomenon in Indian politics has thus drastically changed the traditional political equations. The long-deprived and oppressed labouring people seem to have come up on their own to work for themselves. Whether the released initiative and assertion and the resultant political (electoral) change would also result in enhanced democratic consciousness and solidarity within the labouring classes, irrespective of caste, is yet to be seen. Such socio-political and democratic empowerment would largely depend on sustained movements and *Dalits'* participation in struggles for basic means of production, such as land in rural areas and for a better quality of life in urban areas. The fact, however, remains that socio-political mobilisation of *Dalits* is likely to change the social base of the state. It could now be forced, at least to some extent, to intervene towards fulfilment of at least some of their basic needs.[16]

The increasing share of both vote and seats of regional and smaller parties at the 1996 elections has also its origins in mass movements. The DMK is the offspring of anti-Brahmin politics of Tamil Nadu, Telugu Desam owes to the Telugu pride movement and the Assom Gana Parishad to the student movement against foreigners. As a result of land reforms and the widening of democratic processes, the middle level farmers and the intermediate castes have been able to enter the centre-stage of politics. Their success has changed the balance of power in local and regional and national politics.[17]

Electoral Politics, Cooptation and Dominant Ethos

Dalits are thus emerging as a very significant factor in electoral politics in Indian democracy. Some *Dalit* representatives may get into power in some states and also at the centre. The BSP leader Mayawati, did become the Chief Minister of Uttar Pradesh with the help of the BJP, albiet for a brief period, in 1995. Various political parties would therefore, try to woo *Dalit* voters by making some promises and also by accommodating them in sharing power. How far would such electoral success and promises improve the basic conditions of life of *Dalits*? The upper 'elite' sections of *Dalits*, who are likely to get into power, may themselves learn to behave like other ruling elite and may imbibe some of the Brahminical values. There are apprehensions that such leaders may also indulge, like other ruling elite, in manipulative politics in order to prevent emergence of other competitors (leaders) from among the *Dalit* masses.[18]

One telling evidence of the possibility of such cooptation of *Dalits* into the dominant ethos of the ruling elite is provided by the falling female–male ratio in Uttar Pradesh over the last several decades. In 1901, it was 986 (per 1,000 males) among the *Chamars* (the dominant section and the largest SC group in Uttar Pradesh) and 970 among all SCs (including the *Chamars*) as compared to 887 among the *Kshatriyas* and *Rajputs* and 929 among other upper caste Hindus. By 1981, this ratio came down to 880 for *Chamars* and 892 for all SCs. Thus, this got pulled down very close to the ratio of 878 for the combined group of upper caste Hindus (including *Kshatriyas* and others (Drèze and Sen, 1995, Table 7.2)). Lowering of the female–male ratio among *chamars* as among the upper caste Hindus suggested that the former were giving up their culture of greater gender equality and were catching up with the values of gender discrimination of the latter.

Sex ratio is an important indicator of the cultural and social discrimination obtaining at the household level and in the society in general. The *Chamar* women clearly enjoyed a much better situation in this respect than their counterparts among the higher caste Hindus in 1901. However, some eight decades later, the social situation of *Dalit* women, particularly the *Chamar* women, became as bad as that of the latter. Over this period, conditions worsened not only for the upper caste women but also for the *Chamar* and other SC women. The data are instructive in view of the fact that *Chamars* are the dominant social group among the *Dalits* in Uttar Pradesh. It seems, therefore, that the Dalit movement has not resulted in any improvement in living conditions of the *Dalit* women. If anything, their quality of life seems to have worsened during the period when the Dalit movement was heading towards important electoral victories. It means that the impact of *Dalit* power in the country's competitive politics still remains to be translated into greater access for them in public services such as for literacy, elementary education, health, skill development, employment generation. It remains to be seen whether *Dalits* are able to transform opportunities into social achievements for improving the quality of life for both men and women, particularly the latter.

Democratisation and Collective Action for Activising State Agencies

The recent election results did show that the *Dalits* were on the march. These indicated an increasing sense of political efficacy and assertive behaviour on their part. They have not only shown determination but also skills for forging alliance across caste barriers such as with Dalit Muslims, poorer OBCs and others. However, it is to be seen whether such electoral empowerment would result in their greater participation in mass struggles for achieving socio-economic gains in terms of equality, education, employment, civic rights, etc. Will they be able to create effective political organisation and release public activism in order to channelise their anger for obtaining human development gains and social progress? Such activism is needed to exert pressures from below for activising state agencies for policies and programmes for better schools, primary health centres, public distribution system, for employment generation and equitable income distribution for greater access to other public services and above all, for their civic rights and dignity of life. There is thus a need for them to use their enhanced efficacy and self-esteem to develop a cultural atmosphere in favour of social equality as well as gender equality.

Such collective action would, however, largely depend on the strength of their democratic consciousness. Such political consciousness is essential for motivating them to assert and change the current preference, say, for higher education at the cost of primary education for all and for costly super specialised medical service at the cost of primary health and preventive health service. State priorities and the nature of state functioning during the past few decades have tended to reinforce the traditional entrenched social inequalities and have largely centred around the interests of the elite (Chapter 2). The privileged groups are more educated and politically more organised and powerful. They are thus able to create self-sustaining achievement circles for themselves at the cost of the underprivileged (Tilak, 1991; Weiner, 1991).

The dominant ethos in both, Hinduism as well as in Islam, is traditionally inclined towards elitism with reliance on Brahmin priests and the powerful *mullahs.* The *Dalits'* emerging electoral power needs to be therefore backed by political organisation and informed public activism to be able to break through this entrenched ethos and assertion for their various basic needs and rights. Such organisations and activism are needed even more at the village level (Kohli, 1987, 1990; Mehta, 1995). It is the village society where the *Dalits* have been and are being exploited socially, economically as well as politically by the traditionally entrenched social organisation (Chapter 3). The electoral gains certainly indicate their potentiality as well as readiness to get organised politically.

The new socio-political reality thus provides a growing opportunity for channelising the *Dalit* aspirations to boost meaningful collective action. Such public activism is needed not only for demanding a change in state priorities but also for enhancing the vulnerable people's access to such public services and their basic rights. The need, therefore, is to translate the new-found sense of political efficacy and the assertive voting behaviour into people's movements and mobilisation for collective action in this respect. Such tasks present a formidable challenge also to the concerned political parties, trade unions and other mass organisations.

V

Public Activism for Human Development

One of the urgent requirements in our present situation of poor human development is to pressurise the state to fulfill its Constitutional obligations in order to provide basic services to all people. Since it has been indifferent, if not hostile, to meeting such needs, it is necessary to force it to change direction and to show greater concern for the quality of life of vulnerable people. People's movements and organisations alone can weaken the various inhibiting forces (Chapter 4) and help re-energise the state organs and public institutions for these important tasks. Sustainable human development aims at enhancing an agentive and assertive role in the common people (Chapter 4). Social mobilisation, as discussed above, plays an important role in this respect and contributes to changing the social and political psychology of the common people and to enhancing public activism. Needless to say, such efforts need to be well planned and organised, not sporadic. Studies suggest some interesting conceptual insights which could be used in this regard on the one hand for promoting the desired psychological development of the people, and on the other, for activising state interventions. Such conceptualisation could thus help in planning interventions for promoting both public as well as state activism towards sustainable development. Some such suggested action hypotheses are mentioned next:

Suggested Action Hypotheses

Social mobilisation of people around their basic needs helps break the age-old culture of silence and dependency and promotes in them readiness for articulation and assertion. Participation in socio-political movements promotes a sense of solidarity and organisation in the people for pursuing worthwhile social goals. The collective pursuit of social achievement goals releases their initiative, enhances readiness to take risk, sharpens determination and skills and motives them to 'cause things to happen'. They thus move away from behaving like traditional 'pawns' to be entrenched dominant sections of the society and the related subservient mind-set to emerging an assertive self and being 'origins' and 'actors' on their own. Such psychological development is antithetical to the principle of subordination and superordination and, therefore, helps create conditions for weakening and eliminating the age-old unequal social organisation. Thus: *more the people behave like 'origins', weaker becomes the principle of superordination and subordination and unequal social system.*

Making Public Services More Effective: People's Ability to Command

The capability approach to human development underlines the importance of not just the availability of inputs like foodgrains, primary schools and primary health centres but also people's power to command and to put pressures for proper functioning of and access to such public services. This development principle is best illustrated by the country's serious problem of malnutrition. Nutritional deficiency is not just caused by food deficiency. It also cannot be solved by just the availability of foodgrains. Its sufficiency for children and, particularly, women depends on proper functioning of health care, education, drinking water, sanitation and other such public services and on people's anger, capability and power to command such amenities. Thus: *greater such power and capability, greater is the people's access to and use of public services.*

Invigorating State Interventions: Greater Public Concern

Public awareness about various socio-economic and environmental issues and a sense of concern for development programmes helps provide vigour to state interventions. Adversarial politics, mass media, non-government development organisations, social activists, trade unions and other mass organisations play an important role in inculcating the necessary public awareness and a feeling of a stake in public services. This is all the more important in our context where the state has been indifferent, if not negative, to promoting sustainable and equitable human development. Public perception of such a stake also brings out the inter-relationship between public activism and state interventions in this regard. Thus: *greater the public stake in development programmes, greater is the vigour in state interventions.*

Making Electoral Politics Meaningful: Democratising the Population

Competitive politics plays an important role in promoting active people's participation in elections and in making and breaking power equations. Such electoral mobilisation could, to some extent, change the very nature and character of the state, i. e., the government. In the absence of proper political consciousness for democratisation, such changes may, however, be in danger of getting coopted by the entrenched dominant elites, thus thwarting any basic change in the state. This results in enhanced public cynicism and alienation from politics and more particularly politicians, which in turn could slow down state and other interventions for sustainable and equitable human development. People's movements and mobilisation of various socio-economic and political issues and basic needs contribute to democratising the thinking of the people. Thus: *the greater such democratisation of the vulnerable sections of the population, the more meaningful electoral politics becomes for obtaining equitable human development.*

Making Decentralised Governance More Responsive: People's Creative Action

Decentralisation may make governance more responsive to the needs and problems of common people. The 73rd and 74th Constitutional amendments may help bring about such decentralisation. The *gram sabhas* and the people at the grassroots level, however, need to be prepared to actively and creatively participate in policy-making, action planning and in implementation of programmes. The entrenched ruling elite at the local and higher levels, including the bureaucracy, are likely to resist such changes and retard and distort this process. Comprehensive efforts, including mass mobilisation, education, organisation and training are, therefore, necessary, on the one hand, to develop capability and to release creativity of the people and of the new emerging leaders, on the other, to weakening the inhibiting forces, arising from the entrenched centralised political and social system. Thus: *greater such/creative action, more responsive and democratic is the decentralised governance.*

Making Policies and Programmes More Effective: Greater Political Commitment

In the absence of political commitment, electoral promises, even Constitutional directives remain confined only to paper. Public activism is necessary to compel the ruling elite to translate their promises into practice. People's movements, mass mobilisation and competitive electoral politics promote conditions to put the people's basic needs like education, gender equality, health care, employment, etc., on the political agenda. More importantly, public activism promotes and reinforces commitment in various political parties, particularly in the ruling party to implement such policies and programmes which can obtain a reasonable quality of life for vulnerable people. This is more important in our context of negative political culture and indifferent bureaucracy. Thus: *greater the public activism, greater is the government's political commitment to vulnerable people and greater such commitment, more effective are the public policies and programmes.*

VI

An Alternative Development Strategy Needed

Human development programmes seek to help people develop a positive self-concept, i.e., to weaken their present dependency behaviour and strengthen initiative, hope of success, problem-solving approach, creativity and innovativeness, sense of self-esteem, concern for quality of life and assertion for such social goals (Chapter 4). The resultant subjective (psychological) development of people could become a prime mover for the much desired economic development in the country. Market forces, though necessary for promoting competitiveness among enterprises, are not helpful in creating conditions for such human development. The state has the main responsibility in this respect, as indicated in the Directive Principles of State Policy and also implied in the Preamble and the Fundamental Rights enshrined in our Constitution (Chapter 1). It has however, been, indifferent, if not negative, so far in this respect (Chapter 2). Now, its role is under further attack by the ideology of economic liberalisation and structural adjustment (Chapter 5). It is, therefore, imperative that the people—the disadvantaged and vulnerable people—take initiative for activising the public as well as the state for such vital tasks. Wider socio-political mobilisation and people's movements are important for bringing about changes in the character and direction of the state.

An alternative strategy is thus, required to fire the imagination of the people and to energise the state (i.e., government) functionaries for promoting and obtaining sustainable and equitable human development in the country. We discuss some aspects of such a strategy in the next Chapter.

END NOTES

1. This tendency on the part of state functionaries to subvert and divert public funds to personal accounts is symbolised by the notorious Bihar Fodder Scam. For a story, see *Frontline*, March 8, 1996 : 30–31. The Indian state has been marked by several similar scams such as Securities and Bank Scam, the Jain Hawala Case, etc. For a report, see *Times of India*, titled 'The Year of Trials and Scandals', December 25 1995. See Chapter 5 for discussion.

2. For example, it has been reported that school teachers were busy grazing cows, absenting from schools. See, *Times of India*, September 25, 1996.

3. For land reforms in West Bengal, the PRIs have emerged as grassroots level democracy and as an alternative model of development and poverty alleviation programme. For some details, see Mukherjee (1996).

4. For a report on child labour and related issues, see *Times of India*, May 12, 1996.

5. For widespread and increasing women militancy in several States of the country and on various issues, see a report by R.P. Nailwal, *Times of India*, March 31, 1996 and another report by Bonita Baruah in the same paper dated April 4, 1996.

6. The *Mahasammelan* held in October 1995 at Delhi was attended by 6,777 elected *panchayat* functionaries. It adopted a 19-point charter including devolution of adequate financial and administrative powers and integration of DRDAs with *zila parishads*. For a report, see *Statesman*, October 11, 1995.

7. For articulated resentment of the elected representatives of the *panchayat* institutions in Madhya Pradesh, see a report in *Times of India*, June 3, 1996.

8. Such public activism helped activise the docile state machinery and the Department of Education. One of the gains was that the absentee teachers returned to the school. See, Mehta (1992a).

9. See Suresh (1996) and other contributions cited there.

10. The Ranbir Sena, a private army of *Bhumihars* in Bihar, reportedly gunned down 8 children and 11 women at Bathani Tola on 11 July, 1996. This army of the landlords asserts their right to both land and life of the labouring people. The landless people have been agitating in this Bhojpur area for a long time for their land and other rights. They are now getting increasingly organised. For a report, see *Times of India*, July 12, 1996 and July 25, 1996. See Chapter 2.

11. The President of India declined to issue an Ordinance granting reservation to Christian *Dalits*. See comments on use and abuse of ordinances in *India Today*, April 15, 1996.

12. Kanshi Ram's statement in an interview in *Frontline*, June 28, 1996 and also see a story on the emerging political equation and the role of BSP, *Frontline*, July 26, 1996. This was also borne out by the 1996 Assembly elections in Uttar Pradesh.

13. This is reflected in the changing character of the Lok Sabha. Never before had so many farmers, backward castes and local leaders found a place there. These groups will have a distinct bearing on the business of the House. See a cover story on 'Changing Face of Parliament' in *India Today*, July 15, 1996 : 37–39.

14. See *Frontline*, July 26, 1996.

15. For the first time, regional parties have come to the position of setting the agenda for politics in India. For a story, see *India Today*, July 15, 1996 : 40–44.

16. This is evidenced in the Common Minimum Programme (CMP) of the United Front which promises to address to basic needs, such as drinking water, health, housing, education, literacy and skill development of the people in the country. They have also promised to take measures for developing a humane society and making education a fundamental right under law thereby eradicating child labour in the country. Interestingly, the CMP also pledges to pay attention to proper implementation and management of various programmes. It states that there is a crucial role for public investment, particularly in the social sectors like education and health. However, organisational and management changes in these sectors are as necessary as increase in investment. See United Front, 1996 : 9.

17. See cover story by C. Subramaniam in *India Today*, May 31, 1996 : 77–80.

18. During field work in Rajasthan and Bihar in the early 1980s, several *Dalit* activists told the author that their representatives in the State Assembly and in Parliament, i.e., the *Dalit* MLAs and MPs, did not want them to come up. At best, some of the somewhat educated *Dalits* with high school and other such qualifications were helped only to enter petty government jobs. They were, however, not encouraged to emerge as leaders on their own as this was perceived as a threat to the existing leadership. This is also identified as one of the problems in the functioning of PRIs (Chapter 5). The situation may, however, change under the impact of decentralisation and democratisation which is bound to throw up new local and intermediate leaders.

CHAPTER 7

DEMOCRATISATION AND HUMAN DEVELOPMENT: A PSYCHOLOGICAL STRATEGY FOR ALTERNATIVE ACTION

India's human development performance has been rather meagre. The goal of universal education is still nowhere in sight with about half the population continuing to remain illiterate.[1] The goal of health for all by A.D. 2000 is not possible to achieve. The Supreme Court recently reminded the state of Article 21 of the Constitution which makes it obligatory for the state to provide emergency health care to all citizens and that it cannot abdicate this duty on grounds of financial stringency.[2]

Another worrisome aspect of human development situation in the country is the fact that, some 40 to 50 million women were missing from the Indian population. The sex ratio has been declining over the years. The number of women per 1,000 men was 972 in 1901, which has come down to 927 in 1991. A recent UNICEF report shows that there were 1.4 million missing girls in the age group 0–6 years in the country. Although the overall child mortality rate has been declining, among the girls it has been increasing.[3]

What is even worse is, that our dismal conditions of illiteracy, ill-health and high infant mortality rate have promoted a baby boom. The latest census data show that by the year 2040, India would be the most populous nation in the world where over 18 million people or six Singapores are being added to the population every year. 'While the social and economic compulsions have contributed, the problem has been compounded by a total lack of political will'.[4]

Based on capability indices like percentage of under-weight children under five years, proportion of unattended births, high birth rate, the ratio of children out and in schools, and the low rate of female literacy. It has been estimated that 61.5 per cent of the country's population was poor in 1993 (UNDP, 1996). Recent studies by the National Council of Applied Economic Research show the proportion of people defined as poor on the UNDP's capability poverty measure at 45 to 50 per cent[5] (Chapter 1).

I

The United Front Government:
Promises and Performance

In view of such human development performance, it is no wonder (as discussed in Chapter 5) that our economic performance also has been equally dismal. This is shown dramatically by just one indicator—indebtedness. As the report of the Comptroller and Auditor General of India tabled in the Parliament on May 2, 1995 shows, it increased at the rate of about Rs 214 crore every day or Rs 9 crore every hour during 1993–94. Interest payments swallowed almost one-third of the revenue receipt and one-fourth of the revenue expenditure of the Union Government during the year. As per the CAG report, the country's total external and internal debts from various sources stood at Rs 5,58,421 crore on March 31, 1994 making an increase of Rs 77,954 crore in just one year.[6]

The Common Minimum Programme of the
United Front Government

Viewed in this rather bleak scenario, it was most welcome that the Common Minimum Programme (CMP) of the United Front sought to address some of the pressing issues and committed its government to: empowerment of the under-privileged; skill development and credit for artisans, craft persons, weavers, fishermen and other neglected sections of the working people; conferring ownership rights in respect of minor forest produce to SC/ST rural/tribal workers and to providing equal development opportunities for these people. The UF Government had thus, promised to provide minimum services to all people and to build a just and humane society where children would enjoy the Fundamental Right to free and compulsory elementary education and where child labour in all forms would be eradicated.[7]

The CMP also sought to: raise the rate of investment in agriculture and to augment the rural infrastructure, restructure the rural credit system, particularly for the benefit of small and marginal farmers; enact a comprehensive law for agricultural workers in order to guarantee them minimum wages, fair conditions of work, group insurance and other rights; vigorously implement land reforms and redesign rural development programme to ensure more employment, greater assets and productive skills in order to raising the income of the very poor. The public sector would not only continue to be an important component of Indian industry but would be further strengthened by professional management, workers' participation, job security, re-training and re-deployment. Public investments as well as organisational and management changes would be made in order to ensure basic human needs of drinking water, primary health care and housing for every citizen. Investment in education would particularly be accelerated to six per cent of the GDP of which 50 per cent would be spent on primary education. The mid-day meal scheme would be implemented in all the states and special attention would be paid to the problems of girl children. Most importantly, the United Front Government had sought to fire the imagination of young men and women with idealism and harness their energy for public works like afforestation, repair and restoration of canals, water ways and participation of all citizens for building of a new India of equity, justice and fraternity.[8]

The UF Budget—1996–97

A reliable indicator of government's commitment to a given policy, is its budget outlay. It is, however, only a partial indication, as the real test is its actual performance on the ground. As we are aware, despite some hike in the outlay for the anti-poverty programme in the Eighth Five Year Plan, the number of people living below the poverty line, instead of decreasing, tended to show an increase. There were cases of faulty selection of beneficiaries and widespread leakages at the district and block levels.[9] Despite the emergence of *Dalits* as an important factor in electoral politics, atrocities on them have not only continued but farm labourers were still paid Rs 2 and a bit of *sattu* as daily wages and the dignity of women folk was violated with impunity in many parts of Uttar Pradesh.[10] Because of corrupt implementation, even the entitlements due under the public distribution system do not reach the rural poor. The PDS reaches hardly 36 per cent of the households in most parts of the country.[11]

The actual performance of the UF Government was still to be seen by the time it presented its first ever budget (for the year 1996–97). It showed, however, that its will to translate its promises in terms of budget outlays and provisions, particularly for the basic needs of the people, was not very strong. The Ministry of Health and Family Welfare, Departments of Education and Women & Child Development (under the Ministry of Human Resource Development), Ministry of Rural Areas and Employment and the Ministry of Welfare are directly concerned with some of these basic social needs. The revised estimates (RE) of 1996–97, as presented by the UF Government in July, 1996, showed: only a marginal increase over the previous year's budget estimates (BE) health and family welfare; somewhat greater increase for education and marginal increase for rural development but stagnant situation regarding women and child development and welfare programmes. Most of the increased outlay for elementary education was meant for the National Programme of Nutritional Support to Primary Education, launched in August, 1995 by the previous government. While nutrition is an important strategy for universalising elementary education, it does not improve the much-needed physical infrastructure and quality of education. The scheme of Operation Blackboard, which seeks to provide for at least two all-weather class rooms, two teachers and some minimum learning equipment, remained stagnant at just at an outlay of Rs 279 crore in 1995–96 which remained unchanged in 1996–97. The outlays for these social sector departments as percentage of the total plan expenditure remained constant at 28.52 in BE 1995–96, 30.93 in RE 1995–96 and at 30.26 in the RE for 1996–97 and, which was only a little more than 8 per cent of the total expenditure of the Union Government in the three estimates.[12] The expenditure on rural development, as a proportion of the GDP, also came down in the RE of 1996–97 from the previous year's 0.49 per cent to 0.31 per cent and food subsidy from 0.65 per cent to 0.47 per cent.[13] As we know, even such meagre benefits do not reach the needy weaker sections as these are grabbed by the better-off people because of distorted and inefficient implementation.

Compared to the average increase over the three-year period—1992–93 to 1995–96, the social sector outlays on education, health and family welfare, drinking water, sanitation, housing and on rural development thus showed a decline in RE of 1996–97. For instance, the average increase in outlay on education during the previous three years was 28.99 per cent which came down to 20.89 per cent in the 1996–97 budget. Similarly, the outlay increase in health came down to 8.59 per cent from the previous average of 15.05 per cent. In fact, such increases in the budget outlay for 1996–97 uniformly came down as compared to the average increases for the previous three years in almost all the social sector programmes.[14]

The concerns expressed in the Common Minimum Programme (CMP) of the UF Government were thus, not actualised in their first budget proposal. The assertion that the UF Government would directly address the basic needs of the people instead of waiting for the trickle down effect, thus largely remained on paper, waiting to be translated in action.

The Same Old Values Reflected in the Budget 1996–97

The 'reform' period of 1991–92 to 1995–96 saw a distinct decline in the growth rate of employment in the organised sector. The annual average rate of growth was 2.6 per cent during 1951–52 to 1956–57. This came down to 1.4 during the five-year period of 1986–87 to 1990–91, which declined further to just .08 in the five-year 'reform' period (1991–96). Similarly, there was a fall in the indices of agricultural as well as industrial production and a corresponding rise in the wholesale price index.

The CMP's promise of additional employment by promoting labour intensive growth was also not actualised in their first budget. It continued to show faith in credit as generator of new economic activity. The suggested recipe for employment growth really showed a bias towards larger farmers and commercialisation of agriculture which would not benefit the small farmers nor create jobs in the rural sector. On the contrary, these might even undo the land reforms and contribute to further unemployment. Similar thinking was reflected in the proposal for non-farm employment in the small industry sector by marginally extending the credit facilities of the Small Industrial Development Bank of India (SIDBI). The danger here is that more powerful large industrial borrowers could compete with, and even take over, the small sector units for tax and other benefits.

The social service sector is directly related to human development and fulfilment of basic needs for which the CMP and the UF Government had repeatedly made several promises. However, this objective got limited in the budget to providing an additional outlay (Rs 2,466 crore) for a Centrally-sponsored scheme (in this case to be used mostly for the mid-day meal scheme) and the role of the states was limited to just some flexibility in implementing such central schemes. It was thus clear that despite promises to provide more for basic needs and check the deteriorating human development progress (see Chapter 5), the budget of 1996–97 continued to show the same values which guided the budgets during the reform period of 1991–92 to 1995–96 which pushed the country into a quagmire of non-development.[15]

The UF Government Budget: 1997–98

The UF Government's second and the first full year budget of 1997–98 would be particularly remembered for its proposals of all-round reduction in the rates of individual income tax, corporate tax, import duties and substantial concessions in excise duties for a number of consumer and industrial goods. The corporate sector was, understandably, euphoric with the unprecedented boost in stock prices. The mood was reflected in the Bombay Stock Exchange Sensitive Index which shot up by 176 points in the post-budget session.

The budget also claimed to have made a substantial hike, in pursuance with the Common Minimum Programme, in allocations for social services and rural development. Thus, the outlay for social sector (which includes education, welfare of Scheduled Castes and Tribes, water supply and labour and employment) was increased from 1996–97 (RE) of Rs 11,785.27 crore to Rs 15,707 crore in the BE of 1997–98. It is important, however, to understand that such hikes were with respect to the revised estimates i.e., actual expenditure expected during 1996–97 and not the budgeted estimates for 1996–97.[16] For example, a provision of Rs 1,400 crore was kept for the mid-day meal scheme for 1996–97. It was launched with great fanfare and found a special mention in the Finance Minister's speech. However, the amount actually spent on this important human development programme during 1996–97 was only Rs 800 crore. The allocation for this vital scheme was scaled down to Rs 960 crore in the 1997–98 budget, that is by Rs 440 crore (as compared to the BE of 1996–97). It was, therefore, no wonder that the scheme was not even mentioned in the Finance Minister's second year's speech. The same was the fate of some other schemes of elementary education. Although it was claimed that the budget allocation for it had been raised to Rs 2,543 crore from the previous year's RE of Rs 2,264 crore, the fact, however, was that the actual expenditure on elementary education in that year suffered a cut of Rs 697 crore. Similarly, the actual expenditure of the Ministry of Rural Areas and Employment, including the Department of Rural Development, in 1996–97 represented a cut of Rs 868 crore as compared to the budgeted allocation. The much publicised National Literacy Mission was also not spared from such cuts, allocation for which was scaled down to Rs 129.81 crore in the 1997–98 budget from the previous year's Rs 227 crore.[17]

Expenditure Compression: Scaling Down of the Plan Outlay

A noteworthy feature of the budget of 1997–98, therefore, was that it showed significant expenditure compression in the Central Plan outlay of 1996–97—from the budgeted Rs 87,086 crore to Rs 77,518 crore, thus effecting cuts of Rs 9,568 crore. The revised outlay thus was only 3.9 per cent higher than 1995–96 amounting to sharp contraction in real terms.

Such contraction was effected in agriculture (by Rs 211 crore), rural development (by Rs 856 crore), irrigation and flood control (by Rs 433 crore), energy (by Rs 4,669 crore) and in social service sector (by Rs 538 crore). In this sector, the shortfall in the total expenditure on education was as much as Rs 1,502 crore. Because of such drastic cuts in expenditure in 1996–97, the total budgeted plan outlay in 1997–98 was only 5.5 per cent higher (from Rs 87,086 crore as budgeted in 1996–97 to Rs 91,886 crore). This increase was distinctly lower than the expected inflation rate of 7 to 8 per cent amounting to scaling down of the plan outlay. The plan outlays in the 1997–98 budget, though nominally higher than 1996–97, were significantly lower in real terms. For example, in agriculture it was higher by 4.9 per cent, rural development 2.3 per cent and in the energy sector the plan outlay actually declined from Rs 24,270 crore to Rs 24,234 crore. In irrigation and flood control programmes, the outlays were drastically cut down from the budgetary allocation of Rs 1,248 crore to Rs 813 crore in RE of 1996–97 and further to Rs 323 crore in the BE for 1997–98.[18]

Declining Agricultural Growth

The Economic Survey 1996–97 conceded that the 'post-reform' agricultural performance was extremely disappointing despite an unprecedented run of nine consecutive excellent monsoons. The annual rate of growth of foodgrains in six years between 1991 and 1996–97 was only 1.7 per cent which was lower than the annual population growth of 1.9 per cent during the 1990s and therefore the Survey notes it as a matter of serious concern. It is noteworthy that the total spending on agriculture, irrigation and rural development has been showing a decline over the past years in terms of percentage of GDP. Thus, it was 1.99 per cent in 1989–90, which was gradually cut down to 1.46 per cent in 1995–96 and 1.45 per cent in 1996–97. However, the actual spending on these heads in 1996–97 amounted only to 1.32 per cent of GDP. It was further scaled down to 1.29 per cent in the 1997–98 budget which was contrary to the promises made in the CMP to devolve more funds to the states and to spend more on agriculture and rural development. It was ironical that instead of taking measures to fulfill its promises, the UF budget 1997–98, gave away huge tax cuts (which could amount to Rs 12,500 crore) and at the same time reduced public investments and outlays in agriculture and infrastructure sectors.[19]

Viewed in the perspective of the two budget estimates, the hikes in the allocations for the social sector and rural employment in the 1997–98 budget could be only termed as marginal. In real terms, it could also mean further stagnation in fulfilment of vital basic needs (see Chapter 5). Continuing expenditure compression in programmes like elementary education, child nutrition and employment generation was therefore a very serious matter and showed that the UF Government was not keen about its promises. It also showed that it is not the promises made by the government from time-to-time, not even the provisions shown in the budget allocations, but the actual expenditure and how such resources are utilised which are crucial for human development performance (Chapter 2).

Hoping for Better Tax Compliance

The tax cuts in the 1997–98 budget were unprecedented. The highest personal income tax at 30 per cent was comparable to most East Asian countries. In most European countries, it was still above 50 per cent. The abolition of tax on dividends further reduced the tax burden on the rich and the middle class. Similarly generous was the Voluntary Disclosure of Income Scheme which carried a tax at a flat rate of 30 per cent for individuals and 35 per cent for corporates with no penalty or interest. Those who evaded tax at much higher rates (maybe 40 to 70 per cent or more) were now to reap the benefit of their violation of law.

The underlying assumption for such deep tax cuts and the proposed extended tax net was that lower taxes would ensure better tax compliance and, therefore, greater revenue collection. Given the prevailing political and administrative culture (Chapter 2) and the fact that black money was no longer socially disrespectful, it was too much to expect that the habitual tax dodgers would suddenly change their mentality. The only plausible explanation was that it would be cheaper to pay tax (maximum 30 per cent) than the cost of managing the black money. On the contrary, black money has several distinct advantages with little risk as tax evaders are hardly punished. It could buy favours and patronage, and help in generating more black money and power. Its attraction is, therefore, much more than white money. In the past also, there have been schemes for voluntary disclosure which did not succeed. In fact, the volume of black money has been continuously increasing. Such schemes did not succeed because deterrent actions were not taken to prevent generation of black money.[20] Even the much publicised tax scheme under which the traders could pay just Rs 1,400 a year and avoid regular tax did not succeed and has, there-fore, officially been scrapped.

'Development' Driven by Capital Market

The budget of 1997–98 was thus clearly motivated by faith in the efficacy of the capital market for promoting economic growth, so much so that the repeated promises for fulfilling pressing needs of the people were scaled down. This development strategy, i.e., the one driven by capital market and foreign investments, was reflected in various policy measures contained in the budget. These included: taking out several items reserved for the small scale industry in order to woo multinational companies and large Indian companies; opening of the health insurance sector to private sector; easing of the rules of foreign investment; liberalising oil explora-tion; incentives for private sector investment in infrastructure; and above all, huge cuts and concessions in taxes and custom duties. The budget also showed that the government was not sure of mobilising domestic savings for investment, hence the continuing dependence on foreign capital resources.

The two budgets for 1996–97 and 1997–98, presented and processed by the UF Government, therefore, gave no concrete evidence of their earnestness in meeting the vital and minimum needs of the people. On the contrary, as was widely commented upon in the print media, almost every area of social sector such as agriculture, rural development, ele-mentary education and nutrition witnessed reduction in the Central Government expenditure in the financial year 1996–97 as compared to the budgeted allocation.[21] The finance minister laid great stress (in his budget speech for 1997–98) on the East Asian levels of taxation, but he did not show similar enthusiasm for the East Asian levels of education, health care and land reforms (Chapter 5).

The budget of 1997–98 thus gave hope that the various incentives given to the corporates and the rich would trigger off entrepreneurship and therefore economic growth. Even while recognising that private enterprise is important for various economic and industrial activities, there was no concrete evidence that such 'reforms', particularly when implemented without adequate social development, would usher in sustainable and, more important, equitable growth. On the other hand, experience in our own country shows that such reforms may result in various negative social consequences (Chapter 5). The Common Minimum Programme in a way, gave expression to some of the thwarted aspirations of the common people.

The budget (and the actual expenditure pattern during 1996–97) however, did little to meet such aspirations and the people's basic needs. If the hope of enhanced revenue collection (as a result of the various concessions given in taxes, etc.) did not materialise and the government once again resorted to expenditure compression in social sector and to increasing administered prices such as petroleum products, which would further increase the cost of living. This would only enhance public resentment, alienation and demoralisation among large sections of the population. Such a situation of social unrest along with the scaling down of public sector investments in infrastructure and in agriculture could even jeopardise the intended economic growth itself.

It was clear that the UF Government was not able to modify the development strategy and remove/weaken such structural factors, as discussed in Chapter 4, which have been long inhibiting human development and quality of life of the common people, majority of whom still depended on agriculture and lived in rural areas. Such a development strategy of 'economic reforms' was also not favourable to the urban masses because of growing unemployment and rising prices. The need was to fire the imagination of the people, as promised in the CMP, and to raise their morale and motivation to participate in development efforts. Such participation and involvement was, however, possible only when people at large perceived development policies and plans as beneficial to them and which gave them a hope for better life. Such socio-economic development would require a major paradigm shift in policies and programmes. The fact was that the UF Government which came to power, at least partly, because of people's discontent against the negative consequences of 'economic reforms', was reluctant to change the course of economic policies. For example, it could not initiate policy measures to implement its own promises such as greater investment in agriculture and for rural infrastructure; benefits to small and marginal farmers and agricultural workers; fair conditions of work to industrial and other workers; and for enhancing opportunities for employment and productive work. Such policies were essential for human development in the country. The government's reluctance only underlined the need for organised and sustained people's movements and public activism to 'demand' vigorous state interventions towards the alternative direction. We recall and discuss some related issues in this respect in Section II, some suggested policy interventions for an alternative development strategy in Section III, some dimensions of a composite psychological strategy for challenging people in Section IV and finally the need for creative symbiosis between people and the state for promoting alternative development, particularly for accelerating human development in the country.

II
Role of Public Activism

Huge tax cuts and various concessions given to the rich and the corporate sector, on the one hand, and the expenditure compression in basic needs programme, on the other, also indicated the government's intention to reduce its developmental role. It was also shown by the government's liberal invitation to multinationals, by offering them various concessions such as seven years tax holiday, international price on new discoveries, etc., and incentives to invest in oil exploration. The state's reduced role in productive investment for infrastructure for employment generation and for people's welfare would be in accordance with the ideology of structural adjustment programme (Chapter 5). It would, however, further contribute to slowing down public welfare and human development in the country (Chapter 4).

On top of such pro-rich policies, the nature of state functioning has greatly contributed to the aborted human development in the country. Continuation of the same policies, which have been responsible for poor public welfare and human development performance, suggest the imperative need to pressurise the government and public functionaries for pro-people policies and positive behaviour on the ground, particularly for social development programmes (Chapter 4).

The Need for Activising the State Agencies

Human development, besides being important per se, also plays an important role in promoting economic development. This is borne out by the case of high-performing Asian economies (HPAEs), China and several other countries (Chapter 5). There is also a need to search for new methods to prepare the government for playing a more positive and active role and to create the necessary social environment in the country[22] (Chapter 4). Some rich experience in the country itself can guide us in this regard for creating necessary socio-political environment and for energising the state agencies for better performance in social sector.

The Actor Role of People

Kerala's experience shows that social development can be achieved, even under low level of economic growth through public activism and state interventions, which highlights the importance of 'actor' role of people in their own development. A 'demand' from below works towards energising the state apparatus in favour of the people. The public behaviour thus works as a prime mover of social sector development. The two, i.e., the public and the state, could work in reciprocal relationship and in turn could put pressures on public functionaries for welfare and development goals. Kerala has now launched a state-wide planning and economic development programme, thus energising the people in the state to get actively involved in identifying their needs and problems and in generating ideas for the Ninth Five Year Plan as well as in development of such plans.[23]

Educating, Organising and Activising People

The poor performance of the state, particularly towards fulfilment of basic needs of the people, has also now 'activated' important political functionaries to talk in terms of launching a country-wide campaign to focus attention on people's problems and to force the government to recast its priorities. A thinking is getting crystallised at the national level and also in the States, that if fruits of economic development have to flow to the common man, it is necessary to launch awareness campaigns in the country, particularly to focus attention on institutionalised corruption, compulsory job-oriented education for all children up to the age of 14 years, reservation of some industries for cottage and small scale sector, creation of infrastructure, job-generation and activisation of primary health services in the country.[24] It is interesting in this connection to note the concern in the top political leadership in China for education in 'patriotism' and to foster a national spirit of greater self-respect, self-confidence and self-support in the common people. It is proposed to put greater stress on promoting ideological and moral education among the people as a part of the current stock taking of social development during the past 18 years of reforms.

Poor development performance in the country, particularly in the social sector, underlines the need to think in terms of an alternative strategy. The situation, after 50 years of Independence, reminds us of Gandhiji's famous remark, made as far back as in 1926, that, 'the real India does not live in Bombay, Delhi or Calcutta but in seven lakh villages. If we wish to make these villages self-reliant, the human machine should be activated ...'.

The country's grim situation of poverty and deprivation requires us to ponder over Gandhiji's advice and to take steps to activate the human agency, the people, towards self-reliant development.[25]

III

Alternative Development Strategy

Capability of the People

In the alternative strategy, people need to be the prime movers of development and not tax concessions and financial sector reforms, as emphasised in the 'economic liberalisation'. A concern for capability is integral to this new perspective. The Copenhagen Summit also sought to give 'the highest priority to ... promotion of social progress and the betterment of the human conditions .... To this end, we shall place people at the centre of development and the economy at the service of human needs' (UN, 1995: para 20). On the other hand, policies of liberalisation for economic growth talk about social concerns only on tactical grounds, which is motivated by the need for efficiency rather than by questions of social justice and equity. Without relating development to the ground reality of the poor, the talk about social concerns is only a window dressing (Meike, 1995).

The Common Minimum Programme of the United Front Government only talked about giving primacy to basic needs of the people such as education, health, water, food, skill development, employment, etc. They were, however, reluctant to translate such concerns into concrete policies and programmes. Their policies, despite promises, did not make people the main actors and movers of development. For really fulfilling such promises, there is an urgent need to initiate people-oriented and not just market-oriented development efforts. Such efforts are needed to prepare the people to take on an actor role and to motivate them to release their productive energy and initiative. Contrary to the indications implied in the1997–98 budget proposals, the state has also to play an important and crucial role, as discussed in Chapter 5, in such alternative development. Some policy interventions needed for such a strategy, are briefly discussed next.

Generating Employment and Capability for Poverty Alleviation

An open and competitive economy is helpful for raising productivity and alleviating poverty only when certain social conditions have been met.

The present economic reforms (for promoting economic growth) have not however resulted in reduction of poverty. On the contrary, the extent of poverty may have increased during the reform period of 1991–96[26] (Chapter 5). The East Asian countries, which have managed to reduce/eliminate endemic poverty, have taken care to provide a proper infrastructure in rural areas. Such public investments have also been accompanied by effective land reforms. In these countries and in China, wide access to adult literacy and primary education and drastic reduction in infant mortality rate have contributed to lowering the population growth rate, lower than the rate of economic growth. All such factors greatly help in strengthening the bargaining power of the poor in the labour market and enable them to take advantage of the related market forces and economic liberalisation.

It is necessary, therefore, to pay special attention, as promised in the CMP but not adequately addressed in their actual policies, to creating employment opportunities by strengthening: (*i*) agriculture and the rural infrastructure; (*ii*) implementation of equitable land reforms, and (*iii*) rural industry and crafts. Large investments in agriculture are needed for land regeneration, re-afforestation and regeneration of water resources and for promoting dry land farming and rain-fed agriculture. Such programmes have great potential for the rural economy and for generating meaningful employment in the rural areas. These and other policy related efforts, discussed next, would help bring about some much needed structural changes and in obtaining the goals of human development in the country, as discussed in Chapter 4.

Energising Resource Management for Rural Development

There is a nexus between poverty and poor resource management. For instance, 175 million ha of degraded land is intrinsically capable, if restored to health, of producing additional wealth which could work out to about Rs 1,75,000 crore per annum. Many of our small reservoirs have also gone out of operation on account of premature siltation and many bigger ones are also getting silted up. As the Eighth Five Year Plan document shows, 40 million ha of our land is flood-prone and 7.7 million ha is annually affected (Vohra, 1996). There are, thus, serious economic consequences of poor management of our resources such as land and water, resulting in deforestation, soil erosion, excessive run-off and continuing problems of water logging and salinisation. All these contribute to low productivity and poverty. There is a need, therefore, to make a frontal and determined attack on all aspects of poor resource management and to adopt mini-watershed as a unit for planning as well as implementation of all programmes of land improvement and resource management (ibid.: 1401). Agricultural extension and other support programmes also needed to be augmented to release people's energy and help enhance land productivity.[27]

Public Distribution System

Food prices are intimately related to the index of poverty. As the prices go up, poverty also tends to go up. A public distribution system, therefore, is essential for not only maintaining the prices but for providing food security to all people. Over the last few years, net food availability through the PDS has tended to come down. On the whole, the access to PDS is confined only to one-third of our people. Food security is essential for fighting endemic malnutrition, which is one of the main reasons for raising our capability poverty index. The public distribution system, therefore, needs to be strengthened and food security made more wider. This is needed also because of high prices of food, which have doubled in the last few years. The subsidised food scheme proposed in the 1997–98 budget, as discussed above, although most welcome, was not sufficient as it would, even if implemented properly, provide only a marginal benefit.[28]

Making Markets Accountable to People

The PDS needs to be strengthened also because markets are essentially not democratic in nature. For example, they do not operate on the principle of one person one vote. It requires money to operate on a market. The market is, in fact, controlled by the moneyed people. Civil societies need to exercise control over such institutions so that the local citizens can have a say in advertising and in the nature of investments in order to curb excessive consumerism and speculative practices. In other words, markets need to be made accountable to people—and not people pawns of the market-owners and manipulators.[29]

Public Support for Direct Social Security

The UF Government was reportedly committed to improving the quality of life of the vulnerable people. The government had publicly accepted the fact that it was not possible to achieve this goal by following the principle of trickle-down of economic growth. On the contrary, it was necessary to provide direct public support for social security to the weaker sections of the society. The experience shows that public support-led social security has resulted in much higher human development in China and several other countries (Drèze and Sen 1989:208–209). As there was an agreement on the need for direct social security, the task was to activise the governments at the Centre and in states to translate promises into policy interventions and programmes for fulfilling the basic needs of the people for security, health care, education, employment, etc. Opening of health insurance to the private sector, as discussed above, could benefit some small sections, but would provide no benefit to the large majority of the population, particularly the rural population.[30]

Internal Resources Vs Dependency on External Resources

The development strategy for economic growth and the race for attracting foreign investments and TNCs have released a pernicious vicious circle of consumerism. Inculcation of artificial needs and psychological impulses for acquiring consumer goods directly threaten the age-old habit of saving in the society. While the rate of savings in China was about 35 to 40 per cent and 34 per cent both in Japan and Korea, ours was only 24 per cent of the GDP. Taxation policy also breeds consumerism and many wealthy persons and corporations do not pay any taxes or pay very little. The present tax ratio to GDP is about 10 per cent which leaves considerable scope for a much wider tax net. As the Deputy Chairman of the Planning Commission has said, 'as against 85 per cent of the population in Denmark and Sweden which pays tax, in India only 0.8 per cent pays income tax .... We need to tax the visible expenditure of the creamy layer and include more people in the tax net'. There is thus a need for raising resources from the wealthy sections of the society such as big companies, rich farmers, professionals and others. After all, it is the duty of the state and society to meet people's basic needs which can be done only by raising resources internally. It becomes all the more important in view of the extraordinary tax cuts and other concessions given to the rich in the 1997–98 budget. Internal resource mobilisation would help create conditions for also attracting, absorbing and appropriately retaining and using investments in the country.[31]

Encouraging Investments in Priority Sectors

Along with internal savings and resources, it is equally important to regulate foreign investments as per national priorities. No doubt, we need foreign help and funds for some projects and programmes in the country, particularly for upgrading technology and industrial practices. However, such foreign investments have to be geared to the development priorities of the country and not left to the vagaries of market forces alone. The supporters of economic liberalisation clamour not only for more and more concessions for the capital but for more and more political liberalisation so that vital development decisions are left at the mercy of market forces, which in fact, means large corporations, mostly TNCs. This is the essence of the 'Washington Consensus' which requires the state to withdraw, open up the economy, deregulate and leave the field to the private sector. However, as opposed to this ideological pressure, Japan, and to some extent the 'Asian Tigers' namely, South Korea, Hong Kong, Singapore and Taiwan and then Malaysia, representing the 'East Asian miracle', did try to regulate the financial system and investments by their public policies with active government interventions (Muzumdar, 1996). On the contrary, the ideology of deregulation seeks to empower big corporations, mainly the TNCs, at the cost of the state. It also seeks to promote foreign interventions in the national decision-making, thereby curtailing the sovereign rights of the people.[32]

When market rules without any state regulation and direction, invariably, it is the economically powerful people i.e., the capital, who rule either directly or by proxy. Such policies, which favour a small minority of very wealthy people are, therefore, motivationally dysfunctional as far as common people's involvement in development is concerned. On the other hand, regulation of foreign investments and the TNCs as per the needs of the people along with promotion of self-reliance could motivate them for active involvement in such development efforts.

Decentralisation, Accountability and Information

The 73rd and 74th Constitutional Amendments provide an excellent opportunity for energising *panchayati raj* institutions (PRIs) and municipal bodies towards decentralisation and democratisation of governance in the country (GOI, 1992c, 1992d). The PRIs could facilitate development of capability among the neglected sections of our society and promote their participation in policy-making, regulating, planning and implementing various projects and programmes at the grassroots levels.

The inbuilt inhibiting forces in our social organisation and the administration are, however, not likely to wither away because of Constitutional amendments. These forces have successfully thwarted full implementation of the Directive Principles of State Policy (Chapter 2). It is, therefore, not going to be easy for the dominant elite to accept the emergence of new leadership at the village level which could take away their power over the village society (Chapter 3). Their powers are curtailed when democratisation spreads to villages. It is also not surprising that one of the frequently articulated grievances of the newly elected representatives relates to the attitudes of the entrenched social and political leaders and functionaries like MLAs and the bureaucracy. They have been emphasising the need for a change in their mindset as well as curtailment of their role. It is the duty of the state governments as well as the centre to adequately empower the PRIs and the various municipal bodies to enable them to play their role effectively.[33]

Mobilisation for Decentralisation and Democratisation

Despite the power of inhibiting forces, the West Bengal experience of decentralisation shows that the PRIs have been able to motivate people for increasing agricultural production and to sustain the enthusiasm released by land reforms for further socio-economic development. Organised and planned efforts are, no doubt, required for changing the mindset of the entrenched authorities. There is a need for appropriate administrative and legislative measures, on the one hand, and on the other, for public activism to put pressure from below for greater information and accountability and to obtain the necessary policy changes in this regard. People's movements and organisations, as shown by some success experience in Rajasthan (Roy, 1996), could force the unwilling system of centralised governance for greater devolution of powers, greater transparency and sharing of information and for greater accountability to the people. Such social mobilisation could promote empowerment of the local people and strengthen decentralisation and accountability and transparency (Chapter 6). Such democratised governance could become an effective vehicle for participatory planning and development from the *gram sabha* level upwards, which in turn would greatly facilitate human development in the country (Chapter 4).[34]

Women's Empowerment for Promoting Development

Women hold the key to education, health, population planning, protection of environment and to other areas of social sector development. Like education, women's (and child) health care programmes have also been long neglected in the country. Health care has been more gender blind than even education in our society. Women and girl children get the least attention. Neglect of women's health contributes to transmission of a self-effacing attitude of mothers to daughters resulting in continuing health and nutritional inequality. Health interventions can, therefore, play an important role in mobilising the community to address such stereotypes and in helping women to change attitude to their own health and welfare. This would, however, require planned interventions in order to weaken various social and cultural factors underlying gender discrimination in this respect.

Female Literacy, Population Planning and Related Issues: Education is another significant factor in women empowerment. Even simple literacy, as is well known, contributes to lowering of fertility and birth rate (BR) by increasing the marriageable age of girls. Education also promotes use of contraception and a desire for gainful employment. This is borne out by the experience in our own state of Kerala where both female literacy rate (86.2 per cent) and marriageable age (22.9 years) are high and where they have achieved total fertility rate (TFR) of 1.8. The same is the case with Mizoram, another state with a high female literacy rate, which has achieved a low fertility rate of 2.3 percent only slightly higher than Kerala's. As against this, Uttar Pradesh has TFR of 5.1, Rajasthan 4.6 and Bihar 4.6. Female literacy contributes to women's freedom and motivates them to plan their families.[35]

Along with literacy, employment is another very potent instrument for empowering women. Recent surveys show that a large number of elected women *panchayat* representatives came from households living under the poverty line. These included chairpersons of *panchayat samities* and *zila parishads*. It was obvious that without literacy, women would not be able to play their role effectively. In states like Rajasthan, Bihar, Uttar Pradesh and Madhya Pradesh where female literacy rate was very low, a large number of women representatives were bound to be illiterate. Additionally, very few of such women were likely to possess land or have property of their own. Under such conditions, the dominant males were bound to rule *panchayats* by proxy.[36] Interventions were needed to increase work participation and gainful employment for women. Productive work could contribute to developing a sense of independence and initiative in them which are essential for ensuring proper and effective participation of women in the *panchayat* institutions.[37]

Home-based Vs Community-based Occupations: Women gain self-esteem and capability when they are engaged in some community-based occupations (as against home-based casual work). Women themselves also prefer to work outside their homes.[38] For instance, conditions of women engaged in *beedi* making in the cooperative sector were much better than those engaged in home-based *beedi* making. Community-based occupation provides women with not only much broader exposure to the outside world and brings them in contact with other persons doing similar work in a community setting, but also better income resulting in greater independence and empowerment.[39] With greater awareness about the world of work, women are motivated to overcome the hurdles put on them by the traditionally gender-based work roles. Education and vocational training need to go beyond the traditional skills such as in knitting, lace making, etc., for women as these tend to reinforce gender discrimination in capability development. Such a change in planning skill development in women was urgently needed because, not only government institutions but also some non-government organisations tended to perpetuate such stereotypes through their vocational training programmes. Such training, instead of empowering, may actually hamper capability development in women.[40]

IV

Challenging People for Alternative Development: A Composite Psychological Strategy

The foregoing discussion suggests the need for a composite psychological strategy of structural-cum-behavioural changes for motivating and accelerating human development in the country. The suggested strategy is composed of two essential dimensions: (i) Challenging and socially worthwhile goals in order to motivate the civil society, particularly the vulnerable people; (ii) Creative interaction of people and the state to inculcate empowering and facilitating socio-political environment. The people need to be activated to put pressure on the state for appropriate state interventions, such as the above and for faithful and effective implementation of the given programmes, in order to obtain the desired social objectives. The strategy, thus visualises a symbiotic relationship between state activism and public activism for furtherance of the goals of alternative development, i.e., welfare, capability development and empowerment of the people resulting in shared, participatory and egalitarian economic growth. Some essential elements of these structural-cum-behavioural dimensions of the strategy are briefly recalled and summarised here:

Setting Socially Worthwhile and Challenging Goals

People at large, particularly the vulnerable category, can be challenged to actively participate in development efforts only when they perceive the goals as meaningful and worthwhile for themselves and society. Some such goals, mentioned before, are briefly recalled.

Land Reforms: Equitable distribution of land to large masses of landless agricultural people including the related goals of tenancy registration, enforcement of ceiling laws, etc., have long been the felt-needs of such toiling people. Such land reforms are also highly desirable, from a psychological viewpoint, as these would enhance the people's self-esteem and generate concern for quality of life among the deprived people.[41]

Releasing Creativity and Entrepreneurship at the Grassroots Level: One of the important requirements of faster human development in the country is availability of adequate employment and adequate infrastructural facilities for the weaker people, particularly in rural areas. This would help enhance the morale and motivation of the rural people and to release their entrepreneurship and creativity (Chapter 4).

Supporters of economic liberalisation are never tired of talking about the need for enhancing competition among domestic enterprises and between them and the TNCs. This, we know, does not automatically become a reality as the larger and more powerful TNCs tend to take over the smaller units and become monopolistic, thus excluding healthy and equal competition.[42] Public policies during the reform period (1991–96) crippled the policies followed earlier for providing bank credit to priority sectors like small industry and agriculture. Even the East Asian countries, have used financial policies and banks to boost priority sectors and entrepreneurship at the ground level, (Muzumdar, 1996). In India, on the contrary, policies have made it difficult for the small entrepreneurs to get bank credit (EDII, 1993).

Entrepreneurship plays an important role in creating new enterprises and in promoting excellence, creativity and innovativeness in the economy and in society (McClelland, 1961). One of the important factors in China's and the East Asian countries' faster economic growth was the creation of smaller units and enterprises which in turn helped fire imagination of the enterprising people to compete for excellence and success. This helped in creating job opportunities, fairer distribution of income, thus contributing to more shared and faster economic development. Release and inculcation of creativity, innovativeness and entrepreneurship can play an important role in promoting alternative development.[43]

Suggested Interventions for Restructuring the Workplace: Democratisation of the work-organisation for greater excellence and productivity is thus an important part of the alternative strategy.[44] This, however, required several planned interventions which could aim at: (*i*) Democratic re-orientation of managers for integrative influence. (*ii*) Strengthening managers' and workers' motivation for social achievement. (*iii*) Promoting leadership for managers' and workers' empowerment. (*iv*) Enhancing workers' participation in decision-making and in management. (*v*) Inculcating worthwhile and meaningful goals. (*vi*) Debureaucratisation. (*vii*) Release of innovativeness and creativity. (*viii*) Inculcation of cooperation and promotion of team work. (*ix*) Creating conditions and facilities for skill development. (*x*) Job-security and (*xi*) Promoting a system of accountability and reward for performance. These, and other similar interventions, including the related training interventions, could greatly contribute towards democratisation, enhanced morale and motivation and to increased productivity at the workplace. These, in turn, could help promote democratisation of the larger civil society.[45]

The Goal of Self-Reliance: Pursuit of self-reliance is another important challenging and worthwhile goal and an essential parameter of an alternative development strategy. Readiness to inhibit present needs was an important psychological factor in investing and working for future quality of life and for a better society. Such psychological preparedness is thus an important contributor to sustainable development as the readiness to inhibit present needs reinforces the habit of saving and investment for future (McClelland, 1961:128–29). Market liberalisation, on the contrary, was based on inculcation of artificial needs and unnecessary consumption by corroding the age-old habit of self-reliance and inhibition of present needs for better future. It was necessary, therefore, to curb excessive consumerism and to restore the traditional value of self-reliance in the country.

The culture of saving and reliance on internal resources is greatly strengthened when people participate in a national movement for raising internal resources; self-reliant behaviour as well as tax paying behaviour too are, on the whole, strengthened and reinforced in the society at large. This culture, thus developed, further strengthens the behaviour-pattern of self-reliance and inhibition of present needs for the future.[46] The psychological strategy for alternative development, therefore, requires planned efforts for weeding out unethical business practices and corrupt behaviour and for inculcating the goal of self-reliance and a network of local entrepreneurship in the country.

Promoting a Facilitating and Empowering Social Environment

Fulfilment of People's Basic Needs

Another important and crucial parameter of the alternative strategy is the fulfilment of the basic needs of people. Social sector programmes like those for literacy, elementary education, sanitation, water, housing, social justice and security, gender and social equality, etc., also constitute very powerful social achievement goals. Such activities along with land reforms, development of rural infrastructure, promotion of excellence in manu-facturing and new enterprises, pursuit of self-reliance and such other macro-level policies would greatly contribute to creating the right social and psychological environment. Such an environment is essential for enhan-cing access of the vulnerable people to public services and for motivating them for achieving better quality of life (Chapter 4).

Releasing People's Energy and Reserves in the Economy

As experience has shown, half-hearted, distorted and elite oriented imple-mentation of development policies and programmes creates a sense of cynicism, alienation and anger in people (Chapter 6). On the contrary, people-centred alternative development strategy enhances their assertive power for achieving social achievement. Inculcation of a conducive and empowering social environment is essential for releasing people's creative energy for participatory development.[47]

Such worthwhile programmes, as those for basic needs of the common people, are intrinsically motivational not only for the public but also for those involved in implementing them, such as volunteers, teachers and other government and non-government functionaries. This was borne out by several success stories in Total Literacy Campaigns under the National

Literacy Mission as well as in such other programmes in various parts of the country.[48] Creation of a conducive and empowering socio-psychological environment was thus an important goal of the alternative development strategy.

Political Commitment for People's Welfare

As we know, it is not mere expenditure and the GNP rate per se but commitment to public policies which is crucial for promoting people's empowerment and development. Such a political commitment helps promote conducive social environment and contributes to faster human development as has happened in several countries like China and Sri Lanka (Drèze and Sen, 1989:251–52; Drèze and Sen, 1995:27–51). It indicates values and motivation for social achievement which are necessary for activising various state agencies in favour of the society in general and of weaker sections in particular (Chapter 5).

The Case of Endemic Deprivation

Endemic deprivation in the country illustrated the need for the above alternative model, particularly the importance of facilitating social environment and state's political commitment. Nutrition was one of the minimum needs in the CMP of the UF Government. Deprivation is, however, not only due to chronic deficiency of food intake. The latter is only a means and not an end in itself (Drèze and Sen, 1989:42). In this sense, deprivation was also a socio-political issue rather than merely being a biological and economic issue. It showed values and attitudes of the state and ruling elite towards the poor. The structural-behavioural model, therefore, hypotheses that, greater the pro-people orientation of the state and more driven it is by such values and superordinate goals for improving the quality of life of the common people, the more effective are its various agencies in implementing the related programmes on the ground. Conversely, the less driven it is by such pro-people values and goals, the less sensitive it is toward chronic deprivation of people. Persistence of endemic deprivation, therefore, represents social failures of the state and not just the victims' nutritional biological deficiency. Conceptually, the paradigm (i.e., food alone vs. socio-political inputs in addition to food for eliminating chronic deprivation) was rooted in the overall need for developing an empowering social environment and capability in the people for a healthy life.

The food approach alone failed to eliminate chronic malnutrition, first, because enough food was not made available to such people and second, because they lacked the capability to obtain effective access even to whatever services were available to utilise these for their welfare. Hence the alternative development strategy emphasises the need for greater social sensitivity, positive attitudes towards people, decentralisation and democratisation in the state functioning. These are essential for effective policy interventions in order to promote a facilitative and empowering social environment and capability in people themselves.[49]

Releasing Motivation for Social Achievement and Democratic Influence

The behavioural strategy thus lies essentially in mobilising the people, on the one hand, by motivating them for social achievement goals and for collective action in pursuance of such goals and, on the other, in putting public pressure from below for enhancing political commitment in various state agencies for obtaining similar goals. The strategy thus seeks to release the psychological energy of the people and to empower them to act as prime movers of sustainable development. Various non-government organisations, social activist groups, adversarial politics, people's organisations, mass media and similar other agencies play an important role in this respect. They help to organise and mobilise people to pursue social achievement goals. Such efforts contribute towards strengthening people's self-esteem, efficacy, pride in one's own efforts and their orientation for self-reliance and help release social energy and state intervention for sustainable development.[50]

Promoting a New Mindset at the Workplace and in Governance

Government interventions for the suggested alternative development strategy thus underline the need, as discussed in Chapter 5, for positive and pro-people behavioural characteristics in the state and other functionaries. These need to be, as discussed in Chapter 4, qualitatively different, perhaps the opposite of some typical tendencies which functionaries display from time-to-time on the ground (Chapter 2). The suggested structural and policy changes are likely to create a conducive social environment which could facilitate such behavioral changes at the workplace and in governance. These will, however, not come about automatically and easily.

There is likely to be strong resistance from the entrenched vested interests and from the functionaries' existing values and attitudes. Public activism, as discussed in Chapter 6, can play an important role in bringing about the much needed pro-people commitment in the government. This, in turn, could facilitate the desired behavioural changes in the functionaries. Public activism could also help to promote and obtain effective decentralisation, participatory planning, transparency, accountability and social sensitivity in governance and reinforce vigilant, pro-active, entrepreneurial and result-oriented administration.

Along with democratic public pressure, specifically designed and planned training could also greatly contribute to promoting the desired behavioral changes at the workplace and in administration (Mehta, 1997b). Such training could strengthen pro-active action orientation; readiness to unlearn and learn; and facilitative leadership skills (Chapter 4). Such behavioural changes are further reinforced when functionaries' concern for social achievement and for democratic influence are enhanced (Mehta, 1994c : 58–76). Such planned behaviour modification, in turn, would contribute to implementation of challenging development goals as well as to promoting the desired social environment for accelerating human development in the country.

V

Concluding Remarks

The human development performance in the country in the last 50 years of Independence can only be rated as very low. Despite the Constitutional directives and Fundamental Rights and despite promises made repeatedly, the situation obtaining in the fields of elementary education, literacy, health care and employment and in such other basic areas has been rather pathetic and highly disappointing. The state and its various organs have thus failed even to discharge their minimum Constitutional obligations to the people.

The state agencies in India have been tightly controlled by the 'elite' who have been historically and even educationally conditioned to be insensitive to the needs of the lowly placed labouring people. They have been motivated more by the traditional values of inequality and social power than by the liberal values enshrined in the Constitution of India. Unlike the bureaucracy in some East Asian countries, the functionaries in India have tended to show caste-like rigidity, inflexibility and lack of entrepreneurship and rentier-dole syndrome while discharging their public duties. The administration in the post-Independence period has continued to impose and reinforce negative self-concepts and dependency syndrome on the lowly placed labouring people. The living conditions of the vast sections of Indian population have thus continued to be mired in shameful conditions of illiteracy, ill-health, malnutrition, insanitation and in abysmal poverty.

Under such conditions, human development would require not just some literacy and any casual work but inculcation of positive self-concepts and capability. They have to be helped to move away from dependent pawn-like behaviours to initiative and actor-like behaviours. Participation in organised collective action in people's movements as well as in self initiated development action would greatly help in promoting and reinforcing such positive self-concepts. Public activism is also important for pressuring and activising the unwilling government to act for the welfare of the people and to decentralise and democratise the administration. Repeated electoral verdicts in the past few years indicate, on the one hand, an increasing articulation of pressing socio-economic issues in this respect and, on the other, people's yearning for greater social and political empowerment.

The UF Government came to power in 1996 on the crest of such public resentment and its Common Minimum Programme, in a way, gave expression to the aspirations of the common people. The two budgets, for 1996–97 and 1997–98, presented by the UF Government and the related policies, however, did little to fulfill promises made in the CMP. On the contrary, the 1997–98 budget gave extraordinary concessions to the rich and the corporates including the multinationals and continued to bet on the strong for economic development of the country. It continued to adhere to the capital market and foreign investment-oriented development strategy which was likely to demoralise and alienate the vast sections of the population and which might even jeopardise the economic growth itself. There was a danger that such policies would further hamper capability and human development in the country. There was a need for a paradigm shift where people and not the capital market would be the prime movers of development. The CMP also contained some elements of such an alternative strategy. Some essential policy interventions, though well known and often promised, were not faithfully implemented. The need, therefore, was to pressure the state organs to implement such promises. Creative interaction of people and state was essential to such a strategy.

Creative Interaction of the People and the State

Economic programmes and structural changes such as: strengthening of rural infrastructure; investments in agriculture and rural development; egalitarian land reforms; stress on self-reliance and mobilisation of internal resources as against dependency on foreign investments; interventions designed to promote new enterprises and competitiveness for excellence and quality at the workplace; empowerment and activisation of PRIs and municipal bodies for active participation in planning and in development and similar other superordinate policy goals, all have the potential for raising the morale of the people, thus releasing their productive energy to actively participate in obtaining various achievement goals. Kerala's state-sponsored people's campaign for decentralised planning was a good example of creative interaction between the people and the state.[51]

Creative interaction between the people and the state thus has the potential for motivating the various state agencies as well as the public. This could directly contribute to promoting the desired psychological and social environment for sustainable alternative development. Such development involves a process of social and political empowerment whose long-term objective is to rebalance the structure of power in the society.

Creative and meaningful interaction between people and the state thus helps in releasing people-empowerment and democratisation in the wider society. As the assertive power of the people increases and as they become more and more concerned with social achievement goals, they would also activise the state for similar achievement goals, thus accelerating the process of democratic governance and sustainable human and economic development in the country.

END NOTES

1. See a report by Reeta Dutta in *Times of India*, February 22, 1996. Also see a report by Anita Katyal on a note prepared by the Ministry of Human Resource Development and circulated at the State Education Ministers' Conference which says that key schemes like Adult Literacy, Operation Blackboard, Non-formal Education designed for universalising elementary education by 1999 were in 'a pathetic state'. They suffer from various reasons such as stagnation of projects, lapse of neo-literates into illiteracy for want of effective post-literacy campaign, delay in recruitment of teachers and construction of class rooms, under-utilisation of funds and poor management of the programmes. *Times of India*, August 16, 1996.
2. See reports by Kalpna Jain, *Times of India*, dated 17 November, 1995 and 4, 5, 6 and 7 January, 1996.

3. Quoted in a report by Kalpna Jain, *Times of India*, February 22, 1996. Also see an editorial comment on Missing Girls, *Times of India*, June 17, 1996.

4. See a report on the population situation in India and the editorial comment, *Times of India*, January 23, 1997.

5. A report on the study and also an editorial comment, *Times of India*, December 11, 1996.

6. *Times of India*, May 4, 1996.

7. The former Prime Minister, Shri H.D. Deve Gowda, in his first address to the nation deplored the fact that the country's administration had failed to provide even basic minimum services to all its people. He promised to discuss the matter with the Chief Ministers and finalise a time-bound programme for ensuring basic needs of the people. See the Prime Minister's address to the nation on June 16, 1996 as reported in *Times of India* dated 17 June 1996.

8. See United Front (1996). It has also been reported that infrastructure and social sector development and decentralisation would be the core of Ninth Five Year Plan. See a report by the Business Times Bureau, *Times of India*, August 21, 1996.

9. *Times of India*, February 5, 1996. The statement of Rajiv Gandhi, the then Prime Minister that hardly 15 per cent of such benefits reach the needy masses, is by now well known. The only difference is that the share might have gone further down from 15 per cent.

10. Report by Amresh Mishra, 'Beyond Mandir and Mandal', *Times of India*, March 25, 1996.

11. Findings of research conducted by the National Council of Applied Economic Research and reported in *Times of India*, April 16, 1996. Also see the CAG Report No. 17 mentioned by Praful Bidwai in 'The Social Deficiency: Need for Universalisation and not Targetted PDS', *Times of India*, August 2, 1996. The 1997–98 Budget allocated Rs 7,500/- crore for food subsidy which was only somewhat higher than the previous subsidy of Rs 6,066 crore and lower than Rs 8,300 crore mentioned by the Prime Minister for subsidising food for those living below poverty line. See the cover story 'Budget' 97: Substance and Artifice and also the Editorial, *Frontline*, March 21, 1997. Whether such a scheme would achieve the intended result was highly doubtful in view of the rampant political and bureaucratic pillage going in the name of distributive subsidised goods. (See Chapter 2).

12. See a comprehensive critique of the budget outlays for 1996–97 by Abhay Kumar Dubey, *Jansatta*, July 29, 1996, particularly the table on social sector expenditure. Also for details of the Budget, see Business Times, *Times of India*, July 23, 1996.

13. Prasad (1996, particularly Table 1) for such data culled out from various official economic surveys.

14. Krishnaswamy (1996) for comments on the budget, 1996-97. Stunted economic and social growth have contributed greatly to anarchy, chaos and destruction in Uttar Pradesh and Bihar where human development profile is among the worst in many areas and where only 10 per cent of the rural households in Bihar and 20 per cent in Uttar Pradesh have electricity as compared to the national average of 43 per cent and where net purchase of food in rural households through PDS is Rs 5 each per annum against the national average of Rs 33 per annum. See Sunil Sethi's article 'The Killing Fields of Uttar Pradesh and Bihar', *Times of India*, 17 March, 1977.

15. Krishnaswamy, 1996.

16. *Times of India*, March 1, 1997 (report by Kanwaldeep Singh).

17. *Times of India*, March 2, 1997 (report by Anita Katyal).

18. For comments and data on expenditure compression, see *EPW* (1997).

19. For comments on the budget and agriculture, see Sen (1997).

20. For a review and details of such schemes and aspects of the black economy in India, see *NIPEP* (1986).

21. Editorial comments in *The Hindu*, March 7, 1997.

22. For a discussion of such systemic tendencies found particularly in implementation of various social development programmes, see Chapter 2. For role of public activism in promoting human development and for the changing socio-psychology of the common people, see Chapter 6. Also see Mehta 1994b for motivation of collective action for social achievement.

23. For a report on Kerala's participatory planning for the Ninth Five Year Plan, see Issac and Harilal (1997); Gulati (1996).

24. For example, Mr Chandra Shekhar, the former Prime Minister of India intended to launch such a country-wide campaign. He thought that such a campaign to arouse people's power was necessary as the country was on the brink of chaos due to disturbing economic situation and erosion of people's faith in governmental institutions. For a report, see *Times of India*, January 23, 1997.

25. The recently concluded 6th Plenum of the Central Committee of the Chinese Communist Party took stock of social development during the past 18 years of reforms. It decided to take socio-cultural initiative to curb decadent trends in social behaviour, particularly to counter the host of social trends such as corruption, crime, drug use, growing selfish behaviour of the people. The Plenum emphasised the need for promoting spiritual civilisation and ideological and moral education among the people. For a report, see Manoranjan Mohanty, 'Marxism and Materialism: Middle Path in the Middle Kingdom', *Times of India* 28 December, 1996.; For Gandhiji's quotation, see *Young India*, October 7, 1926, page 348.

26. It has been reported in the media that the percentage of families living below poverty line in the rural areas has risen from 33 per cent in 1987–88 to 49.16 per cent in 1995–96. For details, see *Times of India*, February 2 and 5, 1996.; In the Approach Paper of Ninth Five Year Plan, the Planning Commission has also admitted unabated continuation of poverty in the country. Even the Congress party which initiated economic reforms now seems to be going back on such policies calling for more anti-poor economic programmes. See a report on discussions at the meeting of the Executive Committee of the Congress Parliamentary Party, *Times of India*, January 25, 1997.

27. In a recent survey, agricultural scientists and extension personnel have also identified an urgent need for more effective management of resources, particularly land and water resources as the key issues in Indian agriculture and rural development. See Mehta (1991, 1997a).; The 1997–98 budget brought to fore a difference of opinion between the Ministry of Finance and Ministry of Agriculture with regard to allocation needed for augmentating infrastructure in order to achieve the targetted 4.5 per cent annual rate of growth in agriculture. The Central Plan allocation for agriculture and allied activities was increased from Rs 2,610.75 crore in 1996–97 (revised estimates) to Rs 2,969.13 crore in 1997–98. The Ministry wanted almost 120 per cent hike in their budget allocation. See *Times of India*, March 2, 1997.

28. See Rao, 1995 and Gopalan, 1995. According to the survey by NCAER, 37 per cent of the country's rural population was landless and therefore unable to grow their own crop to fend off hunger. As a consequence of several factors, foodgrain produc-

tion has been declining despite good monsoon—overall from 191 million tonnes in 1994–95 to 185 million tonnes in 1995–96 and in the case of wheat from 65.5 million tonnes to 62.6 million tonnes in the same period. See a report by Sunil Sethi on policy indifference to food security, *Times of India*, January 24, 1997. Also see Sen (1997).

29. For a discussion, see Korten (1995), especially pp. 18–23.

30. See a recent interview by Shri Chidambaram, the then Finance Minister, given to *Newsweek* and reproduced in *Times of India*, July 23, 1996. The Finance Minister said, 'We are clear that the trickle down effect won't work in India. There are too many poor people. It is, therefore, important to address these concerns directly'.

31. See Vardarajan, Siddartha, 'What Thiruvalluvar Really Said', *Times of India*, July 31, 1996. The Approach Paper of the Ninth Five Year Plan takes note of such a situation. For a report and the remarks by Madhu Dandavate, see Mahalingam (1997).

32. This is illustrated dramatically by the recent currency and economic crisis in some of these East Asian Countries publicised as 'miracle economies'. Their limited efforts to regulate the financial sector have not succeeded primarily because of their over-dependence on foreign loans and on big corporations (known as Chaebol in South Korea). Under the stringent conditionalities of the IMF, South Korea is now being forced to lower the rate of economic growth, cut government expenditure, raise interest rates, and to clear up financially shaky banks and conglomerates. These measures would result in large-scale unemployment and in further intrusion of international financial capital and multinational corporations. See *Times of India*, December 24, 1997 and an article by S. Vardarajan, *Times of India*, January 3, 1998. The currency crisis was caused by the 'institutional speculators' and the international banks and financial institutions. They pressured the G-7 governments to implement bail-out operations leading to an absurd situation where they 'financed their own indebtedness' and where the beneficiaries are the same financial institutions. See Michel Chossudovsky, 'Destroying National Currencies', *Frontline*, February 6, 1998 : 100. For discussion of interference of financial power and loss of sovereign rights of people, see Korten (1995 : 126–40) and contributions cited there.

33. For details of the Constitutional amendments, see GOI (1992c, 1992d); for a report on the recommendations of the *Panchayat Mahasammelan* held in October 1995, see *Statesman*, October 11, 1995. For non-implementation of such recommendations particularly concerning the district rural development agency, see an editorial comment on non-implementation of programmes in this regard in *Economic and Political Weekly*, March 2, 1996 : 500–501. Discussing the Raj legacy of 'steel frame', V.Y.D. Raman warns all those interested in preserving the democracy in India that the Indian bureaucracy might become an agent of right reaction unless they are reined in. The civil servants are necessary for smooth functioning of administration but they are no substitute for a democratic government. See, *The Hindu*, 7 March, 1997.

34. For discussion of positive consequences of social mobilisation and people's movement, see Roy (1996). For people's campaign for participatory planning from the *gram sabha* level in Kerala, see Issac and Harilal (1997). It has been reported that the Conference of the Chief Secretaries held on November 20, 1996, demanded a thorough overhaul of the bureaucracy to make it more people-oriented. They discussed the need for accountability, transparency and cleansing the public services. For a report, see Bidwai (1997).

35. See a report 'Female Literacy Abets Baby Boom' by Sundip Talukdar, *Times of India*, July 12, 1996. For another report, see Sudhamai Ragunathan, *Times of India*, March 25, 1996. Also see Drèze and Sen, 1995 : Table 3.3, page 47.

36. For the role of women in *panchayats*, see data given in a report by Mahipal, *Jansatta*, July 19, 1996.

37. For a discussion of various strategies for female education and women development, see May Rihani (1993); and for a discussion of interventions for women in development, see Rose, 1992; UNICEF, 1993a. For gender related human development, see UNDP (1995) and for data on India, Table 3.1 there. Also for programme of action after the World Summit on Social Development, see UNRISD (1995). Also see Batliwala (1996).

38. Mehta (1995 : 65–90 and 166–180).

39. Mohandas and Kumar (1992); Mehta (1994a).

40. In a review study of total literacy project under the National Literacy Mission, women themselves demanded training for marketable skills like radio repair, etc., see Mehta (1987, 1992a).

41. See Kalyan Mukherjee (1996) for discussion of some positive consequences of land reforms such as in Bihar movements for land distribution aim at loosening the semi-feudal hold over the lives of the poor. The basic driving force remained the aspirations of the toiling millions for a decent and free life, see Sinha (1992).

42. *The Economist* recently reported that in consumer durables, the top five firms controlled nearly 70 per cent of the entire world market, a ratio that economists consider highly monopolistic. For discussion of concentration of such money power, see Korten (1995) and other contributions cited there.

43. For impact of ruthless pursuit of profits at the workplace, see Mehta, 1994b. Also see an editorial comment 'Investment in Quality', *Times of India*, November 27, 1996. One of the factors in China's rapid economic growth is attributed to its wide network of small enterprises. The indigenous enterprises have become a dominant economic force there. One of the causes of such successful small enterprises is that these are not driven by foreign investment but by local resources and are known as township and village enterprises. See *Times of India*, September 16, 1995. The 1997–98 budget proposals take out several items from the list of those reserved for small scale industry and open them for large companies including multinational companies. This would profit them greatly but would further impair the employment situation in the country. In fact, the Indian farmers and small-scale manufacturers are being denied the level playing fields similar to the Indian big industrialists. Such a policy can harm the small scale sector and the employment prospects. See Surender Mohan's article, 'Level Playing Fields for Small Sector', *Times of India*, 21 March, 1997.

44. For this principle of zero defect and quality, see Phillip Crosby's remarks in *Times of India*, December 17, 1995. Also see Mehta (1994a). There is a need for developing skill in managing and adapting to change in the whole organisation and to invest in building competence, changing behaviours, and inspire action throughout the workforce. See an article by Peter H. Fuch and Terence V. Naill, 'Managerial Model in Uncertain World', *Times of India*, 26 November, 1996. Also see, a write-up on the need for fadless management and for critical thinking in order to develop a thinking organisation, *Times of India*, 3 February, 1997.

45. For discussion of democratisation of workplace, see Mehta (1992b); for social achievement and democratic influence, see Mehta (1994c); for workers participation and development, see Mehta (1989b) and other contributions cited there.

46. The Approach Paper to the Ninth Five Year Plan proposes to enhance domestic savings from 23.7 per cent of the GDP at market prices in the Eighth Five Year Plan to 26.2 per cent during the Ninth Five Year Plan period of 1997–2002. See Mahalingam (1997). On the contrary, the budget 1997–98 gave away huge concessions in taxes and other duties to corporations and others.

47. See Mehta (1994b). A group of social and environmental activists have suggested an alternative programme of action for managing people's natural resources as an antidote to fragmented bureaucratic regime and also against the bureaucratic monopoly of information. Success of such action depends on people's movements. See Rao and Gadgil (1995).

48. Volunteers and instructors, involved in implementing adult education programmes in remote areas such as villages in western Rajasthan, where literacy rate is very low, have shown great enthusiasm in carrying out such programmes. In fact, their own sense of self-efficacy and self-esteem were enhanced by their involvement in such activities which they perceived as socially relevant and meaningful. See Mehta (1990; 1995 : 17–24).

49. For discussion of the importance of other inputs rather than only food and for the need for necessary state interventions, see Drèze and Sen (1989:214–215; 1995 : 16–26).

50. For discussion on collective action for social achievement, see Mehta (1994b). Also see Mehta (1995 : 161–180).

51. For details of this unique campaign, see Issac and Harilal (1997). op. cit.

APPENDIX

Table 1
Some Select Social Indicators of Development for India Through the Planning Era

Item	Pre-Plan	II Plan	III Plan	IV Plan		V Plan	Annual Plan	VI Plan		VII Plan	Annual Plans		VIII Plan (Projections)	
	1950–51	1960–61	1965–66	1970–71	1973–74	1978–79	1979–80	1980–81	1984–85	1989–90	1990–91	1991–92	1992–93	1996–97
		1956–61	1961–66	1969–71		1974–79								
Mortality														
Death rate (number per thousand):														
Combined	22.8	19.0	18.2	14.9	14.5	14.5	12.8	12.5	11.8	9.7	9.8	10.0	*	8.7
Rural	*	*	*	16.4	15.9	14.1	13.7	13.7	13.0	10.5	10.6	10.8	*	*
Urban	*	*	*	9.7	9.2	8.1	7.9	7.8	7.8	8.8	7.1	7.0	*	*
Infant mortality rate (per thousand live births)	182.5	135.1	151	129.0	129.0	120.0	114.0	110.0	97.0	80.0	80.0	79.0	*	68.0
Male	190.0	142.3	*	129.0	124.0	119.0	113.0	110.0	96.0	*	*	*	*	*
Female	175.0	127.9	*	129.0	134.0	121.0	115.0	110.0	98.0	*	*	*	*	*
Rural Combined	*	*	*	138.0	139.0	130.0	124.0	119.0	114.0	86.0	87.0	85.0	*	*
Male	*	*	*	137.0	133.0	129.0	123.0	119.0	113.0	*	*	*	*	*
Female	*	*	*	138.0	146.0	131.0	125.0	119.0	114.0	*	*	*	*	*
Urban Combined	*	*	*	82.0	80.0	72.0	65.0	62.0	66.0	50.0	53.0	53.0	*	*
Male	*	*	*	83	78	73	65	63	68	*	*	*	*	*
Female	*	*	*	81	82	71	65	62	64	*	*	*	*	*
Under 5 mortality rate (percentage of population in the age group)	*	*	*	51.9	*	51.0	*	41.2	38.4	33.3	*	*	*	*

Continued

Item	Pre-Plan	II Plan	III Plan	IV Plan		V Plan	Annual Plan	VI Plan		VII Plan	Annual Plans		VIII Plan (Projections)	
	1950–51	1960–61	1965–66	1970–71	1973–74	1978–79	1979–80	1980–81	1984–85	1989–90	1990–91	1991–92	1992–93	1996–97
Maternal mortality (per 1,00,000 live births)	*	*	376–418		(1975)	*	500	*	*	550	*	*	*	*
Life expectancy at birth: Overall (years)	32.1	41.3	41.3	45.6	49.7	49.2	52.3	54.4	58.2	58.2	59.9	58.2	*	60.6
Male	32.4	41.9	41.9	46.4	50.5	49.5	52.5	54.1	56.6	58.6	55.9	57.7	*	60.1
Female	31.7	40.6	40.6	44.7	49.0	49.0	52.1	54.7	56.1	59.7	59.9	58.7	*	61.1
Total labour force (millions) Total	140.0	188.7	*	230.4	240.1	255.4	270.8	*	305.4	*	314.9	328.9	383.6	364.3
Male	*	*	*	155.1	161.5	182.2	193.7	*	218.9	*	223.5	*	259.9	*
Female	*	*	*	75.3	78.6	73.2	77.1	*	86.5	*	91.4	*	123.7	*
Rural: Total	*	*	*	192.5	199.6	206.7	215.1	*	237.4	*	249.3	*	304.5	*
Male	*	*	*	124.2	128.7	142.9	148.9	*	164.2	*	167.8	*	196.2	*
Female	*	*	*	68.3	70.9	63.8	66.2	*	73.2	*	81.5	*	108.3	*
Urban: Total	*	*	*	38.0	40.6	48.8	55.6	*	68.0	*	65.6	*	79.1	*
Male	*	*	*	30.9	32.9	39.4	44.8	*	54.7	*	55.7	*	63.7	*
Female	*	*	*	7.1	7.7	9.4	10.8	*	13.3	*	9.9	*	15.4	*
Labour force proportions (per cent of total labour force) Male	*	*	*	67.3	67.3	71.3	71.5	*	71.7	71.8	71.0	*	67.8	*
Female	*	*	*	32.7	32.7	28.7	28.5	*	28.3	28.2	29.0	*	32.2	*
Rural	*	*	*	83.5	83.1	80.7	79.4	*	77.8	75.8	79.2	*	79.4	*
Urban	*	*	*	16.5	16.9	19.3	20.6	*	22.2	24.2	20.8	*	20.6	*
Worker participation rates (in per cent of respective population) (Census and Planning Commission estimates) Total	*	43.0	*	34.0	*	*	*	36.8	*	*	37.6	*	*	*
Male	*	57.1	*	52.7	*	*	*	52.6	*	*	51.6	*	*	*

Female	*	28.0	*	*	13.9	*	*	19.8	*	*	22.7	*	*
Rural													
Total	*	45.0	*	*	36.1	*	*	38.8	*	*	40.2	*	*
Male	*	58.2	*	*	53.6	*	*	53.8	*	*	52.5	*	*
Female	*	31.4	*	*	15.5	*	*	23.1	*	*	27.2	*	*
Urban													
Total	*	33.5	*	*	29.6	*	*	30.0	*	*	30.4	*	*
Male	*	52.4	*	*	48.9	*	*	49.1	*	*	49.0	*	*
Female	*	11.1	*	*	7.2	*	*	8.3	*	*	9.7	*	*
Labour force participation based on usual principal status (NSS estimates), (per cent)													
Rural													
Male	*	*	*	64.6	63.7	*	*	62.6	(61.4) 54.6		*	54.9	54.3
Female	*	*	*	37.7	30.5	*	*	29.1	(29.2) 29.4		*	24.3	24.7
Urban													
Male	*	*	*	60.0	60.1	*	*	60.3	(59.6) 52.4		*	53.2	53.5
Female	*	*	*	16.5	17.1	*	*	14.8	(14.6) 12.9		*	13.0	12.4
Unemployment rates (per 1,000 of labour force)													
Rural													
Male	*	*	*	12	13	*	*	14	(18) 13		*	13	20
Female	*	*	*	5	20	*	*	7	(24) 6		*	4	8
Urban													
Male	*	*	*	48	54	*	*	51	(52) 39		*	45	43
Female	*	*	*	60	124	*	*	49	(62) 27		*	54	56
Income													
Per capita NNP at 1980–81 prices	1126.9	1350.3	1355.3	1519.6	1482.9	1689.3	1550.3	1630.0	1810.7	2160.0	2213.1	2167.1	2215.0

Continued

Item	Pre-Plan	II Plan	III Plan	IV Plan		V Plan	Annual Plan	VI Plan		VII Plan	Annual Plans		VIII Plan (Projections)	
	1950–51	1960–61	1965–66	1970–71	1973–74	1978–79	1979–80	1980–81	1984–85	1989–90	1990–91	1991–92	1992–93	1996–97
Compound growth in per capita income per annum over the preceding period (in per cent)	*	1.9	0.2	2.4	–0.8	2.7	–8.2	5.1	2.7	3.6	2.5	–2.1	2.2	*
Percentage of people living below the poverty line														
Rural														
Planning Commission	*	*	*	*	54.1	51.2	*	*	40.4	33.4	*	*	*	*
Minhas	*	*	*	58.8	56.4	51.5	*	*	50.8	48.7	*	*	*	*
Expert Group	*	*	*	*	54.6	51.2	*	*	43.8	37.6	*	*	*	*
Urban														
Planning Commission	*	*	*	*	41.2	38.2	*	*	28.1	20.1	*	*	*	*
Minhas	*	*	*	46.2	49.5	42.4	*	*	40.2	37.8	*	*	*	*
Expert Group	*	*	*	*	47.5	46.3	*	*	41.7	38.9	*	*	*	*
Combined														
Planning Commission	*	*	*	*	51.5	48.3	*	*	37.4	29.9	*	*	*	*
Minhas	*	*	*	56.3	54.9	49.5	*	*	48.2	45.9	*	*	*	*
Expert Group	*	*	*	*	53.1	50.1	*	*	43.3	38.0	*	*	*	*
Nutrition														
Food and its distribution														
Net availability of foodgrains (in million tonnes)	52.4	75.7	78.5	94.3	97.1	114.9	101.4	114.3	124.3	144.8	158.6	148.9	150.2	*

PDS as a per cent of net availability of foodgrains	15.3	5.3	19.2	8.3	11.1	10.2	14.8	11.4	12.7	11.0	13.1	12.5	10.1	*
Per capita net availability of foodgrains (grams)	394.9	468.7	408.1	468.8	451.2	476.5	410.4	454.8	454.0	476.4	510.1	469.9	465.6	*
Per capita net availability of pulses (grams)	60.7	69.0	48.2	51.2	40.8	44.7	30.9	37.5	38.4	41.1	41.6	34.3	36.6	*
Per capita household consumption expenditure based on NSS rounds (in rupees) (1954–55)														
Rural: Total	15	20	26.4	34.7	53	68.9	*	*	112.5	189.5	*	*	*	*
Food	9.9	14.1	19.3	25.6	39.7	44.3	*	*	73.7	121.3	*	*	*	*
Urban: Total	24.7	27.5	36	50.4	70.8	96.2	*	*	164	298	*	*	*	*
Food	13.7	16.9	22.7	33.1	47.9	57.7	*	*	97	165.5	*	*	*	*
Share of food in per capita household consumption expenditure in per cent 1954–55														
Rural	66.0	70.5	73.1	73.8	74.9	54.3	*	*	65.5	64.3	*	*	*	*
Urban	55.5	61.5	63.1	65.7	67.7	50.0	*	*	59.1	55.5	*	*	*	*
Daily calorie supply (k cal), per capita	*	*	2111.0	*	2296	2366	2404	2404	2481	2283	*	2139	*	*
Daily protein supply (grams), per capita	*	*	*	*	63.6	62.3	62.8	62.8	*	618	*	54.1	*	*

Continued

Item	Pre-Plan	II Plan	III Plan	IV Plan		V Plan	Annual Plan	VI Plan		VII Plan	Annual Plans		VIII Plan (Projections)	
	1950–51	1960–61	1965–66	1970–71	1973–74	1978–79	1979–80	1980–81	1984–85	1989–90	1990–91	1991–92	1992–93	1996–97
Per cent of people with access to water supply and sanitation														
Rural water supply	*	*	*	*	*	*	*	31.0	56.3	73.9	88.0	78.4	*	100.0
Rural sanitation	*	*	*	*	*	*	*	0.5	0.7	2.4	3.0	2.7	*	5.0
Urban water supply	*	*	*	*	*	85.0	*	77.8	72.9	83.8	84.0	84.9	*	94.0
Urban sanitation	*	*	*	*	*	38.0	*	27.0	28.4	45.9	47.0	47.9	*	69.3
Medical Care														
Total number of registered allopathic doctors per 1,00,000 population	17.0	21.0	21.0	27.6	*	31.0	*	39.2	41.8	46.0	47.0	*	*	*
Number of rural allopathic doctors per 1,00,000 rural population	*	6.9	*	13.6	*	*	*	13.8	*	*	*	*	*	*
Number of nursing personnel per 1,00,000 population	5.0	9.0	11.0	14.0	*	18.0	*	21.0	26.0	32.0	*	*	*	*
Number of nurses working in rural areas per 1,00,000 rural population	*	4.9	*	7.3	*	*	*	11.0	*	*	*	*	*	*
Basic health infrastructure														
Total number of beds of all types per 1,00,000 population	32.0	52.0	61.5	64.0	69.0	78.0	83.5	83.0	90.0	97.0	95.0	*	*	*

Number of beds in hospitals and dispensaries in rural areas per 1,00,000 rural population	11.0	14.3	15.1	*	*	*	16.3	17.7	*	*
Number of primary health centres per 1,00,000 rural population	0.22	0.71	1.15	1.16	1.14	*	1.08	2.28	3.33	3.45
Number of rural dispensaries per 1,00,000	1.8	2.1	2.0	*	*	*	2.2	2.4	2.1	*
Number of hospitals per 1,00,000 rural population	0.40	0.31	0.33	*	*	*	0.35	0.28	0.49	*
Education										
Literacy (in per cent terms): Total	18.3	28.3	34.5	*	*	*	(36.2) 43.7	*	*	52.2	52.0
Male	27.2	40.4	46.0	*	*	*	(46.9) 56.5	*	*	64.2	*
Female	8.9	15.3	22.0	*	*	*	(24.8) 29.9	*	*	39.2	*
Population Census data										
Rural	*	*	*	23.7	*	*	29.7	36.1	44.5	*
Male	*	*	*	33.8	*	*	40.8	49.7	57.8	*
Female	*	*	*	13.1	*	*	18.0	21.8	30.4	*
Urban	*	*	*	52.4	*	*	57.4	67.3	73.0	*
Male	*	*	*	61.2	*	*	65.8	76.8	81.1	*
Female	*	*	*	42.1	*	*	47.8	56.4	63.9	*

Continued

National Sample Survey data

Item	Pre-Plan	II Plan	III Plan	IV Plan		V Plan	Annual Plan	VI Plan		VII Plan	Annual Plans		VIII Plan (Projections)	
	1950–51	1960–61	1965–66	1970–71	1973–74	1978–79	1979–80	1980–81	1984–85	1989–90	1990–91	1991–92	1992–93	1996–97
National Sample Survey data														
Rural	*	*	*	*	*	*	*	*	33.9	37.5	*	*	*	*
Male	*	*	*	*	*	41.5	*	*	45.2	48.4	*	*	*	*
Female	*	*	*	*	*	18.4	*	*	22.2	25.9	*	*	*	*
Urban	*	*	*	*	*	*	*	*	61.6	64.5	*	*	*	*
Male	*	*	*	*	*	66.8	*	*	70.1	72.3	*	*	*	*
Female	*	*	*	*	*	50	*	*	52.3	55.9	*	*	*	*
Gross enrolment ratios as per cent to total population					(1975–76)									
Primary schools														
(6–11 years): Total	43.1	62.4	67.0	76.4	*	79.3	*	80.5	93.6	99.9	101.0	102.7	*	*
Male	60.6	82.6	96.3	92.6	*	95.7	*	95.8	110.3	115.5	115.3	116.6	*	*
Female	24.8	41.4	56.5	59.1	*	62.0	*	64.1	76.0	83.6	85.6	88.1	*	*
Middle schools														
(11–14 years): Total	12.9	22.5	30.8	34.2	*	35.6	*	41.9	48.1	59.2	60.1	61.2	*	*
Male	20.6	33.2	44.2	46.5	*	47.0	*	54.3	61.3	73.0	73.4	74.2	*	*
Female	4.6	11.3	17.0	20.8	*	23.8	*	28.6	34.9	44.6	46.1	47.4	*	*
Secondary school														
(14–17 years): Total	5.3	*	*	18.5	*	18.8	21.9	17.3	23.5	26.6	28.6	*	*	*
Male	8.7	*	*	26.8	*	25.6	22.9	23.1	31.7	35.0	37.3	*	*	*
Female	1.5	*	*	9.8	*	11.6	13.9	11.1	14.7	17.7	19.4	*	*	*
Pupil–teacher ratio					(1975–76)									
Primary schools	33.0	36.0	39.0	39.0	37.0	*	38.0	38.0	41.0	43.0	42.0	43.0	*	*

Middle schools	24.0	31.0	33.0	30.0	30.0	*	33.0*	33.0	36.0	37.0	37.0	38.0	*	*
Secondary schools	25.0	25.0	26.0	26.0	26.0	*	26.0	27.0	28.0	29.0	31.0	32.0	*	*
School drop-out rates (per cent)[ii]														
Primary														
Boys	*	65.3	68.6	66.1	58.1	*	*	48.3	*	45.0	*	*	*	*
Girls	*	75.0	78.7	74.4	68.7	*	*	58.2	*	50.0	*	*	*	*
Total	*	*	*	67.0	*	*	*	*	*	43.0	*	*	*	*
Middle														
Boys	*	31.5	34.2	35.1	34.0	*	*	27.6	*	61.0	*	*	*	*
Girls	*	39.0	40.5	40.8	41.4	*	*	34.3	*	70.0	*	*	*	*
Total	*	*	*	79.0	*	*	*	*	*	64.0	*	*	*	*

* denotes information not available.

Source: EPW Research Foundation (EPWRF 1994:Table 1); see this paper for original sources of data included in this table.

Notes: i) Years representing as column heading do not always correspond to respective Five Year, or, Annual periods(e.g., the year 1978–79 for the Fifth Plan period).

ii) Again, the data presented generally pertain to the years indicated in the table though in some cases they pertain to the periods close to those years.

iii) For the sake of brevity, detailed sources of data and their method are not reproduced here.

Table 2
Human Development Index for India and Some other Developing Countries

Country	HDI Rank	Life Expectancy at Birth (Year) 1992	Adult Literacy (%) 1992	Mean Years of Schooling 1992	Literacy Index*	Schooling Index	Educational Attainment 1992	Real GDP Per Capita (PPP$) 1991	Adjusted Real GDP Per Capita	Human Development Index 1992	GNP Per Capita Rank Minus HDI Rank[a]
Republic of Korea	32	70.4	96.8	9.3	0.97	0.62	2.55	8,320	5,233	0.859	4
Chile	38	71.9	93.8	7.8	0.94	0.52	2.39	7,060	5,208	0.848	28
Costa Rica	39	76.0	93.2	5.7	0.93	0.38	2.24	5,100	5,100	0.848	36
Malaysia	57	70.4	80.0	5.6	0.80	0.37	1.97	7,400	5,215	0.794	4
Jamaica	65	73.3	98.5	5.3	0.99	0.35	2.32	3,670	3,670	0.749	22
Cuba	89	75.6	94.5	8.0	0.95	0.53	2.42	2,000	2,000	0.666	21
Sri Lanka	90	71.2	89.1	7.2	0.89	0.48	2.26	2,650	2,650	0.665	38
China	94	70.5	80.0	5.0	0.80	0.33	1.93	2,946	2,946	0.644	49
India	135	59.7	49.8	2.4	0.50	0.16	1.16	1,150	1,150	0.382	12

Source: UNDP (1994), *Human Development Report, 1994*, Table 1, pp. 129–31.

[a]A positive figure shows that the HDI rank is better than the GNP per capita rank.

*For calculation of various indices, see UNDP (1994:108).

Table 3

India's Rank on Human Development Indicators in Comparison with Ranks of some other Developing Countries

Country	HDI Rank Among 172 Countries	HDI Among 97 Countries (1992)	Life Expectancy 1992	Access to Safe Water 1988–91	Infant Mortality Rate 1992	Daily Calorie Supply 1988–90	Child Mal-nutrition 1990	Adult Literacy 1992	Mean Years of Schooling 1992	Radios 1990	Real GDP Per Capita (PPP$) 1991	GNP Per Capita (US$) 1991
Republic of Korea	32	4	18	18	13	21	3	3	2	1	10	8
Chile	38	8	11	24	10	45	2	9	7	19	15	23
Costa Rica	39	9	3	17	5	25	16	11	16	27	23	26
Thailand	54	16	25	33	18	56	34	10	42	48	19	29
Malaysia	57	17	17	36	5	18	45	33	18	12	12	20
Jamaica	65	21	8	1	5	30	14	2	21	13	30	31
Cuba	89	31	4	12	5	5	17	7	6	18	52	43
Sri Lanka	90	32	12	37	17	60	92	17	11	45	44	57
Oman	92	33	22	30	21	36	54	85	81	7	8	9
China	94	34	16	28	19	33	52	32	22	50	39	68
India	135	63	52	67	64	43	96	71	56	74	68	72

Source : UNDP (1994), *Human Development Report*, Annex Table A5.1, pp. 102–03.

Note: Ninety-seven developing countries were given ranks in the original table that reflect their comparative performance in the selected aspects of human development as illustrated in this table. To make the ranks comparable across indicators, countries were ranked only if they had estimates for all the indicators. Countries with equal performance in an indicator were given the same rank.

Table 4
Trends in Human Development and Quality of Life in India and some other Developing Countries

Country	HDI Rank 1992	Life Expectancy at Birth (Years)		Infant Mortality Rate (Per 1000 Birth)		Population with Access to Safe Water (%)		Underweight Children (as % of Children U5)		Adult Literacy Rate (%)		Enrolment Ratio for all Levels (% age 6–23)		Real GDP Per Capita (PPP$)	
		1960	1992	1960	1992	1975–80	1988–91	1975	1990	1970	1992	1980	1990	1960	1991
Republic of Korea	32	53.9	70.4	85	21	66	92	–	–	88	97	66	74	690	8,320
Chile	38	57.1	71.9	114	17	70	88	2	2	89	94	65	66	3,130	7,060
Costa Rica	39	61.6	76.0	85	14	72	92	10	8	88	93	55	56	2,160	5,100
Malaysia	57	53.9	70.4	73	14	–	–	31	18	60	80	54	58	1,783	7,400
Jamaica	65	62.8	73.3	63	14	86	100	14	7	97	99	67	62	1,829	3,670
Cuba	89	63.8	75.6	65	14	–	–	10	8	87	95	72	63	–	–
Sri Lanka	90	62.0	71.2	71	24	19	71	58	42	77	89	58	68	1,389	2,650
China	94	47.1	70.5	150	27	–	–	26	21	–	–	50	53	723	2,946
India	135	44.0	59.7	165	89	–	–	71	63	34	50	50	50	617	1,150

Source: UNDP (1994), *Human Development Report*, Table 4: 136–37.

Bibliography

Abrahamson, L.Y., M.E.P. Seligman and **J.D. Teasadle** (1978), 'Learned Helplessness in Humans: Critique and Reformation', *Abnormal Psychology*, 87: 49–74.

Agarwal, Anil (1985), 'Ecological destruction and the emerging patterns and people's protests in rural India', *Social Action*, 35(1): 54–80.

Agashe, Anand (1992), 'Defying the Drought', *Times of India* (New Delhi),May 31.

Alatas, S.H. (1977), *The Myth of the Lazy Native*. London: Frank Cass.

Ambedkar, B.R. (1945), *What Congress and Gandhi Have Done to the Untouchables*. Bombay: Thacker.

————— (1979–81), B.R Ambedkar: Writings and Speeches, 7 Vols, Bombay: Government of Maharashtra (Edited by Vasant Moon (Vol.2 published in 1981; Vol 5 in 1989).

Arora, Dolly (1994), 'From State Regulation to People's Participation: Case of Forest Management in India', *Economic and Political Weekly*, March 19: 691–98.

Auti, V.B. and **A.S. Chousalkar** (1986), 'Nature and Political Ideas of Jottrao Phuley', in Karlekar and Chousalkar (eds), *Ideas, Movements and Politics in India*. Kolhapur: Ajab Pustakalaya: 9–25.

Bajaj, J.L. and **Rita Sharma** (1995), 'Improving Government Delivery Systems: Some Issues and Prospects', *Economic and Political Weekly*, May 27: M73–80.

Bakshi, Rajni (1996), 'Development, Not Destruction: Alternative Politics in the Making', *Economic and Political Weekly*, February 3: 255–57.

Balagopal, K. (1991), 'Post Chundar and Other Chundars', *Economic and Political Weekly*, October 19: 2399–405.

Bandura, A. (1977), 'Self-efficacy: Toward a Unifying Theory of Behavioural Changes', *Psychological Review*, 84: 191–215.

————— (1982) 'Self-efficacy Mechanism in Human Agency', *American Psychologist*, 37: 127–47.

Bandyopadhyay, D. (1986), 'Land Reforms in India: An Analysis', *Economic and Political Weekly*, 21(25–26): A50–56.

Banerjee, T.K. (1986), 'Girijan Movement in Srikakulam 1967–70', in A.R. Desai, 212–41.

Banerji, Sumanta (1986), 'Naxalbari', in A.R. Desai, 566–88.

Banerji, D. (1992), 'Family Planning in the Nineties—More of the Same', *Economic and Political Weekly*, April 25: 883–87.

Basham, A.L. (1990), *The Origins and Development of Classical Hinduism*. Delhi: Oxford University Press.

Basu, P.K. (1992), 'Strategic Issues in Administrative Reorganisation: Developing Countries Perspective', *Economic and Political Weekly*, May 30: M46–58.

Batliwala, Sri Lata (1996), 'Transforming of Political Culture: Mahila Samakhya Experience', *Economic and Political Weekly*, May 25: 1248–51.

Behera, Chitta (1992), 'Planting Tress Instead of Feeding Brahmins', *Down to Earth*, 20 (June): 41.

Bidwai, Praful (1997), 'Making Government Accountable: A Simple Proposal for Bureaucrats', *Frontline*, January 24, 110–11.

Bowen, Maria, Maureen Miller, Carl R. Rogers and **John K. Wood** (1979), 'Learning in Groups: Their Implications for the Future', *Education*, 100(2): 108–16.

Braibanti, Ralph (ed.) (1966), *Asian Bureaucratic Systems Emergent from the British Imperial Tradition*. Durham, NV: Duke University Press.

Breman, Jan (1986), 'Mobilisation of Landless Labourers: Halpatis of South Gujarat', in A.R. Desai, 362–83.

Casinader, Rex (1995), 'Making Kerala Model More Intelligible: Comparisons with Sri Lankan Experience', *Economic and Political Weekly*, December 2: 3085–92.

Chattopadhyaya, D. (1978), 'Source of Indian Idealism', in Debiprasad Chattopadhyaya (ed.), *History and Society* (Essays in Honour of Professor Niharranjan Ray). Calcutta: K.P. Bagchi & Co.: 239–70.

——————— (1989), *In Defence of Materialism in Ancient India*. New Delhi: Peoples Publishing House.

——————— (1990), *The Global Philosophy for Every Man: The Beginnings*. Bangalore: Navkarnataka.

Centre for Research in Rural and Urban Development (1996), Gender Issues in Population Planning (Report of a National Seminar). Mimeo. Chandigarh: CRRID.

Chaturvedi, Anil (1988), *District Administration: The Dynamics of Discord*. New Delhi: Sage.

Chenery, Hollis and **Moises Syrquin** (1975), *Patterns of Development, 1950–1970*. New York: Oxford University Press for the World Bank.

Cohn, B.S. (1969/1979), 'Structural Change in Indian Rural Society', in R.E. Frykenberg (ed.), *Land Control and Social Structure in Indian History*. Delhi: Manohar: 53–121.

Cohen, G.A. (1993), 'Amartya Sen's Unequal World', *Economic and Political Weekly*, October 2: 2156–60.

Commissioner for Scheduled Castes and Scheduled Tribes (1988), *28th Report, 1986–87*. New Delhi: Office of the Commissioner.

——————— (1990), *29th Report, 1987–89*. New Delhi: Office of the Commissioner.

Dale, Stephen F. (1980), *Islamic Society on the South Asian Frontier: The Mapilas of Malabar*. Oxford: Clarendon Press.

Dalit Panther (1973), *Manifesto*. Translated from Marathi by G. Omvedt. Bombay: Model Art Printing.

Dantawala, M.L. (1987), 'Growth vs. Equity in Agricultural Development Strategy', in B.R. Brahmananda and V.R. Panchmukhi (eds), *The Development Process of the Indian Economy*. Bombay: Himalaya Publishing: 147–60.

Dasholi Gram Samaj Mandal (1982), *Hugging the Himalayas: The Chipko Experience*. Chamoli, Garwal: DGSM.

De, Barun (1978), 'Complexities in the Relationship between Nationalism, Capitalism and Colonialism', in Debiprasad Chattopadhyaya (ed.), *History and Society* (Essays in Honour of Professor Niharranjan Ray). Calcutta: K.P. Bagchi: 479–513.

De Charms, R. (1968), *Personal Causation: The Internal Affective Determinants of Behaviour*. New York: Academic Press.

De Silva, G.V.S., N. Mehta, A. Rahman and **P. Wignaraja** (1979), 'Bhomi Sena—A Struggle for People's Power', *Development Dialogue*: 2.

Desai, A.R. (1986), *Agrarian Struggles in India After Independence*. Delhi: Oxford University Press.

Doyal, Len and **Ian Gough** (1991), *A Theory of Human Need*. New York: Guilford Press.

Drèze, Jean and Amartya Sen (1989), *Hunger and Public Action.* Oxford: Clarendon Press.
—————— (1995), *India: Economic Development and Social Opportunity.* Delhi: Oxford University Press.
Economic and Political Weekly (1997), '1997–98 Budget and State of the Economy: Putting Growth at Stake', Editorial Comment, March 1–8: 431–33.
Elias, N. and J.L. Scotson (1965), *The Established and the Outsiders.* London: Frank Cass.
Entrepreneurship Development Institute of India (1993), *Research Report on Impact of New Economic Policies on Small and Tiny Industries Sector.* Ahmedabad: ED11.
EPW Research Foundation (1994), 'Social Indicators of Development for India-I', *Economic and Political Weekly,* May 14: 1227–40.
Esho, Hideki (1992), 'The Korean Model and the Political Economy of Structural Adjustment', *Journal of International Economic Studies,* No. 8 (March).
Fourth Central Pay Commission (1986), *Report.* New Delhi: Publications Division.
Franke, Richard W. and Barbara H. Chasin (1992), *Kerala: Radical Reforms as Development in an Indian State.* Promilla: New Delhi.
Freire, Paulo (1970), *Cultural Action for Freedom.* Monograph Series No. 1. Cambridge, Mass.: Harvard Education Review.
—————— (1972), *Pedagogy of the Oppressed.* London: Sheed and Ward.
Friedmann, John (1992), *Empowerment: The Politics of Alternative Development.* Cambridge: Blackwell.
Frykenberg, Robert Eric (1969/1979a), 'Traditional Processes of Power in South India: A Historical Analysis of Local Influence', in R.E. Frykenberg (ed.), *Land Control and Social Structure in Indian History.* New Delhi: Manohar: 217–38.
—————— (1969/1979b), 'Village Strength in South India', in Frykenberg (ed.), *Land Control and Social Structure in Indian History.* New Delhi: Manohar: 247–67.
Gayie, Samuel (1994), 'Adjusting to the Social Costs of Adjustment in Ghana: Problems and Prospects'. Mimeo. Geneva: UNRISD.
Geetha, V. and Rajadurai S.V. (1993), 'Dalits and Non-Brahmin Consciousness in Colonial Tamil Nadu', *Economic and Political Weekly,* September 25: 2091–98.
Gopalan, C. (1983), 'Deprivation and Development', *Economic and Political Weekly,* 18: 2163–68.
—————— (1995), 'Toward Food and Nutrition Security', *Economic and Political Weekly,* December 10: A134–141.
Government of India (1966/1971), *Education and National Development: Report of the Education Commission.* New Delhi: NCERT.
—————— (1970), *Fourth Five Year Plan: 1969–74.* New Delhi: Planning Commission.
—————— (1979), *National Adult Education Programme—The First Year.* New Delhi: Ministry of Education.
—————— (1980a), *Sixth Five Year Plan.* New Delhi: Planning Commission.
—————— (1980b), *Report of the Review Committee on National Adult Education Programme.* New Delhi: Ministry of Education.
—————— (1981), *Report of the Working Group on Health for All by 2000 A.D.* New Delhi: Ministry of Health and Family Planning.
—————— (1984), *Adult Education Programme: Policy, Perspective and Strategies for Implementation.* New Delhi: Ministry of Education.
—————— (1985), *Report of the Committee to Review the Existing Administrative Arrangements for Rural Development and Poverty Alleviation Programmes.* New Delhi: Department of Rural Development.

Government of India (1986), *National Policy on Education, 1986.* New Delhi: Department of Education, Ministry of HRD.

————— (1988a), *National Literacy Mission.* New Delhi: Department of Education, Ministry of HRD.

————— (1988b), 'Land Reforms', in Occasional Papers. First Series. New Delhi: Department of Rural Development, Ministry of Agriculture.

————— (1988c), *Jawahar Rozgar Yojana.* New Delhi: Department of Rural Development.

————— (1989), *Jawahar Rozgar Yojana: Guidelines.* New Delhi: Department of Rural Development.

————— (1990a), *Report of the Committee for Review of National Policy on Education: Towards an Enlightened and Human Society.* New Delhi: Ministry of HRD, Department of Education.

————— (1990b), *Annual Report of the Ministry of HRD.* New Delhi: Ministry of HRD.

————— (1991a), *Annual Report, 1990–91.* New Delhi: Department of Education, Ministry of HRD.

————— (1991b), *Literacy Digest.* New Delhi: Ministry of HRD.

————— (1992a), *Eighth Five Year Plan, 1992–97,* Vols I and III. New Delhi: Planning Commission.

————— (1992b), *Jawahar Rozgar Yojana: A Quick Study.* New Delhi: Planning Commission.

————— (1992c), *The Constitution Seventy Third Amendment Act, 1992 on the Panchayat.* New Delhi: Ministry of Rural Development.

————— (1992d), *The Constitution Seventy Fourth Amendment Act, 1992, on the Nagarpalika.* New Delhi: Ministry of Rural Development.

————— (1992e), *Guidelines for Project Formulation.* New Delhi: Department of Education, Ministry of HRD.

————— (1993a), *Education for All: The Indian Scene.* New Delhi: Development of Education, Ministry of Human Resource Development.

————— (1993b), *Report of the Expert Group on Estimation of Proportion and Number of Poor.* New Delhi: Planning Commission.

————— (1994a), *Annual Plan, 1993–94.* New Delhi: Planning Commission.

————— (1994b), *Development of Education in India, 1993–94.* New Delhi: Department of Education, Ministry of HRD.

————— (1994c), *Annual Report.* New Delhi: Ministry of Labour.

Greer, Jed and **Kavaljit Singh** (1996), *TNC and India: An Activists Guide to Research and Campaigns on Transnational Corporations.* New Delhi: Public Interest Research Group.

Gulati, I.S. (1996), *Power to the People: Decentralised Planning Movement.* Thiruvananthapuram: State Planning Board, Government of Kerala.

Gupta, S.K. (1985), *Scheduled Castes in Modern Indian Politics.* Delhi: M.M. Publications.

Gupta, S.P. (1995), 'Economic Reform and Its Impact on Poor', *Economic and Political Weekly,* June 3: 1295–313.

Gupta, Tirth and **Amar Guleria** (1982), *Non-Wood Forest Products in India.* New Delhi: Oxford and IBH.

Habib, Irfan (1963), *Agrarian Structure in Mughal Empire.* Bombay: Popular Prakashan.

————— (1974), 'The Social Distribution of Landed Poverty in Pre-British India (A Historical Survey)', in R.S. Sharma (ed.), *Indian Society: Historical Probings.* New Delhi: People's Publishing House: 264–316.

Haggard, Stephen and Robert Kauffman (eds), (1992), *The Politics of Economic Adjustment*. Princeton: Princeton University Press.

Haldipur, R.N. (1984), 'Bureaucracy's Response to New Challenges', in L.N. Chaturvedi, S.P. Verma and S.K. Sharma (eds), *Development Administration*. New Delhi: IIPA: 97–109.

Hargopal, G. (1994), 'Bureaucracy, Rule of Law and Human Rights', *Indian Journal of Public Administration*, XL(3), July–September: 305–15.

Hasan, Nurul S. (1969/1979), 'Zamindars Under the Mughals', in Frykenberg, R.E. (ed.), *Land Control and Social Structure in Indian History*. New Delhi: Manohar: 17–32.

————— (1973), *Thoughts on Agrarian Relations in Mughal India*. New Delhi: Oxford University Press.

Higginbotham, Stanley J. (1975), *Cultures in Conflicts: The Four Faces of Indian Bureaucracy*. New York: Columbia University Press.

Hussain, Athar (1993), 'Reform of the Chinese Social Security System', Discussion Paper No.24, Research Programme on the Chinese Economy. London: London School of Economics.

————— (1994), 'Social Security in Present Day China and Its Reforms', *American Economic Review*, 84.

Illaiah, Kancha (1992), 'Andhra Pradesh's Anti Liquor Movement', *Economic and Political Weekly*, November 7: 2406–08.

Illich, I. (1981), *Shadow Work*. London: Marion Boyars.

Indian People's Human Rights Commission (1993), *The People's Verdict: An Inquiry into the December '92 and January '93 Riots in Bombay*. Bombay: IPHRC.

Issac, Thomas (1985), 'From Caste Consciousness to Class Consciousness: Alleppey Coir Workers during the Inter War Period', *Economic and Political Weekly*, 20(4): PE5–PE18.

Issac, Thomas and Michael Tharakan (1995), 'Kerala—The Emerging Perspectives: Overview of the International Congress on Kerala Studies', *Social Scientists*, 23: 1–3, 3–36.

Issac, Thomas and K.N. Harilal (1997), 'Planning for Empowerment: People's Campaign for Decentralised Planning in Kerala', *Economic and Political Weekly*, January 4–11: 53–58.

Iyer, K.Gopal and R. Vidyasagar (1986), 'Agrarian Struggle in Tamilnadu', in A.R. Desai, 508–37.

Iyer, K. Gopal and R.N. Maharaj (1986), 'Agrarian Movement in Tribal Bihar (Dhanbad) 1972–80', in A.R. Desai, 330–61.

Kala, Maju, R.N. Maharaj and K. Mukherjee (1986), 'Peasant Unrest in Bhojpur: A Survey', in A.R. Desai, 255–80.

Kashtakari Sanghatna (1986), 'Kashtakari Sanghatna (The Warli Uprising Revisited)', in A.R. Desai, 255–80.

Kawakami, Tadao (1992), 'Markets and Government: The Korean Case', *Journal of International Economic Studies*, March, No. 6.

Kohli, Atul (1987), *The State and Poverty in India: The Politics of Reform*. Cambridge: Cambridge University Press.

————— (1990), *Democracy and Discontent*. Cambridge: Cambridge University Press.

————— (1991), *Democracy and Discontent: Growing Crisis of Governability*. Cambridge: Cambridge University Press.

Kolodner, Eric (1994), 'Transnational Corporations: Impediments or Catalysts of Social Development', Occasional Paper No.5, UNRISD. Geneva: UNRISD.

242 • **A Strategy for Alternative Human Development**

Korten, David C. (1995), *When Corporations Rule the World.* Connecticut: Kumarian Press.
Kosambi, D.D. (1956/1975), *An Introduction to a Study of Indian History.* Bombay: Popular Prakashan.
Kothari, Rajni (1993), *Growing Amnesia.* New Delhi: Viking.
———— (1995), 'Globalisation and Revival of Tradition: Dual Attack on Model of Democratic Nation Building', *Economic and Political Weekly,* March 25: 625–33.
Krishnaji, N. (1986), 'Agrarian Relations and the Left Movement in Kerala: A Note on Recent Trends', in A.R. Desai, 255–80.
Krishnan, S. (1996), 'The Appropriation of Dissent: The State vis-a-vis People's Movements', in T.V. Satyamurthy (ed.),*Class Formation and Political Transformation in Post-colonial India.* New Delhi: Oxford University Press: 238–57.
Krishnaswamy, K.S. (1993), 'For Panchayats the Dawn is Not yet', *Economic and Political Weekly,* October 9: 2183–86.
———— (1996), 'Continuity with No Change: Budget 1996–97', *Economic and Political Weekly,* July 27: 2001–03.
Kumar, Ravinder (1986), *Essays in the Social History of Modern India.* Delhi: Oxford University Press.
Kurien, C.T. (1987), 'Planning and the Institutional Transformation of the Indian Economy', *Social Scientist,*17: 3–29.
La Palombara, Joseph (1963), 'An Over-view of Bureaucracy and Political Development', in Joseph La Palombara (ed.), *Bureaucracy and Political Development.* Princeton: Princeton University Press.
Leipziger, Danny M. (1988a), 'Editor's Introduction to Korea's Transition to Maturity', *World Development,* January.
———— (1988b), 'Industrial Restructuring in Korea', *World Development,* January.
Mackintosh, Maureen (1994), 'Competition and Contracting in the Process of Selective Social Provisioning'. Mimeo. Geneva: UNRISD.
MacMillan, Margret (1986), *Women of the Raj.* London: Thames and Hudson.
Mahalingam, Sudha (1997), 'Aspiring for Growth: The Ninth Plan Approach Paper', *Frontline,* January 24: 23–24.
Mandelbaum, David (1972), *Society in India.* Bombay: Popular Prakashan.
May, Rihani (1993), *Strategies for Female Education in Middle East and North Africa* (MENA), Creative Associates International, Washington for UNICEF.
McClelland, David C. (1961), *The Achieving Society.* Princeton , N.J.: D. Van Nostrand Co.
———— (1965), 'Toward a Theory of Motive Acquisition', *American Psychologist,* 20(5): 321–33.
McClelland David C. and **David Winter** (1969), *Motivating Economic Achievement.* New York: Free Press.
Mehta, Prayag (1969), *The Achievement Motive in High School Boys.* New Delhi: NCERT.
———— (1975), *Election Campaign: Anatomy of Mass Influence.* New Delhi: National.
———— (1976), *Managing Motivation in Education.* Ahmedabad: Sahitya Mudranalaya.
———— (1977),'Efficacy, Participation and Politics', *ICSSR Research Abstract Quarterly,*VI (3–4): 88–89.
———— (1981), 'Political Processes and Behaviour', in Udai Pareek (ed.), *A Survey of Research in Psychology, 1971–76,* Part II. New Delhi: ICSSR and Popular Prakashan: 577–615.
———— (1983), 'Mortgaged Child Labour of Vellore: Women Beedi Workers, Tale of Woe', *Mainstream,* 22(3): 15–17.

Mehta, Prayag (1985), 'Participative Management of Rural Development', *Administrator*, 30(1): 73–90.
———— (1987), 'Integrated Education for Urban Poor: A Review Study of Shramik Vidyapeeths'. Mimeo. New Delhi: PADC.
———— (1988a), 'Energizing Resource for National Literacy Mission: A Review Study of State Resource Centres'. Mimeo. New Delhi: PADC.
———— (1988b), 'Organisation of the Poor: A Case Study of Some Non-government Efforts'. New Delhi: PADC.
———— (1989a), *Bureaucracy, Organisational Behaviour and Development*. New Delhi: Sage.
———— (1989b), *Participation and Organisation Development*. Jaipur: Rawat.
———— (1990), 'Integrate Adult Education with Life: Feedback from Rajasthan'. Mimeo. New Delhi: PADC.
———— (1991), 'Energizing Agriculture Extension: Involvement of Voluntary Agencies'. Mimeo. New Delhi: PADC.
———— (1992a), 'Movement for Total Literacy: The Case of Sonebhadra'. Mimeo. New Delhi: PADC.
———— (1992b), 'Democratising the Workplace' in Udai Pareek(ed.), *Managing Transition: The HRD Response*. New Delhi: Tata McGraw Hill: 111–30.
———— (1994a), 'New Economic Policy, Workplace and Human Development', *Economic and Political Weekly*, 22, May 28: M75–82.
———— (1994b), 'Empowering the People for Social Achievement', in R. Kanungo, and Manuel Mendoca (eds), *Work Motivation: Models for Developing Countries*. New Delhi: Sage: 161–83.
———— (1994c), *Social Achievement Motivation: Needs, Values and Work Organisation*. New Delhi: Concept Publishing Co.
———— (1995), *Education, Participation and Empowerment: Studies in Human Development*. New Delhi: Concept Publishing Co.
———— (1996), 'Gender Issues in Population Planning: (Content Analysis of Ideas Generated at a National Seminar'. Mimeo. Chandigarh: CRRID.
———— (1997a), 'Managing Motivation in Agricultural Research Organisations: Some Indian Perceptions, Needs, Strategies and Interventions', *Man and Development*, March: 117–24.
———— (1997b), 'Promoting Motivation and Leadership for Democratising Governance and the Workplace'. Mimeo. New Delhi: PADC.
Meike, Sheilah (1995), 'Toward a Social Perspective in Development', *DPU News*, No. 33, December: 2–4.
Mies, Maria (1986), 'The Shahada Movement: A Peasant Movement in Maharashtra (India)—its Development and its Perspective', in A.R. Desai, 401–22.
Ministry of Home Affairs (1986), 'The Census and Nature of Current Agrarian Tensions', in A.R. Desai, 36–43.
Mitra, Amit (1992), 'Weaving a Common Destiny', *Down to Earth*, June. 30: 40.
Mitter, Swasti (1986), 'Peasant Movement in Sonarpur', in A.R. Desai, 589–617.
Mohandas, M. and **P.V. Praveen Kumar** (1992), 'Impact of Cooperativisation on Working Conditions: Study of Beedi Industries in Kerala', *Economic and Political Weekly*, June 27: 1333–338.
Moore, Barrington, Jr (1967), *Social Origins of Dictatorship and Democracy: Lord and Peasant in the Making of the Modern World*. London: Penguin.

Mukherjee, Kalyan (1996), 'Power to People Panchayats and Rural Development', *Frontline*, June 28: 107–11.

Mukherjee, Nirmal (1985), 'Democracy and Development', *Future*, December 6–13.

————— (1993), 'The Third Stratum', *Economic and Political Weekly*, May 1: 859–62.

Mukherjee, N. (1994), 'Restructuring the Bureaucracy: All India Services', *Economic and Political Weekly*, December 17–24: 3193–95.

Muzumdar, N.A. (1996), 'Public Policy and the Financial System: A Dilemma of Two Cultures', *Economic and Political Weekly*, December 14: 3237–40.

Myrdal, G. (1968), *Asian Drama: An Enquiry into the Poverty of Nations* (Three Volumes). New York: Twentieth Century Fund.

NABARD (1984), 'Study of Implementation of Integrated Rural Development Programme'. Mimeo. New Delhi: NABARD.

Nandi, Ramendra Nath (1986), *Social Roots of Religion in India*. New Delhi: K.P. Bagchi & Co.

National Council of Educational Research and Training (1994), *Research Based Interventions in Primary Education: The DPEP Strategy*. New Delhi: NCERT.

National Institute of Public Finance and Policy (1986), *Aspects of Black Economy in India*. New Delhi: NIPFP.

National Labour Institute (1979), *National Survey on the Incidence of Bonded Labour: Preliminary Report*. New Delhi: NLI.

NLI (1986). 'Post Independence Peasant Movement in Ryotwari Areas of Andhra Pradesh', in A.R. Desai, 242–54.

Neale, Walter (1969/79), 'Land is to Rule', in R.E. Frykenberg. (ed.), *Land Control and Social Structure in Indian History*. Delhi: Manohar.

Nehru, Jawaharlal (1946/1982), *The Discovery of India*. New Delhi: Jawaharlal Nehru Memorial Fund and Oxford University Press.

————— (1953), *Autobiography*. London: Methaen (Revised Edition).

Omvedt, Gail (1986), 'Caste, Agrarian Relations and Agrarian Conflicts', in A.R. Desai: 168–95.

————— (1993), *Reinvesting Revolution: The New Social Movement and the Socialist Tradition in India*. London: M.E. Sharpe.

————— (1996), 'The Anti-Caste Movement and the Discourse of Power', in T.V. Satyamurthy (ed.), *Region, Religion, Caste, Gender and Culture in Contemporary India*: New Delhi: Oxford University Press: 335–54.

Panandikar, V.A. and **S.S. Kshirsagar** (1978), *Bureaucracy and Development Administration*. New Delhi: Centre for Policy Research.

Parekh, Bhikhu (1989), *Colonialism, Tradition and Reform: An Analysis of Gandhi's Political Discourse*. New Delhi: Sage.

Patnaik, Prabhat and **C.P. Chandrasekhar** (1995), 'Indian Economy under Structural Adjustment', *Economic and Political Weekly*, November 25: 3001–13.

Pinto, Ambrose (1995), 'Badanvalu: Energizing Dalit Paradigm', *Economic and Political Weekly*, April 15: 797–99.

Potter, David C. (1986), *India's Political Administrators*. Oxford: Clarendon Press.

Prabhu, Seeta K. (1994), 'The Budget and Structural Adjustment with Human Face', *Economic and Political Weekly*, April 16–23: 1011–28.

Prabhu, Seetha and **P.C. Sarkar** (1994), 'Measuring Human Development', *Journal of Educational Planning and Administration*, 7(1): 103–24.

Pranjape, H.K. (1966), 'Trojan Inheritance', *Seminar*, August: 32–33.

Prasad, Pradhan, H. (1996), 'Union Budget: Neglect of Employment in Organised Sector', *Economic and Political Weekly*, July 27: 2003–4.

Premchand (1992), *Statistical Database for Literacy*. New Delhi: NIAE.

————— (1993), *Statistical Database for Literacy: Final Population and Literacy — 1991*. New Delhi: NIAE.

Radhakrishnan, P. (1991), 'Ambedkar's Legacy to Dalits: Has the Nation Reneged on Its Promises?', *Economic and Political Weekly*, August 17: 1911–22.

Radhakrishnan, P. and **R. Akila** (1993), 'India's Educational Efforts: Rhetoric and Reality', *Economic and Political Weekly*, November 27: 2613–19.

Rao, Hanumantha (1995), 'Structural Adjustments, Markets and the Poor', in *Economic Policies Development and Social Justice: Proceedings of AITUC Workshop*, March 22–24. New Delhi: AITUC: 31–49.

Rao, R. (1989), 'Dalit Movements in Contemporary India', *Kerala Sociologist*, 17 (June): 1, 7–19.

Rao, V.M. (1992), 'Land Reforms Experience: Perspective for Strategy and Programmes', *Economic and Political Weekly*, June 27: A50–64.

Rao, S.P.R. and **Madhav Gadgil** (1995), 'People's Bill on Nature, Health and Education', *Economic and Political Weekly*, December 7: 2501–12.

Rath, N. (1985), 'Garibi Hatao: Can IRDP Do it', *Economic and Political Weekly*, February 6: 238–46.

Registrar General and Census Commissioner (1992), *Census of India, 1991*, Paper 3 of 1991. New Delhi: Government of India.

Rose, Kalima (1992), *Where Women are Leaders: The SEWA Movement in India*. London: Zed Books.

Rosenthal, R. and **L. Jacobson** (1968), *Pygmalion in the Classroom*. New York: Holt, Rinehart and Winston.

Roy, Bunker (1996), 'Right to Information, Profile of a Grass Roots Struggle', *Economic and Political Weekly*, May 11: 1120–21.

Saligman, M.E.P. (1975), *Helplessness: On Depression, Development and Death*. San Francisco: Freeman.

Sarkar, Krishnakanta (1986), 'Kakwip Peasant Insurrection', in A.R. Desai, 255–80.

Sathyamurthy, T.V. (1996a), *Region, Religion, Caste, Gender and Culture in Contemporary India*. New Delhi: Oxford University Press.

————— (1996b), 'Centralised State Power and Decentralised Politics: Case of India', *Economic and Political Weekly*, March 30: 835–43.

Sen, Abhijit (1997), 'Agriculture Policy: The Wages of Neglect, Agriculture and the Budget', *Frontline*, April 4: 97–98.

Sen, Amartya (1990), 'Development as Capability Expansion', in K.Griffin and J. Knight (eds), *Human Development and International Development Strategy for 1990s*. London: Macmillan.

————— (1992a), *Inequality Reexamined*. Oxford: Clarendon Press.

————— (1992b), 'Capability and Well-being', in Martha C. Nusabaum (ed.), *The Quality of Life*. Oxford: Clarendon Press.

Sengupta, Nirmal (1986), 'Bataidari Movement (I)', in A.R. Desai, 281–99.

Sengupta, Nirmal, Anil Sinha and **T. Vijayendra** (1986), 'Bataidari Movement (ii)', in A.R. Desai, 300–29.

Sengupta, Chandan and **M.N. Roy** (1996), 'Sociological Impact of Total Literacy Campaign: The Case of Midnapore', *Economic and Political Weekly*, February 24: 483–88.

Sheth, D.L. (1996), 'Changing Terms of Elite Discourse: The Case of Reservation for other Backward Classes' in T.V. Sathyamurthy (ed.), *Region, Religion, Caste, Gender and Culture in Contemporary India*. Delhi: Oxford University Press: 314–33.

Singh, Rajendra (1986), 'Agrarian Social Structure and Peasant Unrest: A Study of Land Grab Movement in District Basti, East U.P.', in A.R. Desai, 538–65.

Singh, Trilok (1963), 'Administrative Assumptions in the Five Year Plans', *Indian Journal of Public Administration* IX: 336–43.

Singh, M. P. (1994), *V.N. Shukla's Constitution of India*. Lucknow: Eastern Book Co.

Singh, S.N. (1982), 'A Study of the Recruitment Pattern of IAS', *Administrator*, 27(2): 339–44.

Sinha, A.K. (1979), 'Organisation building in a developing country: A study of the central Department of Food in India', *International Review of Administrative Sciences*, 45: 176–82.

Sinha, B.P. (1992), 'Empowering Poor Farmers for Cooperative Action'. Mimeo. New Delhi: Indian Institute of Agricultural Research.

Shah, Tushaar (1993), 'Agriculture and Rural Development in 1990s and Beyond: Redesigning Relations between State and Institutions of Development', *Economic and Political Weekly*, September 25: A74–85.

Shankar, Kripa (1994), 'Jawahar Rozgar Yojana: An Assessment in U.P.', *Economic and Political Weekly*, July 16: 1845–48.

Shuhatme, P.V. (1993), 'Supplementary Note', in *Report of the Expert Group on Estimation of Proportion and Number of Poor*. New Delhi: Planning Commission.

Suresh, V. (1996), 'The Dalit Movement in India' in T.V. Satyamurthy (ed.), *Region, Religion, Caste, Gender and Culture in Contemporary India*. New Delhi: Oxford University Press: 355–87.

Sinha, Arvind (1996), 'Social Mobilisation in Bihar: Bureaucratic Feudalism and Distributive Justice', *Economic and Political Weekly*, December 21: 3287–89.

Society for Promotion of Wasteland Development (1992), *Joint Forest Management: Regulations Update*. New Delhi: SPWD.

Talib, B.D. (1986), 'Agrarian Tensions and Peasant Movement in Punjab', in A.R. Desai, 454–73.

Team of Researchers (1991), 'Upper Caste Violence: Study of Chunduru Carnage', *Economic and Political Weekly*, September 7 (Report of Team who visited Tenali and Chunduru on August 10, 1991): 2079–84.

Third Pay Commission (1973), *Report*. New Delhi: Ministry of Finance, Government of India.

Tendulkar, Suresh and **L.R. Jain** (1995), 'Economic Reforms and Poverty', *Economic and Political Weekly*, June 10: 1373–77.

Thapar, Romila (1989), 'Imagined Religious Communities/Ancient History and the Modern Search of a Hindu Identity', *Modern Asian Studies*, 23(2): 209–19.

Tilak, J.B.G. (1991), 'Human Development Index for India', *IASSI Quarterly*, October–December: 132–38.

Trivedi, P. (1994), 'Improving Government Performance: What Gets Measures, Gets Done', *Economic and Political Weekly*, August 27: M109–114.

UNICEF (1993a), 'Interventions for Women in Development in Bangladesh: A Country Strategy Paper'. December. Mimeo. Dhaka: UNICEF.

——————— (1993b), *The State of the World's Children*. New Delhi: Oxford University Press.

United Nations (1995), 'Report of the World Summit for Social Development', A/Conf. 166/9, 19 April. New York: UN.

United Nations Research Institute for Social Development (1994), *Structural Adjustment in the Changing World*, Briefing Paper, Series 4. Geneva: UNRISD.

——— (1995), *After the Social Summit: Implementing the Programmes of Action*, Report of the UNRISD Round Table Seminar held on July 4, 1995. Geneva: UNRISD.

United Nations Development Programme (1990), *Human Development Report, 1990 (Concept and Measurement of Human Development)*. New York: Oxford University Press.

——— (1992), *Human Development Report, 1992*. New York: Oxford University Press.

——— (1993), *Human Development Report, 1993*. New York: Oxford University Press.

——— (1994), *Human Development Report, 1994*. New York: Oxford University Press.

——— (1995), Human *Development Report, 1995*. Delhi: Oxford University Press.

——— (1996), *Human Development Report*, 1996. Delhi: Oxford University Press.

United Front (1996), *The Common Minimum Programme*. New Delhi: UF.

Vandergeest, Peter (1991), 'Gifts and Rights: Cautionary Note on Community Self-help in Thailand', *Development and Change*,22(3): 421–43.

Vieux,Steve and James Petras (1996), 'Selling Structural Adjustment: Intellectuals in Uniform', *Economic and Political Weekly*, January: P23–28.

Vivian,Jessica (1994), 'Social Safety Nets and Adjustments in Developing Countries', Occasional Paper No.1. Geneva: UNRISD.

Vohra, B.B. (1996), 'Resource Management for Poverty Alleviation', *Economic and Political Weekly*, June 8: 1397–404.

Vyas, V.S. (1994), 'The New Economic Policy and the Vulnerable Sections: Rationale for Public Interventions', WP/93–94(2). Jaipur: Institute of Development Studies.

Wade, Robert (1990), *Governing the Market Economic Theory and the Role of the Government in East Asian Industrialisation*. Princeton: Princeton University Press.

Wallerstein, Nina (1992), 'Powerlessness, Empowerment and Health: Implications for Health Promotion Programmes', *American Journal of Health Promotion*,6(3): 197–205.

Walsh, James (1993), 'Isle of Despair', *Time*, March 15.

Wasterston, Albert (1965), *Development Planning: Leasons of Experience*. Baltimore: The John Hopkins University.

Waterbury, John (1989), 'The Political Managment of Economic Adjustment and Reform', in Joan Nelson (ed.), *Fragile Coalitions*. New Brunswick: Transaction Books.

Weiner, Myron (1991), *The Child and the State in India*. Delhi: Oxford University Press.

Weiner, Ronald (1992), *What is the Matter with Liberalism*. Berkeley: University of California Press.

Williamson, John (1990), *Latin American Adjustment*. Washington: Institute for International Economics.

Wolfe, Marshall (1981), *Elusive Development*. Geneva: UNRISD/ECCLA (Economic Commission For Latin America).

World Bank (1991), *World Development Report 1991: The Challenge of Development*. Washington, D.C.: WB.

——— (1993), *The East Asian Miracle*. New York: Oxford University Press.

INDEX

ABOUT THE AUTHOR

Prayag Mehta is currently Director, Participation and Development Centre, New Delhi. In a distinguished career spanning several decades, Professor Mehta has held numerous positions at universities and development institutes in India and abroad and with international organisations. He has also worked with several non-government organisations as an academic and social activist.

Among his many publications are *Bureaucracy, Organisational Behaviour and Development* (1989), *Social Achievement Motivation: Needs, Values and Work Organisation* (1994) and *Education, Participation and Empowerment* (1995).

Structural Adjustment, Global Trade and the New Political Economy of Development

BY

Biplab Dasgupta

The World Bank's policies, known collectively as structural adjustment, supplemented by the IMF's stabilisation package, were introduced in the early 1980s as a short-term remedy to rectify the severe imbalances in the internal and external accounts of many developing countries. However, once initiated, very few countries grow out of this package. Collating global experience, with case-studies from East and Southeast Asia, Subsaharan Africa and Latin America, Professor Dasgupta provides a comprehensive and critical account of the implications of these policies for the economies of the less developed countries. He analyses competently the changing role of the World Bank and the IMF in today's world economy, the conditionalities which are part and parcel of structural adjustment, global trade issues, restrictive trade practices, the implications of the activities of the multinationals for the third world and the relationship between structural adjustment and environmental issues.

With its broad global coverage and holistic approach the book will be essential reading for scholars in the fields of economics, political science, political economy, development studies, international trade and environmental studies.

Contents: *List of Tables* ● *List of Abbreviations* ● *Prologue* ● Introduction ● The New Political Economy of Development ● Structural Adjustment ● GATT, WTO and the World Trade System ● Environment and Structural Adjustment ● The East Asian Development Experience ● A Global Overview: East and Southeast Asia, Sub-Saharan Africa, Latin America and India ● Conclusions ● *Epilogue* ● *References and Select Bibliography* ● *About the Author* ● *Subject Index* ● *Author Index*

220 x 140 mm ● HB ● 1998 ● 432 pp

Sage Publications
New Delhi/Thousand Oaks/London